공무원 9급 공개경쟁채용 필기시험

응시번호
성 명

문제책형
다

【시험과목】

과 목	영 어

응시자 주의사항

1. **시험시작 전에 시험문제를 열람하는 행위나 시험종료 후 답안을 작성하는 행위를 한 사람은** 「공무원임용시험령」 제51조에 의거 부정행위자로 처리됩니다.

2. **답안지 책형 표기는 시험시작 전 감독관의 지시에 따라 문제책 앞면에 인쇄된 책형을 확인한 후, 답안지 책형란의 해당 책형(1개)에 "●"와 같이 표기하여야 합니다.**

3. **답안은 반드시 문제책 표지의 과목순서에 맞추어 표기하여야 하며, 과목순서를 바꾸어 표기한 경우에도 문제책 표지의 과목순서대로 채점되므로 유의하시기 바랍니다.**
   - 특히, **선택과목의 경우 원서접수 시 선택한 과목이 아닌 다른 과목을 선택하여 답안을 표기하거나, 선택 과목 순서를 바꾸어 표기한 경우에도 응시표에 기재된 선택과목 순서대로 채점되므로 유의하시기 바랍니다.**

4. **시험이 시작되면 문제를 주의 깊게 읽은 후, 문항의 취지에 가장 적합한 하나의 정답을 고르며,** 문제내용에 관한 질문을 하실 수 없습니다.

5. **답안을 잘못 표기하였을 경우에는 답안지를 교체하여 작성하거나 수정테이프만을 사용하여 수정할 수 있으며**(수정액 또는 수정스티커 등은 사용 불가), **부착된 수정테이프가 떨어지지 않도록 눌러주어야 합니다.**
   - **불량 수정테이프의 사용과 불완전한 수정처리로 인해 발생하는 모든 문제는 응시자 본인에게 책임이 있습니다.**

6. **시험시간 관리의 책임은 응시자 본인에게 있습니다.**

   ※ 문제책은 시험종료 후 가지고 갈 수 있습니다.

2024 심우철 실전 동형 모의고사 1회

심슨영어연구소

SEASON I

※ 밑줄 친 부분의 의미와 가장 가까운 것을 고르시오. [문 1. ~ 문 4.]

문 1.
Mattel, the world's largest toy manufacturer, apologized for its products identified as a health hazard. The company issued an urgent recall of the products, prioritizing customer safety.

① pressing
② selective
③ extensive
④ mandatory

문 2.
The government announced that eligible war veterans can receive special benefits, including housing assistance and educational grants.

① injured
② qualified
③ disciplined
④ established

문 3.
It is important for actors not to let on any details about the thrilling plot twist before the release of the movie.

① alter
② conceal
③ exclude
④ disclose

문 4.
After a lengthy debate, the committee had to yield to the majority opinion and proceed with the proposed plan.

① ignore
② uphold
③ represent
④ surrender

문 5. 밑줄 친 부분 중 어법상 옳지 않은 것은?

The days leading up to Christmas are practically a celebration in their own right, ① offering various ways to savor the holiday season. Trees are decorated, carols are sung, and gingerbread houses rise and fall. There is a sense of goodwill ② which takes root in the soil of childhood memories and ③ blossom annually — a kind of magic too powerful ④ to be limited to just one day.

문 6. 어법상 옳지 않은 것은?

① I would rather go for a hike than spend the day indoors.
② We will have our picnic if the weather improves tomorrow.
③ The master key believed to have lost was finally found by them.
④ A number of books on social philosophy are available at the library.

문 7. 우리말을 영어로 잘못 옮긴 것은?

① 그 놀이터는 과거에 훨씬 더 조용했었다.
   → The playground used to be much quieter in the past.
② 그녀가 집을 나서자마자 비가 오기 시작했다.
   → No sooner had she left the house than it started raining.
③ 그 소프트웨어는 모든 장치에 쉽게 설치할 수 있게 설계되었다.
   → The software is designed to be easy to install it on any device.
④ 물을 마시면 갈증이 경기력에 영향을 미치지 않게 할 수 있다.
   → Drinking water can keep thirst from affecting your performance.

문 8. 다음 글의 내용과 일치하지 않는 것은?

Rosa Parks was born in 1913 in Tuskegee, Alabama. Early in life, she experienced racial discrimination and attended a segregated school. Though she had to leave school at 16, she returned to high school to obtain a diploma after her marriage to Raymond Parks. Her defining moment came on December 1, 1955, when she rejected the bus driver's order to give up her bus seat to a white passenger. For this, she was arrested and fined under Montgomery's segregation laws. This sparked the Montgomery bus boycott by 17,000 Black citizens that led to a U.S. Supreme Court decision declaring that segregation on buses was illegal. Even before her brave act on the bus, she was active in the civil rights movement, supporting Black voting rights despite many obstacles. Her devotion to racial equality earned her the title of "Mother of the Civil Rights Movement."

① Rosa got married before she earned a high school diploma.
② Rosa was arrested for not offering her seat to a white person.
③ Due to the bus boycott, segregation on buses became illegal.
④ Rosa began fighting for Black voting rights after the bus boycott.

문 9. 다음 글의 내용과 일치하는 것은?

Intermittent fasting is a type of eating pattern that involves cycling between periods of fasting and eating. The most common type of intermittent fasting is the 16/8 method, where individuals fast for 16 hours and eat within an 8-hour period for 3 or 4 days a week. Other types include alternate-day fasting where you fast every other day, and the eat-stop-eat method which involves choosing two days of the week on which you don't eat for a full 24-hour period. You can consume beverages during fasting as long as they don't contain sugar, like unsweetened tea or black coffee. Intermittent fasting has been shown to have many health benefits. But it is important to note that it may not be suitable for everyone, especially those with certain medical conditions or who are pregnant or breastfeeding.

① The 16/8 method requires fasting for 16 hours every day.
② You fast every other day for the eat-stop-eat method.
③ Drinking black coffee is allowed during the fasting period.
④ Breastfeeding moms particularly benefit from intermittent fasting.

공무원 9급 공개경쟁채용 필기시험

응시번호

성 명

문제책형
다

【시험과목】

| 과 목 | 영 어 |

응시자 주의사항

1. 시험시작 전에 시험문제를 열람하는 행위나 시험종료 후 답안을 작성하는 행위를 한 사람은 「공무원임용시험령」 제51조에 의거 부정행위자로 처리됩니다.

2. 답안지 책형 표기는 시험시작 전 감독관의 지시에 따라 문제책 앞면에 인쇄된 책형을 확인한 후, 답안지 책형란의 해당 책형(1개)에 "●"와 같이 표기하여야 합니다.

3. 답안은 반드시 문제책 표지의 **과목순서에 맞추어** 표기하여야 하며, 과목순서를 바꾸어 표기한 경우에도 문제책 표지의 과목순서대로 채점되므로 유의하시기 바랍니다.

   - 특히, 선택과목의 경우 원서접수 시 선택한 과목이 아닌 다른 과목을 선택하여 답안을 표기하거나, 선택과목 순서를 바꾸어 표기한 경우에도 응시표에 기재된 선택과목 순서대로 채점되므로 유의하시기 바랍니다.

4. 시험이 시작되면 문제를 주의 깊게 읽은 후, 문항의 취지에 가장 적합한 하나의 정답을 고르며, 문제내용에 관한 질문을 하실 수 없습니다.

5. 답안을 잘못 표기하였을 경우에는 답안지를 교체하여 작성하거나 수정테이프만을 사용하여 수정할 수 있으며(수정액 또는 수정스티커 등은 사용 불가), 부착된 수정테이프가 떨어지지 않도록 눌러주어야 합니다.

   - 불량 수정테이프의 사용과 불완전한 수정처리로 인해 발생하는 모든 문제는 응시자 본인에게 책임이 있습니다.

6. 시험시간 관리의 책임은 응시자 본인에게 있습니다.

   ※ 문제책은 시험종료 후 가지고 갈 수 있습니다.

2024 심우철 실전 동형 모의고사 2회

심슨영어연구소

SEASON I

※ 밑줄 친 부분의 의미와 가장 가까운 것을 고르시오. [문 1. ~ 문 4.]

문 1.
Departing from convention, the artist deliberately abandoned traditional methods. She made use of avant-garde techniques and created a groundbreaking masterpiece after several experiments.

① ceased
② resisted
③ adopted
④ inverted

문 2.
Following successful negotiations, the nations signed a perpetual treaty aimed at peaceful relations and closer cooperation in various domains.

① formal
② lasting
③ inclusive
④ definitive

문 3.
Despite her fear of violence, Julia surprised herself by taking up boxing, drawn to the sport's mental challenges.

① mastering
② instructing
③ undertaking
④ appreciating

문 4.
The developers were able to iron out bugs in the new software through continuous testing.

① settle
② exploit
③ identify
④ reproduce

문 5. 밑줄 친 부분 중 어법상 옳지 않은 것은?

Climate change is a broad topic ① that includes periodic alterations in Earth's climate caused by natural forces — biological, chemical, ② geologic and meteorological factors — ③ combined with the effects of various human activities. Over the last 100 years, however, the collective weight of human activities ④ emerged as an important factor in guiding the trajectory of global climates.

문 6. 어법상 옳지 않은 것은?

① The child asked his parents if he could have a pet.
② It is of no use to complain without proposing solutions.
③ A student who put a bandage on her finger has just had it taken off.
④ The customer demanded that the product replaced due to a structural defect.

문 7. 우리말을 영어로 잘못 옮긴 것은?

① 그는 아무 일도 없었다는 듯이 나를 향해 미소를 지었다.
→ He smiled at me as if nothing had happened.
② 보고서를 제시간에 제출할 것을 기억하는 것이 중요하다.
→ It's important to remember submitting the report on time.
③ 집을 나서기 전에 창문이 모두 닫혀 있는지 확인해라.
→ Make sure that all windows are closed before leaving the house.
④ 그녀의 재능은 노래보다는 악기 연주에 있다.
→ Her talent is not so much in singing as in playing musical instruments.

문 8. 다음 글의 내용과 일치하지 않는 것은?

The Booker Prize, formerly known as the Man Booker Prize, is one of the most prestigious literary awards in the world. Established in 1969, the prize aims to recognize outstanding works of fiction written in the English language. Initially limited to writers from the Commonwealth, Ireland, and Zimbabwe, it was later expanded in 2013 to include authors from any nationality, provided their work is originally written in English and published in the UK or Ireland. The influence of the prize is such that the winner will almost certainly see the sales increase significantly, besides the £50,000 that comes with the prize. A sister prize, the International Booker Prize, is awarded for a book translated into English and published in the UK or Ireland. For this award, the £50,000 prize money is split evenly between the author and the translator of the winning novel.

① The Booker Prize awards remarkable works of fiction.
② To win the Booker Prize, novels must be written in English.
③ The scope of authors eligible for the Booker Prize widened in 2013.
④ The winning author of the International Booker Prize receives £50,000.

문 9. 다음 글의 내용과 일치하는 것은?

A rack jobber is a vendor who rents space in a retail store or supermarket to display and sell products. Some rack jobbers are distributors, bringing in products from larger wholesale companies to sell in local stores. Others actually make or manufacture their own items and contract with store owners to use their floor space. Before contracting with a retailer, a rack jobber conducts market research to try to predict if the store's regular customers will be interested in his or her goods. The jobber determines what quantities of items to stock and what percentage of profits should be given to the retailer. As the job title implies, a rack jobber usually brings his or her own rack to display goods.

① Rack jobbers don't manufacture their own products.
② Market research is conducted after contracting with a retailer.
③ Rack jobbers decide how much of the profit goes to the retailer.
④ Rack jobbers generally use the store's rack to display their items.

공무원 9급 공개경쟁채용 필기시험

응시번호	
성 명	

문제책형: 다

【시험과목】

과 목	영 어

응시자 주의사항

1. 시험시작 전에 시험문제를 열람하는 행위나 시험종료 후 답안을 작성하는 행위를 한 사람은 「공무원임용시험령」 제51조에 의거 부정행위자로 처리됩니다.

2. 답안지 책형 표기는 시험시작 전 감독관의 지시에 따라 문제책 앞면에 인쇄된 책형을 확인한 후, 답안지 책형란의 해당 책형(1개)에 "●"와 같이 표기하여야 합니다.

3. 답안은 반드시 문제책 표지의 과목순서에 맞추어 표기하여야 하며, 과목순서를 바꾸어 표기한 경우에도 문제책 표지의 과목순서대로 채점되므로 유의하시기 바랍니다.
   - 특히, 선택과목의 경우 원서접수 시 선택한 과목이 아닌 다른 과목을 선택하여 답안을 표기하거나, 선택과목 순서를 바꾸어 표기한 경우에도 응시표에 기재된 선택과목 순서대로 채점되므로 유의하시기 바랍니다.

4. 시험이 시작되면 문제를 주의 깊게 읽은 후, 문항의 취지에 가장 적합한 하나의 정답을 고르며, 문제내용에 관한 질문을 하실 수 없습니다.

5. 답안을 잘못 표기하였을 경우에는 답안지를 교체하여 작성하거나 수정테이프만을 사용하여 수정할 수 있으며(수정액 또는 수정스티커 등은 사용 불가), 부착된 수정테이프가 떨어지지 않도록 눌러주어야 합니다.
   - 불량 수정테이프의 사용과 불완전한 수정처리로 인해 발생하는 모든 문제는 응시자 본인에게 책임이 있습니다.

6. 시험시간 관리의 책임은 응시자 본인에게 있습니다.

※ 문제책은 시험종료 후 가지고 갈 수 있습니다.

2024 심우철 실전 동형 모의고사 3회

심슨영어연구소

SEASON I

※ 밑줄 친 부분의 의미와 가장 가까운 것을 고르시오. [문 1. ~ 문 4.]

문 1. The company's resources were insufficient to handle the surge in demand for its products.

① short
② abundant
③ exhausted
④ distributed

문 2. In response to valuable customer feedback, the enterprise announced an initiative to introduce innovative features and significantly enhance the overall user experience.

① pledge
② scheme
③ objection
④ investigation

문 3. Mary had to turn down the request for additional information.

① fulfill
② review
③ refuse
④ manage

문 4. Michael had to stand in for the manager in overseeing daily operations.

① assist
② imitate
③ substitute
④ acknowledge

문 5. 밑줄 친 부분에 들어갈 말로 가장 적절한 것은?

The politician has shown _____ to transparency in governance, consistently engaging in open communication with citizens in person.

① distortion
② corruption
③ alternative
④ commitment

문 6. 밑줄 친 부분 중 어법상 옳지 않은 것은?

Although only ① a few of the 70-80 species of poisonous mushrooms are fatal when ② ingesting, many of these deadly fungi ③ bear a particularly deceptive resemblance to edible species, making identification ④ challenging and increasing the risk of accidental ingestion.

문 7. 밑줄 친 부분이 어법상 옳지 않은 것은?

① The sale prices will be valid until the end of the week.
② After hearing the arguments, she convinced of their logic.
③ They have been living in the city since they graduated from college.
④ I look forward to discussing potential partnerships with your company.

문 8. 우리말을 영어로 잘못 옮긴 것은?

① 당신의 주말 계획이 어떻게 되는지 알려주세요.
→ Let me know what your plans are for the weekend.
② 어떤 이유로도 중요한 마감일을 놓쳐서는 안 된다.
→ On no account should important deadlines be missed.
③ 그곳의 분위기는 긴장되어 있어 모두가 눈을 마주치길 피하는 것 같다.
→ The atmosphere there seems tense, with everyone avoiding eye contact.
④ 그 소설은 내가 최근에 읽은 그 어떤 책보다 더 흥미진진하다.
→ The novel is more fascinating than any other books I have read recently.

※ 밑줄 친 부분에 들어갈 말로 가장 적절한 것을 고르시오. [문 9. ~ 문 10.]

문 9.
A: Did you know that bedbugs were found in our neighborhood?
B: Oh no, you've got to be kidding me! What should we do if they get inside our homes?
A: In that case, it's best to call a pest control expert.
B: _____
A: Even so, getting help from an expert will be a lot better than trying to handle the situation by yourself.

① But I haven't found any in my house yet.
② How did the bedbugs get inside your house?
③ I heard even specialists have difficulties, though.
④ Do you know the specific location they were found?

문 10.
A: What do you feel like having for lunch?
B: Hmm. I was thinking of pasta. How about you?
A: Funny you should say that. I was thinking the same. _____?
B: There's a nice one that I frequently visit just around the corner, actually.
A: Alright, let's go there then.

① Where did you have lunch today
② Which restaurant should we go to
③ What kind of pasta is your favorite
④ Who else is joining us at the restaurant

공무원 9급 공개경쟁채용 필기시험

응시번호	
성 명	

문제 책형
다

【시험과목】

과 목	영 어

응시자 주의사항

1. 시험시작 전에 시험문제를 열람하는 행위나 시험종료 후 답안을 작성하는 행위를 한 사람은 「공무원임용시험령」제51조에 의거 부정행위자로 처리됩니다.

2. 답안지 책형 표기는 시험시작 전 감독관의 지시에 따라 문제책 앞면에 인쇄된 책형을 확인한 후, **답안지 책형란의 해당 책형(1개)에 "●"와 같이 표기**하여야 합니다.

3. 답안은 반드시 문제책 표지의 **과목순서에 맞추어** 표기하여야 하며, 과목순서를 바꾸어 표기한 경우에도 문제책 표지의 과목순서대로 채점되므로 유의하시기 바랍니다.
   - 특히, **선택과목**의 경우 원서접수 시 선택한 과목이 아닌 다른 과목을 선택하여 답안을 표기하거나, 선택과목 순서를 바꾸어 표기한 경우에도 응시표에 기재된 선택과목 순서대로 채점되므로 유의하시기 바랍니다.

4. 시험이 시작되면 문제를 주의 깊게 읽은 후, 문항의 취지에 가장 적합한 하나의 정답을 고르며, 문제내용에 관한 질문을 하실 수 없습니다.

5. 답안을 잘못 표기하였을 경우에는 답안지를 교체하여 작성하거나 수정테이프만을 사용하여 수정할 수 있으며(수정액 또는 수정스티커 등은 사용 불가), 부착된 수정테이프가 떨어지지 않도록 눌러주어야 합니다.
   - 불량 수정테이프의 사용과 불완전한 수정처리로 인해 발생하는 모든 문제는 응시자 본인에게 책임이 있습니다.

6. 시험시간 관리의 책임은 응시자 본인에게 있습니다.

   ※ 문제책은 시험종료 후 가지고 갈 수 있습니다.

2024 심우철 실전 동형 모의고사 4회

심슨영어연구소

SEASON I

※ 밑줄 친 부분의 의미와 가장 가까운 것을 고르시오. [문 1. ~ 문 4.]

문 1. In many cultures, the belief in certain myths is prevalent, shaping daily practices.

① sincere
② absolute
③ constant
④ widespread

문 2. The volunteers helping others without expecting anything in return inspired admiration. And this has led to more people getting involved in meaningful activities.

① esteem
② hostility
③ gratitude
④ sympathy

문 3. During the busy workweek, Jane makes time to lay aside stress.

① sustain
② dismiss
③ tolerate
④ confront

문 4. The change in the system gave rise to much speculation within the organization.

① contradicted
② intensified
③ confirmed
④ triggered

문 5. 밑줄 친 부분에 들어갈 말로 가장 적절한 것은?

The collaborative project resulted in a fragmented final product as team members persisted in their _____ opinions.

① respective
② considerate
③ respectable
④ considerable

문 6. 밑줄 친 부분 중 어법상 옳지 않은 것은?

The word *nerd* first ① appeared in the book *If I Ran the Zoo*, ② where one of the zoo creatures ③ was called a "nerd." A 1951 Newsweek article also used the word *nerd* to refer to "a drip or a square," ④ that is closer to modern stereotypes regarding nerds.

문 7. 밑줄 친 부분이 어법상 옳지 않은 것은?

① We should have booked our tickets earlier to get better seats.
② I learned about cutting-edge technology while attending the conference.
③ By the time we reach the summit, we will have hiked for several hours.
④ The achievement of the team is something you cannot help but applauding.

문 8. 우리말을 영어로 잘못 옮긴 것은?

① 어떤 이들은 그가 예술계에서 경력을 쌓았다는 것에 놀라워한다.
→ Some find it surprised that he pursued a career in art.

② 이번 주말에 같이 요가 수업을 받는 게 어때?
→ What do you say to getting a yoga class together this weekend?

③ 가이드북은 여행객들이 그 도시의 길을 쉽게 찾도록 돕기 위해 설계되었다.
→ The guidebook is designed to help travelers navigate the city easily.

④ 운동을 통해 다져진 그녀의 몸은 스트레스에 더욱 회복력 있게 되었다.
→ Strengthened through exercise, her body became more resilient to stress.

※ 밑줄 친 부분에 들어갈 말로 가장 적절한 것을 고르시오. [문 9. ~ 문 10.]

문 9.
A: Just look at this view. I'm so glad I took a trip here. I haven't seen anything so beautiful in my life.
B: I know! We should take an extra day off from work and look around some more. What do you think?
A: Hmm. Trust me, I'd love to do that as much as you do. But that seems like an impulsive decision.
B: Okay, you're right. I was too caught up in the moment. _____

① You need to stop being so impulsive.
② The view here isn't as great as I expected.
③ I'll tell my boss I'm taking an extra day off.
④ Let's make the most of our time here, then.

문 10.
A: Hey, do you make any investments with your money?
B: Yes, I invest in stocks. How about you?
A: I'm thinking of starting stock investments as well. _____
B: Only if you invest a small portion of your income. I don't advise putting too much money into it.
A: I see. That seems like a wise way to approach stock investments.

① Do you think it's a good idea?
② How much money are you investing?
③ What other investments do you make?
④ Since when have you started stock trading?

공무원 9급 공개경쟁채용 필기시험

응시번호	
성 명	

문제책형: 다

【시험과목】

과 목	영 어

응시자 주의사항

1. 시험시작 전에 시험문제를 열람하는 행위나 시험종료 후 답안을 작성하는 행위를 한 사람은 「공무원임용시험령」 제51조에 의거 부정행위자로 처리됩니다.

2. 답안지 책형 표기는 시험시작 전 감독관의 지시에 따라 문제책 앞면에 인쇄된 책형을 확인한 후, 답안지 책형란의 해당 책형(1개)에 "●"와 같이 표기하여야 합니다.

3. 답안은 반드시 문제책 표지의 과목순서에 맞추어 표기하여야 하며, 과목순서를 바꾸어 표기한 경우에도 문제책 표지의 과목순서대로 채점되므로 유의하시기 바랍니다.

  - 특히, 선택과목의 경우 원서접수 시 선택한 과목이 아닌 다른 과목을 선택하여 답안을 표기하거나, 선택과목 순서를 바꾸어 표기한 경우에도 응시표에 기재된 선택과목 순서대로 채점되므로 유의하시기 바랍니다.

4. 시험이 시작되면 문제를 주의 깊게 읽은 후, 문항의 취지에 가장 적합한 하나의 정답을 고르며, 문제내용에 관한 질문을 하실 수 없습니다.

5. 답안을 잘못 표기하였을 경우에는 답안지를 교체하여 작성하거나 수정테이프만을 사용하여 수정할 수 있으며(수정액 또는 수정스티커 등은 사용 불가), 부착된 수정테이프가 떨어지지 않도록 눌러주어야 합니다.

  - 불량 수정테이프의 사용과 불완전한 수정처리로 인해 발생하는 모든 문제는 응시자 본인에게 책임이 있습니다.

6. 시험시간 관리의 책임은 응시자 본인에게 있습니다.

  ※ 문제책은 시험종료 후 가지고 갈 수 있습니다.

2024 심우철 실전 동형 모의고사 5회

심슨영어연구소

SEASON I

영 어

※ 밑줄 친 부분의 의미와 가장 가까운 것을 고르시오. [문 1. ~ 문 3.]

문 1.
> The young inventor showcased his ingenious device at the science fair, leaving judges and attendees impressed.

① striking
② intricate
③ inventive
④ convenient

문 2.
> Overreliance on single-use plastics continues to curtail the biodiversity of marine ecosystems.

① threaten
② diminish
③ sacrifice
④ devastate

문 3.
> After the celebrity appeared on a series of late-night talk shows, most of his mysteries seemed to come to light.

① become trivial
② remain unsolved
③ get a lot of attention
④ become widely known

※ 밑줄 친 부분에 들어갈 말로 가장 적절한 것을 고르시오. [문 4. ~ 문 5.]

문 4.
> Social media platforms play a vital role in preventing the _____ of online interactions by implementing measures to combat cyberbullying and the spread of harmful content, essential for fostering a safe digital environment.

① abuse
② scarcity
③ isolation
④ complexity

문 5.
> The hikers agreed to _____ each other, emphasizing the importance of safety.

① break off
② look after
③ fall behind
④ play up to

문 6. 어법상 옳은 것은?

① How busy I am, don't hesitate to ask for assistance.
② The couple are having trouble to find a reliable babysitter.
③ The black cat chasing a bird was seen to climb the tall tree.
④ He told me the Battle of Gettysburg had brought a turning point in the Civil War.

문 7. 다음 글의 내용과 일치하지 않는 것은?

> Bats don't just live in caves — they could find their way into your place of lodging. If you find a bat in your room after you wake up, you should see a medical professional as rabies can be transmitted through a bat bite. Though most bats don't have rabies, bats are the leading cause of rabies deaths in the United States. Because bat bites are small and don't cause much pain, some people neglect them. Don't make this mistake! Always seek medical advice if you've been bitten by a bat or think you may have been bitten by one. It's imperative to act right away because once a person shows any signs of the illness, rabies is almost always fatal. Bats are normally unaggressive and avoid contact with humans, but bats with rabies can bite without being provoked. So if a cave is inhabited by bats, it's best to avoid it.

① It is not common for a bat to have rabies.
② Though bat bites are small, they are very painful.
③ Being highly dangerous, rabies must be treated instantly.
④ Bats that don't have rabies generally don't attack humans.

문 8. 밑줄 친 부분 중 어법상 옳지 않은 것은?

> The first dinosaur fossils with structures that could be considered ① as feathers were found in the 1990s. Other discoveries ② followed. By 2011 some studies were even suggesting that all dinosaurs had some type of feathery covering on at least some parts of their bodies — in much the same way ③ which all mammals have hair but not all mammals are hairy. ④ Despite the first dinosaurs being thought to have emerged some 245 million years ago, dinosaurs with feathers have been dated to only 180 million years ago.

문 9. 다음 글의 제목으로 가장 적절한 것은?

> The devil's advocate technique is a critical thinking approach where someone deliberately takes on an opposing viewpoint to challenge and question prevailing opinions within a group. Its origin lies in the practice of the Roman Catholic Church when considering a candidate for sainthood. Understandably, the Church doesn't want to make a mistake. They don't want to learn later that the candidate behaved in ways that were not saintly. Thus, in 1587, they introduced a practice of exploring everything negative about the candidate, which was what the devil's advocate was assigned to do. His job was to find any evidence that would cast doubt on the candidate's holiness by questioning witnesses, scrutinizing documents, and uncovering potential flaws. By employing the devil's advocate, the Church aimed to ensure that only truly deserving individuals were declared saints.

① The Origin of the Devil's Advocate Technique
② Does the Devil's Advocate Technique Really Work?
③ How the Church Eliminated the Devil's Advocate Practice
④ The Controversy over Who Should Play the Devil's Advocate

공무원 9급 공개경쟁채용 필기시험

응시번호

성 명

문제책형 ⓒ

【시험과목】

| 과 목 | 영 어 |

응시자 주의사항

1. 시험시작 전에 시험문제를 열람하는 행위나 시험종료 후 답안을 작성하는 행위를 한 사람은 「공무원임용시험령」 제51조에 의거 부정행위자로 처리됩니다.

2. 답안지 책형 표기는 시험시작 전 감독관의 지시에 따라 문제책 앞면에 인쇄된 책형을 확인한 후, 답안지 책형란의 해당 책형(1개)에 "●"와 같이 표기하여야 합니다.

3. 답안은 반드시 문제책 표지의 **과목순서에 맞추어** 표기하여야 하며, 과목순서를 바꾸어 표기한 경우에도 문제책 표지의 과목순서대로 채점되므로 유의하시기 바랍니다.
   - 특히, **선택과목**의 경우 원서접수 시 선택한 과목이 아닌 다른 과목을 선택하여 답안을 표기하거나, 선택 과목 순서를 바꾸어 표기한 경우에도 응시표에 기재된 선택과목 순서대로 채점되므로 유의하시기 바랍니다.

4. 시험이 시작되면 문제를 주의 깊게 읽은 후, 문항의 취지에 가장 적합한 하나의 정답을 고르며, 문제내용에 관한 질문을 하실 수 없습니다.

5. 답안을 잘못 표기하였을 경우에는 답안지를 교체하여 작성하거나 수정테이프만을 사용하여 수정할 수 있으며(수정액 또는 수정스티커 등은 사용 불가), 부착된 수정테이프가 떨어지지 않도록 눌러주어야 합니다.
   - 불량 수정테이프의 사용과 불완전한 수정처리로 인해 발생하는 모든 문제는 응시자 본인에게 책임이 있습니다.

6. 시험시간 관리의 책임은 응시자 본인에게 있습니다.

※ 문제책은 시험종료 후 가지고 갈 수 있습니다.

2024 심우철 실전 동형 모의고사 6회

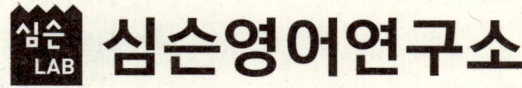

SEASON I

※ 밑줄 친 부분의 의미와 가장 가까운 것을 고르시오. [문 1. ~ 문 3.]

문 1.
Most subordinate tasks were assigned efficiently to team members, maximizing productivity in the workplace.

① secondary
② appropriate
③ independent
④ sophisticated

문 2.
The indigenous communities are actively engaging in preserving and promoting their precious heritage.

① ritual
② legacy
③ integrity
④ commodity

문 3.
Successful project management requires teams to take into account potential risks in multiple ways.

① become aware of
② previously remove
③ be ready to suffer
④ think carefully about

※ 밑줄 친 부분에 들어갈 말로 가장 적절한 것을 고르시오. [문 4. ~ 문 5.]

문 4.
The COVID-19 pandemic led to _____ job losses, which means that a lot of businesses were forced to close or reduce operations. Even employees of companies that were originally large and stable could not avoid layoffs.

① precise
② inevitable
③ distinctive
④ confidential

문 5.
To promote a balanced lifestyle, you should _____ unhealthy habits.

① hold on
② hold by
③ keep up with
④ keep away from

문 6. 어법상 옳은 것은?

① His speech is often thought as a powerful message of inspiration.
② The more goals you set, the more motivated you'll be to achieve them.
③ The theory requiring vast statistical analyses are likely to be proven credible.
④ The director encouraged the actors to rise their voices during the performance.

문 7. Arnold Schwarzenegger에 관한 다음 글의 내용과 일치하지 않는 것은?

Arnold Schwarzenegger's political career began in 2003 when he ran for the Governor of California and won a seat in a special election, marking a remarkable transition from Hollywood to public service. Despite lacking prior political experience, Schwarzenegger brought his charisma to the forefront and demonstrated his competence in managing the responsibilities of public office. He successfully implemented measures to improve California's economic situation by working to bridge political parties and emphasize cooperation. He's also notable for his efforts to address environmental issues, including the passage of the Global Warming Solutions Act. As a result, he was able to secure an easy win in the 2006 reelection.

① His experience in politics contributed to his win in the 2003 election.
② He tackled California's economic issues by promoting cooperation.
③ He dedicated efforts to confronting environmental issues.
④ He faced little difficulty in winning the 2006 reelection.

문 8. 밑줄 친 부분 중 어법상 옳지 않은 것은?

On November 29, 1947, the UN voted to partition the British mandate of Palestine into a Jewish state and an Arab state, ① which immediately caused clashes between Jews and Arabs in Palestine. As British troops prepared to withdraw from Palestine, conflict continued to escalate. Among the most infamous events ② were the attack on the Arab village on April 9, 1948. The news of a massacre there spread ③ widely and inspired both panic and revenge. Days later, Arab forces attacked a Jewish convoy ④ approaching a hospital, killing 78.

문 9. 다음 글의 제목으로 가장 적절한 것은?

The reason the human race has been so successful is not because we're the strongest animals — far from it. Size and might alone do not guarantee success. We've succeeded as a species because of our ability to form groups that share a common set of values and beliefs. And when we share values and beliefs with others, we form trust. In these trust circles, we rely on others to help protect our children and ensure our personal survival. The ability, for example, to leave the den to hunt or explore with confidence that the community would protect your family until you returned was one of the most important factors in the survival of our species. Through mutual trust, we pool our resources, keep each other safe, and take on challenges that we could not deal with on our own. It is through trust that we create a network of support for the betterment of all.

① Diverse Aspects of World Cultures
② How to Earn Trust from Other People
③ Wisdom Beats Strength in Survival Games
④ Power of Human Prosperity: Trust in Others

공무원 9급 공개경쟁채용 필기시험

응시번호

성 명

문제책형
ⓒ

【시험과목】

| 과 목 | 영 어 |

응시자 주의사항

1. 시험시작 전에 시험문제를 열람하는 행위나 시험종료 후 답안을 작성하는 행위를 한 사람은 「공무원임용시험령」 제51조에 의거 **부정행위자**로 처리됩니다.

2. 답안지 책형 표기는 시험시작 전 감독관의 지시에 따라 문제책 앞면에 인쇄된 책형을 확인한 후, **답안지 책형란의 해당 책형(1개)**에 "●"와 같이 표기하여야 합니다.

3. 답안은 반드시 문제책 표지의 **과목순서**에 맞추어 표기하여야 하며, 과목순서를 바꾸어 표기한 경우에도 문제책 표지의 과목순서대로 채점되므로 유의하시기 바랍니다.

 - 특히, 선택과목의 경우 원서접수 시 선택한 과목이 아닌 다른 과목을 선택하여 답안을 표기하거나, 선택과목 순서를 바꾸어 표기한 경우에도 응시표에 기재된 선택과목 순서대로 채점되므로 유의하시기 바랍니다.

4. 시험이 시작되면 문제를 주의 깊게 읽은 후, 문항의 취지에 가장 적합한 하나의 정답을 고르며, 문제내용에 관한 질문을 하실 수 없습니다.

5. 답안을 잘못 표기하였을 경우에는 답안지를 교체하여 작성하거나 **수정테이프만**을 사용하여 수정할 수 있으며(수정액 또는 수정스티커 등은 사용 불가), 부착된 수정테이프가 떨어지지 않도록 눌러주어야 합니다.

 - 불량 수정테이프의 사용과 불완전한 수정처리로 인해 발생하는 모든 문제는 응시자 본인에게 책임이 있습니다.

6. 시험시간 관리의 책임은 응시자 본인에게 있습니다.

 ※ 문제책은 시험종료 후 가지고 갈 수 있습니다.

2024 심우철 실전 동형 모의고사 7회

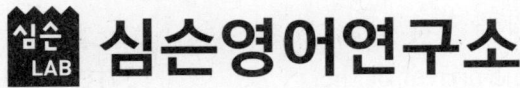
심슨영어연구소

SEASON I

※ 밑줄 친 부분의 의미와 가장 가까운 것을 고르시오. [문 1. ~ 문 3.]

문 1.
The architects considered how to confine the modern elements within the historical structure.

① reflect ② remove
③ restrict ④ embrace

문 2.
The new policy is highly adverse to the interests of the workers.

① inferior ② advantageous
③ opposed ④ corresponding

문 3.
The ecosystem is on the verge of collapse, requiring conservation efforts.

① owing to ② at the point of
③ relating to ④ in the event of

문 4. 밑줄 친 부분에 들어갈 말로 가장 적절한 것은?

The chef was careful not to _____ all ingredients before the reserved guests arrived.

① use up ② stand by
③ stick to ④ make out

※ 어법상 옳지 않은 것을 고르시오. [문 5. ~ 문 6.]

문 5. ① The city has widely known for its iconic landmarks.
② Scarcely had he entered the hall when everyone got silent.
③ Each of the volunteers is expected to follow the guidelines.
④ The streets crowded with visitors during the annual festival are lively.

문 6. ① She found joy in that others perceived as a boring job.
② The program aims to provide the elderly with social activities.
③ So shocked were they by the news that they couldn't believe it.
④ Predicting when a pandemic will end requires constant analysis.

※ 우리말을 영어로 잘못 옮긴 것을 고르시오. [문 7. ~ 문 8.]

문 7. ① 그들이 결혼한 지 10년이 되었다.
→ It is ten years since they got married.
② 그는 오류가 생기지 않도록 계산을 두 번 확인했다.
→ He checked the calculations twice lest there be an error.
③ 나는 그 웹 사이트에서 보여주는 업데이트된 메뉴를 자주 확인한다.
→ I frequently check the updated menu displaying on the website.
④ 우리는 행사를 준비한 후, 손님들이 도착하기를 기다렸다.
→ Having organized the event, we awaited the arrival of the guests.

문 8. ① 적절한 안전 조치를 시행하는 것이 필수적이다.
→ It is essential that proper safety measures be implemented.
② 그 선수는 팬들의 관심을 유지하기 위해 때때로 그들과 대화를 나눈다.
→ The player talks to the fans now and then to keep them engaged.
③ 갑작스러운 사태 전환으로 인해 나는 신중하게 세운 계획을 변경해야 했다.
→ The sudden turn of events made me change my carefully laid plans.
④ 그곳은 다양한 액티비티를 제공했는데, 그중 대부분이 패키지에 포함되어 있었다.
→ It offered various activities, most of them were included in the package.

문 9. 두 사람의 대화 중 가장 어색한 것은?
① A: It's so hard to get through to you these days.
B: I know, I'm just so busy. Let's catch up soon.
② A: The tip you gave me is coming in handy for me.
B: Oh, I'm sorry to hear it's not working out for you.
③ A: Would you like your food for here or to go?
B: To go, please. Could you also pack in extra napkins?
④ A: Who's in charge of our next project?
B: It's up to our boss to decide but he hasn't yet.

문 10. 밑줄 친 부분에 들어갈 말로 가장 적절한 것은?

A: Ugh, my computer just crashed!
B: What? What happened?
A: I downloaded something silly from the internet which must have been a virus.
B: Oh, no. _____?
A: It's my work computer so all my work-related files were on there. This is so frustrating!
B: I feel you. But don't worry, I had a similar issue last year, and this technician worked wonders. He even recovered all of my files. Here, I'll give you his number.

① What was it that you downloaded
② Did you try restarting your computer
③ Have you tried calling someone to fix it
④ Was there anything important on your computer

문 11. 주어진 글 다음에 이어질 글의 순서로 가장 적절한 것은?

In 425 BCE, Athens was in a long and destructive war with Sparta.

(A) Some of them were morally wrong, like killing all the citizens of a conquered city, while others were strategically bad, such as launching a doomed expedition to Sicily. Athens eventually lost the war.
(B) Athens rejected this proposal and the war continued. However, as the war went on, Sparta increasingly gained the advantage, turning the game around. This was just one of many poor decisions made by Athens.
(C) During the Battle of Pylos, Athens succeeded in capturing many of Sparta's top soldiers. When Spartan leaders realized this, they asked for peace with favorable terms.

① (B) — (A) — (C) ② (B) — (C) — (A)
③ (C) — (A) — (B) ④ (C) — (B) — (A)

공무원 9급 공개경쟁채용 필기시험

응시번호	
성 명	

문제책형
Ⓒ

【시험과목】

과 목	영 어

응시자 주의사항

1. 시험시작 전에 시험문제를 열람하는 행위나 시험종료 후 답안을 작성하는 행위를 한 사람은 「공무원임용시험령」 제51조에 의거 부정행위자로 처리됩니다.

2. 답안지 책형 표기는 시험시작 전 감독관의 지시에 따라 문제책 앞면에 인쇄된 책형을 확인한 후, **답안지 책형란의 해당 책형(1개)에 "●"와 같이 표기하여야 합니다.**

3. 답안은 반드시 문제책 표지의 **과목순서에 맞추어** 표기하여야 하며, 과목순서를 바꾸어 표기한 경우에도 문제책 표지의 과목순서대로 채점되므로 유의하시기 바랍니다.
   - 특히, 선택과목의 경우 원서접수 시 선택한 과목이 아닌 다른 과목을 선택하여 답안을 표기하거나, 선택과목 순서를 바꾸어 표기한 경우에도 응시표에 기재된 선택과목 순서대로 채점되므로 유의하시기 바랍니다.

4. 시험이 시작되면 문제를 주의 깊게 읽은 후, 문항의 취지에 가장 적합한 하나의 정답을 고르며, 문제내용에 관한 질문을 하실 수 없습니다.

5. 답안을 잘못 표기하였을 경우에는 답안지를 교체하여 작성하거나 수정테이프만을 사용하여 수정할 수 있으며(수정액 또는 수정스티커 등은 사용 불가), 부착된 수정테이프가 떨어지지 않도록 눌러주어야 합니다.
   - 불량 수정테이프의 사용과 불완전한 수정처리로 인해 발생하는 모든 문제는 응시자 본인에게 책임이 있습니다.

6. 시험시간 관리의 책임은 응시자 본인에게 있습니다.

   ※ 문제책은 시험종료 후 가지고 갈 수 있습니다.

2024 심우철 실전 동형 모의고사 8회

심슨영어연구소

SEASON I

영어

※ 밑줄 친 부분의 의미와 가장 가까운 것을 고르시오. [문 1. ~ 문 3.]

문 1. In the creative writing workshop, participants focused on developing <u>coherent</u> narratives.

① novel
② central
③ consistent
④ compelling

문 2. In the park, the gardener uses organic methods to <u>nurture</u> the plants.

① rear
② exhibit
③ classify
④ protect

문 3. The application was rejected <u>on the grounds of</u> lack of experience.

① in spite of
② in place of
③ in virtue of
④ in search of

문 4. 밑줄 친 부분에 들어갈 말로 가장 적절한 것은?

We should value diversity rather than _____ those with different lifestyles.

① carry out
② depend on
③ look down on
④ come down to

※ 어법상 옳지 않은 것을 고르시오. [문 5. ~ 문 6.]

문 5. ① My parents have gone to Europe, so I'm alone now.
② Should she study abroad, she could gain valuable experiences.
③ The cake he baked is as delicious as the one from the bakery.
④ Trust your instincts to avoid taking advantage of in any situation.

문 6. ① He finally noticed the small note left on his desk.
② It takes me three hours to get to work every day.
③ The film received acclaim for its intense, humor, and sensitivity.
④ Participating in a coding class, we practiced developing applications.

※ 우리말을 영어로 잘못 옮긴 것을 고르시오. [문 7. ~ 문 8.]

문 7. ① 협업에 있어서 성공은 정직함에 달려있다.
→ Success relies on honesty when it comes to collaborating.
② 그녀는 수영 초보자임에도 불구하고 물에 빠진 아이를 구했다.
→ Beginner swimmer as she was, she saved a drowning child.
③ 나는 지난주에 들었던 강의에서 얻은 통찰을 공유할 것이다.
→ I'm going to share insights from the lecture I listened to last week.
④ 토론을 유발하는 소설을 쓴 그 작가의 영향력이 커졌다.
→ The writer whose novels spark discussions have become influential.

문 8. ① 그들은 높은 수준에서 경쟁할 수 있을 정도로 열심히 훈련했다.
→ They trained enough hard to compete at a high level.
② 그는 계속 정보를 얻도록 업계 뉴스를 읽는 것을 원칙으로 삼는다.
→ He makes a point of reading industry news to stay informed.
③ 두 후보 모두 경험이 부족하다는 비판을 받았다.
→ Both of the candidates were criticized for their lack of experience.
④ 그녀의 공연에 감동한 관객들은 앙코르를 외쳤다.
→ Touched by her performance, the audience cried out for an encore.

문 9. 두 사람의 대화 중 가장 어색한 것은?

① A: Could you help me organize these files?
   B: Yes I can, since my hands are tied at the moment.
② A: BTS raised the bar for Korean pop music.
   B: Yeah, they definitely set a new standard.
③ A: Why does your brother pick on you all the time?
   B: I think he finds it enjoyable to watch me get angry.
④ A: Would you like to see a baseball game this weekend?
   B: I'd love to, but I can't. Can I take a raincheck on that?

문 10. 밑줄 친 부분에 들어갈 말로 가장 적절한 것은?

A: I'm in trouble. My biology exam is tomorrow and I haven't even started studying yet.
B: What? Didn't you have plenty of time?
A: Yeah, but you know, I have a habit of cramming for tests.
B: You should really plan out your studies next time.
A: _____

① No, I didn't get a good grade on the exam.
② You're right. There's no need to break my habit.
③ Yeah, I'm seeing the importance of that right now.
④ I beg to differ. I'll make sure to follow your advice.

문 11. 주어진 글 다음에 이어질 글의 순서로 알맞은 것은?

Dan Ariely, an MIT professor of psychology, used self-imposed restriction and rewards in his own life to rid himself of hepatitis C.

(A) To ensure he'd withstand these side effects and go through with the treatment, Ariely, a movie lover, allowed himself to watch an unlimited number of movies on the days of his injections, only after he had taken the dose.
(B) That way, he made a full recovery, and, in fact, was the only patient to stick to the treatment plan. Introducing a positive association with the injection allowed him to tolerate short-term agony to achieve long-term health.
(C) To treat himself, Ariely had to inject himself three days a week with Interferon, a drug known for its extreme side effects, including fever, vomiting, nausea, and headaches.

※ hepatitis: 간염

① (A) ― (C) ― (B)
② (B) ― (A) ― (C)
③ (C) ― (A) ― (B)
④ (C) ― (B) ― (A)

문 12. 주어진 문장이 들어갈 위치로 가장 적절한 곳은?

But the Pluto/planet link cannot be rapidly erased and will likely remain deep-rooted in my brain circuits for the rest of my life.

One day in 2006 I was informed that some powerful people had decided that Pluto was no longer a planet. (①) After a lifetime of being told that Pluto was a planet, my brain had created strong links between the neural representation of "planets" and the celestial object "Pluto." (②) But now I was being told that this link was incorrect. Unfortunately, the brain is well-designed to form new links between concepts, but the converse is not true: there is no specific mechanism for "unlinking." (③) Of course, my brain may adjust to the new turn of events by creating new links between "Pluto" and "not a planet." (④) And there may come a day late in my life in which I will return to my first belief and insist to my grandchildren that Pluto is a planet.

문 13. 다음 글의 제목으로 가장 적절한 것은?

Juries are a big deal in the legal world. They force lawyers and judges to break down the law so that ordinary people can understand it. If we didn't have juries, the legal people in the courtroom might talk in confusing ways. That would make it hard for people on trial to understand what they're being accused of and how the trial works. Although jurors aren't legal experts, they bring a down-to-earth viewpoint that expert panels may lack. This prevents the legal proceeding from being overly technical and ensures a more balanced setting. So juries are there to provide different points of view. They help keep the law clear and fair. With juries, we get a mix of perspectives that keeps things in check and makes sure everyone gets a fair shot.

※ juror: (한 사람의) 배심원

① Benefits and Drawbacks of Incorporating Juries
② Why Juries Exist: Their Role in the Legal System
③ How to Resolve Conflicts between Different Jurors
④ Common Problems Found during the Trial Process

문 14. 글의 흐름상 가장 어색한 문장은?

A strategic alliance, the newest form of international business structure, is a partnership formed between two or more organizations to create competitive advantage on a worldwide basis. ① The number of strategic alliances is growing at an estimated rate of about 20 percent per year. ② In fact, in the automobile and computer industries, strategic alliances are becoming the predominant means of competing. Why is this happening? ③ International competition is so fierce and the costs of competing on a global basis are so high that few firms have all the resources needed to do it alone. ④ Increasing international competition makes creativity more important than ever in the battle for technological leadership. Thus, individual firms that lack the internal resources essential for international success may seek to collaborate with other companies to gain a competitive edge.

※ 다음 글의 내용과 일치하지 않는 것을 고르시오. [문 15. ~ 문 16.]

문 15.

Soviet astronaut Valentina Tereshkova was born on March 6, 1937, in Russia. She started school at eight and left school at sixteen, but continued her education through correspondence courses while working. Since a young age, she developed skills in parachute jumping, which eventually led to her selection as an astronaut. In 1962, she was recruited into a space program and selected for spaceflight training with four other candidates. Tereshkova was the sole individual to complete that training. On June 16, 1963, Tereshkova made history as the first woman to fly in space when she was launched aboard Vostok 6. In this historic 70.8-hour flight, she orbited Earth 48 times. Her achievement earned her the title "Hero of the Soviet Union." Although she never went to space again, Tereshkova became a Soviet spokesperson, and received the United Nations Gold Medal of Peace while in office.

① 젊은 시절에 Tereshkova는 일하면서도 학업을 계속하였다.
② 1962년에 Tereshkova는 우주 비행 훈련에 혼자 선발되었다.
③ Tereshkova는 1963년에 우주 비행을 한 최초의 여성이 되었다.
④ Tereshkova는 첫 우주 비행 이후로 다시는 우주에 가지 않았다.

문 16.

Austria has a relatively low youth criminal rate compared to other European countries, and the rate is declining according to Austrian crime statistics. However, what's concerning is the increasing brutality displayed by these young perpetrators: "today, they don't stop when the other one starts bleeding," researchers reported. One contributing factor to the rising brutality is the involvement of a significant proportion of young offenders in substance abuse, which often acts as a pathway to further criminal behavior. However, despite the urgency of the problem, the authorities including the police, prosecutor's office, youth welfare offices, and family courts, seem to pass the responsibility of dealing with these young offenders back and forth. This is creating a fragmented framework for handling youth offenders, hindering any viable solutions.

① The criminal rate of Austrian youths is decreasing.
② The level of violence young Austrian offenders show is intensifying.
③ Increasing brutality of youth criminals is linked to substance abuse.
④ Austrian authorities are effectively dealing with youth criminal issues.

문 17. 다음 글의 요지로 가장 적절한 것은?

It is widely believed that by 2030, up to two-thirds of the world's countries will face severe water shortages, leading to water stress. Water is a scarce resource, and its mismanagement can lead to conflict between nations that share the same river. To address water issues, countries must work together to share data, knowledge, and best practices, and to establish treaties and agreements to allocate water resources equitably and sustainably. International organizations such as the United Nations and the World Bank can play a critical role in facilitating this cooperation by providing funding, technical assistance, and policy guidance. By working together, nations can ensure that all people have access to clean water and that water resources are used efficiently and effectively to promote economic growth and environmental sustainability.

① Conflict over water is increasingly pulling nations apart.
② International cooperation is needed to solve water problems.
③ Water shortage will worsen the economies of developing nations.
④ International organizations should have ownership of water resources.

문 18. (A)와 (B)에 들어갈 말로 가장 적절한 것은?

Polycarbonate is a transparent plastic material invented in 1898 which wasn't commercialized until 1953. It is prized for its tough, shatter-resistant strength and its resistance to heat and flame.   (A) , polycarbonate is a safer choice than glass and other plastics, making it ideal for a wide range of products from baby bottles to Blu-ray disks. About one billion kilograms of polycarbonate are produced annually.   (B) , although polycarbonate is not likely to shatter and physically harm users of these products, it is less clear whether the plastic might chemically harm them. Polycarbonate can contain traces of bisphenol A (BPA), a harmful chemical, from the manufacturing process and can release that BPA as the plastic ages or is exposed to heat, cleansers, or other substances.

	(A)	(B)
①	As a result	Yet
②	Therefore	Thus
③	Nevertheless	Likewise
④	By contrast	Instead

※ 밑줄 친 부분에 들어갈 말로 가장 적절한 것을 고르시오. [문 19. ~ 문 20.]

문 19.

In a recent book entitled *Scarcity*, Sendhil Mullainathan, an economist from Harvard University, and Eldar Shafir, a psychologist from Princeton University, detail what they refer to as the 'scarcity mindset.' When people experience resource pressures, whether they're short of money, time, friends or food, they tend to automatically focus their attention on making the most effective use of the resources they already have. While this focus may increase productivity and efficiency, it also comes at the cost of what they refer to as 'tunnelling.' That is, the tendency for people in a scarcity mindset to miss out on important peripheral details in their decision-making. In an effort to only give full consideration to that which is in the tunnel — and therefore to what appears to be the most pressing concern — they no longer attend to other, broader factors. Understood in this way, scarcity serves to _____.

① reduce trust
② identify details
③ narrow attention
④ sacrifice efficiency

문 20.

If you believe in an afterlife, you have less reason to fear your own death than if you don't — provided, of course, that the afterlife is likely to be a pleasant one and not eternal damnation. For those who believe in an afterlife, death is not the end of everything. However, Greek philosopher Epicurus argued that those who don't believe in an afterlife and consider death as completely final also have no reason to fear death. According to Epicurus, fear of death arises from imagining that we will be there after our deaths to mourn our own loss. But when we are alive, death is absent; and when we are dead, we no longer exist to be harmed. So either we are alive, and death isn't harming us; or we are dead, and then there is nothing to be harmed. Furthermore, he argued, we don't worry about the eternity of our nonexistence before birth, so we shouldn't worry in the least about it after death. His conclusion was that fear of death is _____.

① harmless
② universal
③ irrational
④ beneficial

문 12. 주어진 문장이 들어갈 위치로 가장 적절한 곳은?

If you are clearly of a higher status than they are, they will conceal their envy by appearing to admire your success.

As social animals we humans are very sensitive to our rank and position within any group. (①) We constantly measure our status by monitoring differences and comparing ourselves with others. (②) And for some people, status is more than a way of measuring social position — it is the most important determinant of their self-worth. (③) These people will try to measure their status against yours by asking about how much money you make, whether you own your home, and all of the other little things that can be used as points of comparison. (④) In contrast, if they sense a potential rivalry, they will attack you in secret and dishonest ways, trying to undermine your position within the group.

문 13. 다음 글의 제목으로 가장 적절한 것은?

In the historical past, children were ill-treated and often regarded as the property of their parents. In Roman times, the father had the absolute power of life and death over his children. As possessions of their father, children were left unprotected by the law, subject to the practice of maltreatment. In medieval and early modern Europe, although conditions for children were not so severe, the property concept continued to apply. Parents still had almost unlimited power over their children, and children remained subject to abandonment and abuse. Even in the 17th and 18th centuries, children still had the status of property. They could be cared for in a relatively humane way by their parents, but they were typically seen as parental possessions and the private domain of their parents.

① The Definition and Elements of Possession in Law
② The Advancement of Parental Rights over Children
③ Kids in Ancient Times: A Source of Family Support
④ Children as Property: A Prevalent Notion in the Past

문 14. 글의 흐름상 가장 어색한 문장은?

The universe contains immense amounts of water. In our solar system alone, the interiors of many planets and moons have enormous quantities of water. ① Mars has ice caps on its poles, just like Earth, as well as belts of glaciers in its southern and northern latitudes. ② The moons of Saturn and Jupiter also have oceans beneath their icy surfaces. ③ The radar reflections observed on the icy moons of Jupiter and Saturn exhibit unique characteristics that could potentially suggest the existence of extraterrestrial life. ④ But what makes Earth's water unique is that it exists in a glorious liquid state between ice and vapor, and it's not too salty or too acidic or too alkaline. And we have a lot of it. The Earth's oceans cover about 70 percent of the surface of our planet. Without this vast reserve of water, life as we know it would not exist.

※ alkaline: 알칼리성의

※ 다음 글의 내용과 일치하지 않는 것을 고르시오. [문 15. ~ 문 16.]

문 15.

For decades, India suffered from what was called the "Hindu rate of economic growth" which was a little more than 1 percent per capita. But this slow rate of economic growth turned out to owe less to Hindu culture than to imported British socialist economic planning. After independence in 1947, India followed an inward-looking policy focused on heavy industry. Then, after market-oriented reforms in the 1990s, the pattern changed and growth rates rose to 7 percent, with projections of double-digit rates in the future. British columnist Martin Wolf calls India a "premature superpower," saying that the Indian economy will be bigger than Britain's in a decade and bigger than Japan's in two. That India has an emerging middle class of several hundred million, and that English is an official language spoken by some 50-100 million people position India to play a major role in global markets.

① 힌두 경제 성장률은 주로 영국의 사회주의 경제 계획에서 비롯되었다.
② 인도는 독립 이후에 중공업 중심의 산업 구조로부터 탈피하였다.
③ 1990년대 시장 중심의 개혁 이후 인도의 경제 성장률이 높아졌다.
④ 많은 신흥 중산층 인구는 세계 시장에서 인도에 이점이 된다.

문 16.

Learning plays a large part in making honeybees such efficient foragers. When honeybees find a profitable flower patch, they learn the location so they can find it again. Other honeybees can also learn the location from the dances of recently returned foragers. As some flower species are better sources of nectar, they pay special attention to learning the shape, colour, and scent of those flowers. They even learn the optimal time of day to visit particular flower patches. Learning is rapid and accurate: in the first five seconds of a nectar sip, the bee learns to accurately associate the nectar reward with the features of the flower. This association is remembered for days, and, if the learning is repeated, the association will influence the bee's choices for the rest of its three-week-long life of foraging.

① Honeybee dances provide information to other bees.
② Honeybees learn the best time to visit specific flowers.
③ The nectar-flower link is inexact when made in a few seconds.
④ Associations honeybees learn can last for days and even weeks.

문 17. 다음 글의 요지로 가장 적절한 것은?

Intelligence is often seen as a critical factor in determining one's success in life. It is generally assumed that those with high IQs are destined for greatness and are more likely to achieve great things in their careers. However, intelligence alone is no guarantee of success. While a high IQ may give individuals an advantage in certain areas, it does not necessarily translate into exceptional skills or accomplishments. In fact, many individuals with high IQs may not necessarily be considered gifted, as there are other factors that contribute to success, such as creativity, determination, and hard work. Therefore, it is important to recognize that intelligence is only one piece of the puzzle, and that other qualities are equally important in achieving success in life. In the end, it is the combination of intelligence, hard work, and personal qualities that determines an individual's success in life, not just their IQ.

① IQ can be increased by persistent repetition and training.
② Intelligence is not the only factor that determines success.
③ Success in life is meaningless if it is gained without effort.
④ Intelligence is mostly determined in childhood and fixed thereafter.

문 18. (A)와 (B)에 들어갈 말로 가장 적절한 것은?

Stress is often very helpful. The classic stress response mobilizes energy to your muscles by increasing your heart rate, blood pressure, and breathing. High stress also helps your sensory system. __(A)__, policemen report that during shoot-outs their visual acuity and focus improves, leading the mind to focus intently on the task at hand for a short burst. This reaction is valuable in extraordinary circumstances. Stress has an adverse effect, __(B)__, if it is constant. Unfortunately, most human stress comes from the chronic, emotional strains of job deadlines, financial worries, and relationship issues. These kinds of ongoing stress pose health risks overtime. While mobilizing your body to respond to a short-term threat is an amazing feat, the same response is detrimental to your health if it is always on.

	(A)	(B)
①	For example	however
②	For example	therefore
③	Instead	furthermore
④	Instead	conversely

※ 밑줄 친 부분에 들어갈 말로 가장 적절한 것을 고르시오. [문 19.~문 20.]

문 19.

Most mothers would say that being a good mother is extremely important to them; most mothers believe they act in the best interests of their children, at least most of the time. Yet, sometimes as hard as they try to do right by their kids, bad things happen; sometimes they say or do things that hurt the very kids they so desperately love; sometimes they get uncontrollably angry with their kids and they behave badly. So often, thus, they feel burdened by the weight of guilt over their mothering. Even the best moms — those gracious, calm magicians, perfectly dressed, bringing home-baked brownies and clean-faced toddlers to their older child's school events in between their jobs — have feelings of regret about some aspects of their mothering. Indeed, it seems that _____.

① moms benefit from emotional space when angry
② guilt is an inseparable companion of motherhood
③ every child feels some guilt towards their mother
④ juggling between career and parenting is inevitable

문 20.

Great evolution can be achieved in the face of tremendous constraints, and one of the best examples of this is the vertebrate wing. Wings have been invented in many separate lineages. The wings of bats, birds, and pterosaurs all evolved separately and therefore have big structural differences. However, in all of those cases, the wing evolved from a forelimb. Those animals lost many uses of their forelimbs in order to get wings. Neither birds nor bats can grasp things very well; they have to use their feet and mouths to manipulate objects, which is obviously uncomfortable. It would have been far better for those animals to grow wholly new wings while retaining their forelimbs, but evolution rarely works that way. For an animal with a complex body plan, the option was to slowly reshape existing limbs. In light of this, a conclusion can be drawn that evolution is a constant game of _____.

※ vertebrate: 척추동물

① defense
② probability
③ compromise
④ accumulation

문 10. 다음 글의 흐름상 가장 어색한 문장은?

Many runners, believing that arm movements help propel them forward, use rather expansive arm swings while running. Scientific research convincingly shows that this is not a good strategy. ① Swinging the arms in big movements like across the front of the body is energy-consuming and inefficient. ② Faster, more economical runners actually tend to have less arm movement than slower runners. ③ It is common for runners to find it challenging to alter their established running form during a run. ④ Quick, *little* arm movements carried out in synchrony with the swings of the legs appear to be the ones that produce the most economical running. The key to efficient running lies in minimal, not maximal, arm movements.

※ 밑줄 친 부분에 들어갈 말로 가장 적절한 것을 고르시오. [문 11. ~ 문 12.]

문 11.
A: Good evening, this is Shim's Steakhouse.
B: Hi, I'd like to book a table for four people for Saturday evening.
A: I'm sorry, but all tables are fully booked during that time as of now.
B: Oh, that's a shame. _____
A: Sure, absolutely. We tend to have a few cancellations on Saturday evenings, so I'll give you a call as soon as a table becomes available.

① How would you like your steak?
② Which times are available that evening?
③ Could you put me on the waiting list then?
④ Would it be okay if I cancel my reservation?

문 12.
A: Are you coming to the class reunion this Friday?
B: _____
A: What's making you hesitate?
B: Well, it could be fun but I haven't been in touch with a lot of people after graduating. It'll probably be really awkward for me.
A: Hey, you have me, right? And I have no doubt you'll be able to mingle easily. You won't regret coming.
B: Hmm. Okay, but promise you'll stick with me.

① Count me in.
② I'm on the fence.
③ I'd like to make a toast.
④ I'm planning to show up.

※ 우리말을 영어로 잘못 옮긴 것을 고르시오. [문 13. ~ 문 14.]

문 13. ① 당신의 부주의가 하마터면 재앙을 불러올 뻔했다.
→ Your carelessness came near to causing a disaster.
② 그 팀은 소프트웨어 개발 프로젝트를 완수하려고 노력했다.
→ The team tried to get the software development project completed.
③ 이 걸작들을 그린 예술가가 전시회를 열고 있다.
→ The artist who painted these masterpieces is holding an exhibition.
④ 그 회사는 확장되었을 뿐만 아니라, 공로로 상을 타기도 했다.
→ Not only has the firm expanded, but it has also awarded for its contribution.

문 14. ① 한 소년이 던진 공이 호수에 떨어졌다.
→ The ball thrown by a boy landed in the lake.
② 내가 정보를 찾은 웹 사이트는 평판이 좋다.
→ The website on which I found the information is reputable.
③ 만약 내가 결과를 알았다면 그런 위험을 감수하지 않았을 것이다.
→ If I had known the results, I wouldn't have taken such a risk.
④ 그들이 인터넷에서 보는 모든 것을 믿는 것은 어리석은 짓이다.
→ It's stupid for them to believe everything they look at on the internet.

문 15. 밑줄 친 (A), (B)에 들어갈 말로 가장 적절한 것은?

Cancer is a major cause of human deaths worldwide. Most cancers generally follow an exponential increase with age, being prevalent mostly during the post-reproductive period of the lifespan. Thus, aging is the most straightforward risk factor for cancer. __(A)__, some specific types of cancer disobey this pattern. The incidence of testicular cancer is mostly concentrated within the reproductive portion of life, when spermatogenic cells are most active. Bone cancers also have a substantial peak of incidence during early ages when the skeleton is growing. __(B)__, the natural incidence of cancers can be significantly influenced by risk factors related to lifestyle choices. Smoking, alcohol abuse, and obesity are among the many factors linked with elevated cancer risk.

	(A)	(B)
①	However	That is
②	However	Additionally
③	For instance	Instead
④	For instance	As a result

문 16. 밑줄 친 부분에 들어갈 말로 가장 적절한 것은?

Social psychologist Stanley Milgram's groundbreaking study on obedience aimed to investigate the extent to which individuals would comply with authority figures. In his experiment, he asked participants to give electric shocks to another person, believed to be a fellow participant, whenever they answered questions incorrectly. The person receiving the shocks was actually an actor, and no real harm was inflicted. The shocks were progressively increased in intensity and the actor would react with increasing signs of distress, pleading for the experiment to stop. Many participants continued to give the shocks as instructed even when they believed the shocks could be lethal, although they reported feeling guilty and disturbed. Milgram found that approximately 65% of participants obeyed the authority figure and continued to deliver shocks until the maximum voltage. This demonstrated the power of authority to _____ personal moral beliefs and individual conscience.

① boost
② restore
③ surpass
④ combine

문 17. 다음 글의 제목으로 가장 적절한 것은?

In 1993, a major flood in Missouri caused roughly $15 billion worth of damage and fifty deaths. 10,000 homes were totally destroyed, and hundreds of towns were hit hard, with at least seventy-five towns completely under flood waters. And yet today, more than $2.2 billion worth of new development stands on that land. Why so much development in an area that was severely flooded only less than two decades ago? The federal government, both through disaster relief and by providing flood insurance, has led developers to feel comfortable building in a zone that is really unsafe. The building boom did bring jobs, services, and tax revenue to the region, which was what the government had intended. But many are concerned this could lead to more damage in future floods. Encouraging development in a flood plain is risky, but that's exactly what the federal government's actions did.

① The Outcome of Federal Efforts on Flood Prevention
② Flood Plain Development: Federal Promotion of Danger
③ Disaster Recovery as a Prescription for Economic Growth
④ How Can We Reduce Flood Risk in Development Projects?

문 18. 주어진 문장이 들어갈 위치로 가장 적절한 곳은?

Once they got the animal's attention, a researcher modeled an action — either touching the object with their nose or hand.

Dr. Fugazza and her team tested whether puppies and other young animals might imitate people's actions. They gathered 42 puppies, 39 kittens and 8 young wolves, all of which lived with human families. (①) In each test, the researchers showed an animal an object. (②) Then, the scientists watched whether the animal copied it. (③) It often took a while to get the attention of kittens and young wolves, Fugazza says. (④) But "the dog puppies were immediately looking at the human even before we started to call their attention." After showing the actions, cats rarely mimicked what humans did. Wolves sometimes copied, but the dogs were much more reliable.

문 19. 다음 글의 요지로 가장 적절한 것은?

Receiving criticism, even constructive criticism, can be a difficult experience. It's natural to feel defensive or hurt when someone points out areas where we can improve. However, feeling this way can be counterproductive and prevent us from learning and growing. It's important to try to approach criticism with an open mind and a willingness to learn. Instead of reacting immediately, take some time to process the feedback and consider its validity. It may be helpful to ask clarifying questions to better understand the feedback and find solutions to the problem. Remember that healthy criticism can help you grow and learn new skills. By being open to feedback, you can be more successful in your personal and professional life.

① Accept healthy criticism as an opportunity to improve.
② Stand up for yourself when you receive unfair criticism.
③ Never hesitate to question authority if you want to grow.
④ Don't criticize anyone without offering practical solutions.

문 20. 주어진 글 다음에 이어질 글의 순서로 가장 적절한 것은?

Imagine that seven out of ten working Americans got fired tomorrow. What would they all do? It's hard to believe you'd have an economy at all if you laid off more than half the labor force.

(A) Since then, wave upon wave of new occupations have arrived — appliance repair person, food chemist, photographer, web designer — each building on previous automation. Today, the majority of us are doing jobs that no farmer from the 1800s could have imagined.

(B) But that, in slow motion, is what the industrial revolution did in the early 19th century. Two hundred years ago, 70 percent of American workers were farmers. Today automation has eliminated all but 1 percent of their jobs, replacing them with machines.

(C) But the displaced workers did not sit idle. They found new jobs in factories that manufactured farm equipment, cars, and other industrial products as automation created hundreds of millions of jobs in entirely new fields.

① (B) — (A) — (C) ② (B) — (C) — (A)
③ (C) — (A) — (B) ④ (C) — (B) — (A)

문 10. 다음 글의 흐름상 가장 어색한 문장은?

Bonding is so good for us that the most reliable way to extend one's life expectancy is to marry and stay married. The flip side is the risk we run after losing a partner. ① The death of a spouse often leads to despair and a reduced will to live, which can trigger social isolation and depressive symptoms. ② It can also leave a physical vulnerability, including a statistically higher risk of developing diseases like heart complications or cancer. ③ It is actually known that mortality remains elevated for about half a year following a spouse's death. ④ In coping with the death of a spouse, it is important to lean on others for support, whether they are family, friends, or counselors. It is worse for younger than older people, and worse for men than women.

※ 밑줄 친 부분에 들어갈 말로 가장 적절한 것을 고르시오. [문 11. ~ 문 12.]

문 11.
A: Rick, did you burn something in the microwave?
B: How did you know?
A: _____
B: Really? I cleaned up everything and left it open for quite a while, though.
A: You must have burnt something pretty badly. What did you burn anyway?
B: A sweet potato. I'll be more careful next time.

① Not that I know of.
② It's stinking in there.
③ The microwave works fine.
④ I microwaved it for too long.

문 12.
A: Um, Mr. Royko, I was wondering if I could transfer to a different department.
B: Oh, is there any problem?
A: I feel that I'm showing a poor performance at the sales department, and that I could contribute more elsewhere.
B: Well, it's only been 3 months since you started. No one is good at their job at first, and your performance isn't actually that bad. _____
A: Wow, I didn't expect to hear that. I will. Thank you.

① I'm glad I've been doing well in sales.
② Your performance here has been declining.
③ How about you take some time to reconsider?
④ Which department would you like to be transferred to?

※ 우리말을 영어로 잘못 옮긴 것을 고르시오. [문 13. ~ 문 14.]

문 13. ① 이제 우리가 다가오는 행사 계획을 세우기 시작할 때이다.
→ It is about time we start planning for the upcoming event.
② 현재 상황을 고려하면, 그 계획은 재고되는 것이 당연하다.
→ Given the current circumstances, the plan may well be reconsidered.
③ John은 시험 결과에 만족하지 못했고, 그의 부모님도 마찬가지였다.
→ John wasn't satisfied with the exam results, and neither were his parents.
④ 새는 날개를 엄청 빠르게 움직여 공중에 떠 있을 수 있다.
→ The bird moves its wings incredibly fast, allowing itself to float in the air.

문 14. ① 학생의 3분의 1은 도서관에서 공부하는 것을 선호한다.
→ One third of the students prefer studying in the library.
② 예산안이 부결된 이유를 제게 설명해 주실 수 있나요?
→ Can you explain to me why the budget proposal was rejected?
③ 베개에 머리를 대고 누우면 수면의 질이 향상될 수도 있다.
→ Lying with your head placing on a pillow may improve sleep quality.
④ 직무 능력 평가는 4개월마다 시행된다.
→ Employee performance evaluations are conducted every four months.

문 15. 밑줄 친 (A), (B)에 들어갈 말로 가장 적절한 것은?

Social surveys are powerful tools that offer a quick and efficient means of collecting valuable information from a sub-sample of the population. However, to do this effectively is expensive, because of the time and cost involved in drawing up sampling frames, selecting a sample and then carrying out the fieldwork. Much survey work, __(A)__, doesn't need to meet these demanding standards as it is typically done on a one-time basis by organizations that want quick snapshots of particular groups of people, such as employees or local residents. In these instances, the conclusions drawn from the survey data are often difficult to generalize. __(B)__, the results do provide basic descriptions of the people involved in the survey, which gives some indication of the prevalence of behaviours and attitudes in the particular group.

	(A)	(B)
①	however	For instance
②	however	Nevertheless
③	therefore	By contrast
④	therefore	In addition

문 16. 밑줄 친 부분에 들어갈 말로 가장 적절한 것은?

A poor farmer had a lot of moldy hay. Instead of wasting it, he tried to feed it to his cows, but the cows would rather go hungry than eat the bad-tasting grass. So the farmer mixed the moldy hay with some fresh hay and gave it to his cows. The cows simply separated the good hay from the bad and ate the good stuff. Still, the moldy hay remained. Then the farmer noticed something strange. Even though there was plenty of grass in the paddock, the cows would often be seen pushing their heads between the wires of the fence to eat the grass just outside the paddock. So the farmer left the moldy hay just outside of the fence, close enough for a cow to reach with a stretch. The moldy hay was all eaten in a couple of days. _____ hay, even when moldy, tastes sweet.

※ paddock: 울타리를 쳐 놓은 들판

① Mixed
② Wasted
③ Borrowed
④ Forbidden

문 17. 다음 글의 제목으로 가장 적절한 것은?

Drug addiction is an old problem for society, leading to crime, diminished productivity, mental illness and, more recently, to an expanding prison population. Most countries deal with the problem of drug addiction by criminalizing it. A few decades ago, 38,000 Americans were in prison for drug-related offenses. Today, it's half a million. On the face of it, that might sound like success in the War on Drugs but this mass imprisonment hasn't slowed the drug trade. This is because, for the most part, the people in jail aren't the cartel bosses, the mafia dons, or the big-time dealers. Instead, the prisoners have been locked up for possession of a small amount of drugs, usually less than two grams. They're just the users, the addicts. Simply locking them up in prison doesn't solve the problem.

① The Legal Basis for Criminalizing Drug Abuse
② How Jail Became a Major Route for Drug Trades
③ Is Imprisonment the Answer to the War on Drugs?
④ The Vicious Cycle of Drug Use and Crime: How It Works

문 18. 주어진 문장이 들어갈 위치로 가장 적절한 곳은?

In contrast, other athletes may view success purely in terms of comparisons with others; their standard for a high perception of ability and achievement is beating the opposition.

Task-involved athletes are concerned with the development of their competence and use levels of effort and task completion to assess their competence in a self-reflective manner. (①) They view ability as something that is improvable. (②) Therefore, they are satisfied if they perform at a level that extracts the best of their current ability by mastering a particular technique, increasing tactical awareness, or making personal improvements in a given skill. (③) In other words, to feel successful and competent, these athletes have to demonstrate ability superior to somebody else, regardless of personal improvements or developments that may have occurred in the process. (④) In this case, the athletes are ego-involved.

문 19. 다음 글의 요지로 가장 적절한 것은?

In today's world, we are constantly bombarded with information. With the Internet and social media at our fingertips, we have access to an infinite amount of information about anything and everything. While this may seem like a good thing, it can actually be overwhelming and lead to indecision. When we have too much information, we may feel that we need to gather more and more information before we can make a decision. This can get us stuck in a cycle of constantly researching and analyzing without actually taking action. In addition, in a state of information overload, we struggle to process and retain all the information we receive, making it difficult to prioritize information and determine what is truly relevant to our decision-making process. As a result, we may become overwhelmed with details and fail to make a clear decision.

① Information overload can lead to decision paralysis.
② It's important to check the validity of every information.
③ Access to vast amount of information facilitates learning.
④ Details should not be overlooked when making a decision.

문 20. 주어진 글 다음에 이어질 글의 순서로 가장 적절한 것은?

When people can witness the work done for them, they believe more effort is involved and see the service provider as more skilled. Furthermore, showing the process can make people prefer even "delayed" results.

(A) By doing this, they show how hard they're working for those using the site, making them wait until the search is finished. As a result, people trust *Kayak.com* to deliver a better outcome for travelers.

(B) Researchers call this observed pattern *operational transparency*. Ryan Buell and Michael Norton report in their article that the travel website *Kayak.com* is beloved in part because of this psychological principle.

(C) When searching for a holiday, the site laboriously illustrates which airline is being examined, providing visual updates of results throughout the search rather than offering an instantaneous reveal.

① (A) ― (C) ― (B) ② (B) ― (A) ― (C)
③ (B) ― (C) ― (A) ④ (C) ― (A) ― (B)

문 11. 두 사람의 대화 중 자연스럽지 않은 것은?

① A: You know, it was my birthday yesterday.
　B: Oh no, I'm sorry. It completely slipped my mind.
② A: The new employee makes so many mistakes.
　B: You should give him some slack. He's new, after all.
③ A: I heard Nicole didn't make it on the soccer team.
　B: No wonder she seemed so upset.
④ A: I am sick of having the same food for lunch every day.
　B: You should see a doctor and get some medicine.

문 12. 다음 글의 제목으로 가장 적절한 것은?

Anyone interested in the biology of trust has probably heard of the supposed magic of oxytocin, the hormone of trust, love, and basically anything that sounds warm and fuzzy. However, it is also known to have a darker side. To understand why, we need to take a look at one of its key roles — strengthening a mother's bond with her baby. If you think about it, there are two sides to this bond. She loves that baby dearly, and as a result believes the baby to be perfect and worth her undying nurturing efforts. But on the flip side, this means the mother sees her child as more perfect than any other baby and to be extremely protective. So, yes, oxytocin might increase attachment and willingness to trust those close to us, but it also might result in greater discriminatory behavior toward those we see as different. In the end, it may make us see the world in a slightly polarized way.

① The Meaning of Trust in a Polarized World
② Oxytocin: A Barrier to Maternal Bonding
③ How Oxytocin Increases Affection
④ The Two Faces of Oxytocin

문 13. 다음 글의 주제로 가장 적절한 것은?

We encounter many people in our day-to-day lives and, like many stimuli, this can sometimes lead to cognitive overload. We cope with this overload by making cognitive shortcuts that help us simplify and classify the stimuli we encounter. One such shortcut is the use of stereotypes; employing this technique probably gave us an advantage in our evolutionary past as it would have allowed us to establish very quickly who was friend (a member of our own in-group) and who was foe (a member of the out-group). Stereotypes can thus help us make sense of the world. They are a form of categorization that helps to simplify and systematize information. This makes information easier to identify, remember, predict, and respond to.

① positive aspects of using stereotypes
② ways biased information forms stereotypes
③ instances where stereotypes can be dangerous
④ inevitability of having cognitive overload in our lives

문 14. 다음 글의 요지로 가장 적절한 것은?

The ongoing global financial crisis has led some countries to consider reducing their commitment to international food aid. This has raised concerns that another food crisis could occur next year. The Director-General of the Food and Agriculture Organization of the United Nations has urged governments to continue their support for developing countries in need of external assistance due to crop failures, civil unrest, insecurity or escalating food costs. Currently, 36 countries are still in need of such assistance. Access to nutritious food is a fundamental human right; it's essential that everyone has access to adequate and healthy food, regardless of their circumstances or location. It's critical that we continue to provide food aid, as the global food crisis remains a pressing issue that cannot be overlooked.

① Conflicts within nations must end to solve the food crisis.
② Food aid should not stop despite the global financial crisis.
③ The global financial crisis is intensified by rising food costs.
④ Food aid is key in fostering positive relations among nations.

문 15. 다음 글의 내용과 일치하지 않는 것은?

Uruk is a well-studied Mesopotamian city. By 3,500 BCE, its population was around 10,000 people, which grew to a peak of 50,000. Surrounding Uruk was a massive brick wall seven meters high, its numerous gates and guard towers suggesting that Uruk was a city very conscious of defense. Monumental architecture included a prominent feature called a ziggurat, a pyramidal temple built to serve religious purposes. Commoners as well as slaves built and maintained the monumental buildings, showing the collective efforts that shaped the city's cultural and historical significance within the ancient world.

① Uruk는 인구가 최대 5만 명에 달하는 도시였다.
② Uruk 사람들은 도시를 방어하고자 하는 의식이 강했다.
③ Ziggurat는 주거 목적을 위해 세워진 기념비적인 건축물이다.
④ 노예뿐만 아니라 평민들도 기념비적인 건물을 건축하는 데 참여했다.

문 16. 다음 글의 흐름상 어색한 문장은?

Trend spotting is one popular use for data. ① Essentially, this comes down to spotting and monitoring patterns online, and using that information to predict where things might go in the future. ② In understanding and predicting trends, social media and the Internet play a large role. ③ Through social media like Instagram or blogs, we're used to sharing vast amounts of data about ourselves, our interests, habits, likes and dislikes, which companies use to spot the latest trends. ④ Before making use of any data, one must first be able to distinguish between good data and bad data. With individuals openly contributing data about their lives, companies are able to identify evolving trends and foresee future developments.

문 17. 주어진 글 다음에 이어질 글의 순서로 가장 적절한 것은?

In 1994, a young woman asked for an order of restraint against her husband and filed for divorce.

(A) It was through writing fantasies that she was able to battle through the depression and eventually turn her life around. The woman's name was Joanne, but the world would come to know her as J.K. Rowling.

(B) But they were not enough to sustain her and her child, and she was constantly under financial pressure, suffering from depression and at times even having thoughts of suicide.

(C) With no job and little money to live on, she signed up for welfare benefits so that she could afford to care for her baby.

① (A) ― (C) ― (B) ② (B) ― (A) ― (C)
③ (C) ― (A) ― (B) ④ (C) ― (B) ― (A)

문 18. 주어진 문장이 들어갈 위치로 가장 적절한 것은?

But labor economists have been pessimistic about the possibility that middle-aged adults can be effectively retrained for a new career.

In our cities, many middle-aged adults are out of the labor force — and often for prolonged periods. (①) An optimist would presume that at any given moment, such displaced workers can be retrained so they can work in a booming sector. (②) We often hear, for example, about retraining coal miners to be computer programmers. (③) Their core argument is that, as we age, most of us have less ability to reinvent ourselves and learn new skills. (④) Also, the fact that unemployment periods tend to be longer in middle-aged adults than younger groups adds to the problem because a person's inclination and ability to find a job decrease the longer the person has been unemployed.

※ 밑줄 친 부분에 들어갈 말로 가장 적절한 것을 고르시오. [문 19. ~ 문 20.]

문 19.

The estimates of others' attractiveness may change depending on the circumstances. In a study of singles bars, as closing time neared, both men and women showed increased ratings of attractiveness towards remaining individuals. Presumably, as the time deadline approached, people's freedom to decide on a possible partner was reduced and their liking for those remaining increased. This is an example of *reactance*, a response to reduced freedom of choice that leads to increased liking. This is common in marketing with advertisements such as "a one-day sale" or "supplies are limited." It is also applied in relationships where people intentionally act disinterested to avoid appearing too eager. In all of these cases, attraction toward a possible choice typically increases, as its _____ decreases.

① appeal
② reliability
③ availability
④ uniqueness

문 20.

Our respiratory system _____.
The air we breathe goes down a single tube in our throat, and then divides into many smaller branches in our lungs. These branches end in small dead-end spaces filled with air sacs that allow gas exchange across a thin membrane. When we exhale, air follows the same pathway in reverse. This breathing process is not very efficient because stale air remains in our lungs even when fresh air is taken in. The old and new air mix together and reduce the oxygen content of the air that reaches our lungs. This means that the presence of stale air in our lungs limits the amount of oxygen that can be delivered to our body. To compensate for this, we need to go through the trouble of breathing deeper, especially during times of increased oxygen demand such as during exercise.

① decreases in efficiency as we age
② is not ideally designed for breathing
③ works to maximize our body's efficiency
④ closely interacts with organs outside its system

문 11. 두 사람의 대화 중 자연스럽지 않은 것은?

① A: May I use your computer for a second?
   B: Sure, go ahead. I don't mind.
② A: What is it like to run your own business?
   B: A pet shop I've been running for three years now.
③ A: Aren't we supposed to have a meeting today?
   B: It was postponed to tomorrow, remember?
④ A: One of the flight attendants on the plane was so rude.
   B: I know who you're talking about. I want to file a complaint.

문 12. 다음 글의 제목으로 가장 적절한 것은?

The American author H. L. Mencken wrote in his book that a man is satisfied so long as he is earning more than his brother-in-law. This is because relatives are the closest individuals with whom we can compare our fortunes. Relativity also explains why people become discontented when they learn that their colleagues earn a higher salary. Industrial disputes are less about wages and more about what others in the company are earning in comparison. When we discovered what the bankers were earning during the recent financial crisis, we were outraged. But the bankers could not see the problem with their high salaries and bonuses because they were comparing themselves to other bankers who were prospering.

① Contentment Is Based on Comparison
② Comparison Makes People Work Harder
③ Always Keep Your Negative Emotions in Check
④ Salary Increases and Promotions: Why We Work

문 13. 다음 글의 주제로 가장 적절한 것은?

Prescription and over-the-counter medicines have greatly improved the treatment of many health conditions. They help relieve pain, reduce inflammation, and manage chronic diseases. However, like any other substance, medicines can be dangerous and even deadly if misused. People often take more than the recommended dose or mix different types of medicines. This behavior can lead to serious health consequences, including addiction, overdose, and even death. The negative aspect of medication misuse is not limited to illegal drugs; even the most commonly used medications, such as pain relievers, can be dangerous if misused. This concern becomes a reality when we don't take medications as prescribed by a healthcare professional.

① dangers of drug abuse
② symptoms of drug overdose
③ widespread use of illegal drugs
④ ways to avoid misusing medication

문 14. 다음 글의 요지로 가장 적절한 것은?

Defensive pessimism is a cognitive strategy used by some individuals to achieve positive outcomes by taking a seemingly negative approach. Such individuals anticipate and prepare for worst-case scenarios. By considering all possible negative outcomes, defensive pessimists create a plan to mitigate any potential damage. Defensive pessimists do not dwell on the negative thoughts; instead, they use them as a tool to prepare for any obstacles that may arise. While defensive pessimism may seem counterintuitive, it can be a valuable strategy for succeeding in challenging situations. With this mindset, people can develop effective coping mechanisms and perform better under pressure.

① Optimism can make people neglect their duties.
② Expecting the worst can lead to positive results.
③ Negative thoughts can reinforce negative emotions.
④ Challenging situations bring out one's true character.

문 15. 다음 글의 내용과 일치하지 않는 것은?

Black-footed ferrets are North America's only native ferret species. They measure 18 to 24 inches and weigh less than three pounds. Their coats are yellow-beige, adorned with distinct black markings that blend into their natural habitat. In the early 1900s, it was believed that there were up to 5 million black-footed ferrets in the United States. However, due to habitat fragmentation and the decline of prairie dogs which constitute 90% of their diet, they were considered extinct by the 1970s. Fortunately, the species was rediscovered in 1981, leading to concerted efforts by various partners to give black-footed ferrets a second chance at survival. Through initiatives such as captive breeding and habitat protection, their population has been restored to around 300 in the wild. Biologists estimate that successful recovery of this endangered species would require about 3,000 adult ferrets.

① 검은발족제비의 털은 자연 서식지 환경에 잘 녹아든다.
② 1970년대에는 검은발족제비가 멸종했다고 여겨졌다.
③ 검은발족제비는 1980년대 초에 다시 발견되었다.
④ 현재 야생에는 약 3천 마리의 검은발족제비가 있다.

문 16. 다음 글의 흐름상 어색한 문장은?

Preferences for sweets are found during infancy and childhood and peak in early adolescence. One study found that more than 40 percent of calories eaten by children came from sugar and fat. ① This preference declines in later years, which reduces their significance in food choice. ② The opposite is true for bitterness, which is strongly disliked by most children. ③ Research shows that some compounds found in bitter foods can be toxic when consumed in large amounts. ④ The ability to detect bitterness decreases with age, however, and many adults consume foods with otherwise unpleasant taste. There are some who remain especially sensitive to certain bitter compounds, in which case this tendency does not apply.

문 17. 주어진 글 다음에 이어질 글의 순서로 가장 적절한 것은?

Homages are not simply scenes that copy or plagiarize previous films. Rather, homages deliberately evoke another film in order to show respect to that film and its filmmaker.

(A) A scene strikingly similar to this where a baby's stroller rolls down the steps during a crossfire was originally famously filmed in 1925 by the influential Soviet filmmaker Sergei Eisenstein, in *Battleship Potemkin*.

(B) By recreating this famous scene, De Palma pays tribute to Eisenstein's extraordinary skill as a filmmaker capable of creating compelling images.

(C) In Brian De Palma's gangster film *The Untouchables*, there is a scene on the steps of a train station in which, during a shoot-out, a stroller containing a baby rolls down the steps coming dangerously close to the bullets.

① (B) — (A) — (C)
② (B) — (C) — (A)
③ (C) — (A) — (B)
④ (C) — (B) — (A)

문 18. 주어진 문장이 들어갈 위치로 가장 적절한 것은?

As a result, specialization emerged; farmers started focusing on their strengths, growing only specific crops and trading surplus produce for other goods.

Humans have existed for 200,000 years. During the first 99% of our history, our activities mainly revolved around survival and reproduction. (①) This was largely a response to the challenging global climactic conditions, which eventually stabilized only about 10,000 years ago. (②) Subsequently, people discovered the benefits of farming and irrigation, abandoning their nomadic lifestyle to cultivate stable crops. (③) However, not all farmlands were identical; regional differences in sunlight, soil quality, and other factors meant that certain farmers excelled in growing onions, while others thrived in cultivating apples. (④) This shift to individual crop production and surplus generation brought about the development and expansion of marketplaces and trade.

※ 밑줄 친 부분에 들어갈 말로 가장 적절한 것을 고르시오. [문 19. ~ 문 20.]

문 19.
If you aim to transform a disagreement into an opportunity for connection, it's crucial to differentiate between the past, present, and future. When disagreements revolve around what happened in the past, it's easy to get caught up in a cycle of "you said this, I said that." Focusing on what did or didn't happen in the past, or what past events led to the current situation, usually increases tension and decreases connection. A critical first step is to shift the focus to "Where are we now?" and the most important turning point comes when we focus on the road ahead. What are we trying to accomplish for the future? What are our long-term goals? What are our desires for our family, team, faith community, or industry? This _____ thinking shifts blame to a joint understanding about a shared future that we want to create together.

① cyclical
② analytical
③ progressive
④ multidimensional

문 20.
Parents often persuade their children to enter vocations upon the tiniest possible excuses. Almost every child takes a pencil and tries to draw, yet there are many parents who spend thousands of dollars in trying to make great artists of children who have only the most mediocre artistic ability. Mere purposeless drawing of faces and figures is an entirely different thing from the years of hard work necessary to become a great artist. The mere writing of little essays and stories is quite a different thing from the long, arduous training necessary to become a writer of any acceptability. Just because a child finds it more amusing to idle the hours away with a pencil or a brush than to go into the harvest field or into the kitchen doesn't mean that this preference _____.

① illustrates the parents' passion for art
② is an indication of either talent or genius
③ blocks the opportunities for physical activity
④ has little to do with the child's innate ability

※ 밑줄 친 부분에 들어갈 말로 알맞은 것을 고르시오. [문 10. ~ 문 11.]

문 10.
A: I heard someone came in for an interview yesterday.
B: Yes, I interviewed her for the senior manager position.
A: Oh, how was she?
B: She has a lot of experience in the field, and she seemed very responsible. She's definitely a candidate.
A: _____
B: Yes, I need to choose between three people. It's a very hard decision to make.

① Do you think you'll get the job?
② Who else interviewed her with you?
③ Is she the only candidate for the position?
④ Are there others you're considering as well?

문 11.
A: Did you apply for the audition for the play Macbeth?
B: No, and I don't plan to either.
A: Why not? You've been preparing so hard for it.
B: Well, I've failed at every audition I've had so far. I must be horrible at acting. There's no chance I'll make it anyway.
A: Oh, come on. _____ You need to leave the past behind. Things might turn out differently this time.

① I second that.
② Snap out of it.
③ Don't give it a shot.
④ The audition will be in vain.

문 12. 두 사람의 대화 중 자연스럽지 않은 것은?

① A: Is the date for the conference set?
   B: I'll check right now and get back to you.
② A: May I ask what you do for a living?
   B: I live just a few streets down from here.
③ A: I'm meeting up with Wendy tomorrow.
   B: Oh, you are? Tell her I say hi.
④ A: When are you going to start packing your luggage?
   B: I'll get to it eventually. There's no need to rush.

문 13. 다음 글의 제목으로 알맞은 것은?

Over the years, scientists have developed a variety of technologies and techniques for detecting lies. Topping the list are polygraph machines, often called lie detectors, which relate changes in heart rate, blood pressure and electro-dermal reactivity to a subject's truthfulness. Widely used by law enforcement agencies and businesses, however, lie detectors have increasingly come under critical scrutiny. In 2002, a National Academy of Sciences panel reviewed data from several decades of polygraphs and concluded that there was "little basis for the expectation that a polygraph test could have extremely high accuracy." In fact, the panel estimated that if polygraphs were administered to a group of 10,000 people that included 10 spies, nearly 1,600 innocent people would fail the test — and two of the spies would pass.

① Polygraphs Make Lying Powerless
② Polygraph Machines: Highly Controversial
③ Ways to Improve the Lie Detector's Accuracy
④ Characteristics of People Prone to Lie Detection

문 14. 다음 글의 주제로 알맞은 것은?

The medical community is beginning to realize how important the hospital environment is to patient recovery. Specifically, art can create a calming and positive environment in the hospital, which can reduce stress and anxiety, ultimately promoting faster healing and better overall well-being. To make hospitals more welcoming, famous artists are being asked to decorate old hospitals and modernize new ones. About 100 of the National Health Service's 2,500 hospitals have acquired collections of modern art to display in corridors and treatment rooms. The effect has been amazing, as patients have reported a noticeable improvement in their overall mood and reduction in stress levels. Incorporating art into the hospital environment has become a widely accepted method of enhancing the holistic health and well-being of patients.

① doubts about the healing power of art
② positive effects of bringing art into hospitals
③ absolute necessity of building more hospitals
④ various attempts to find places to display art

문 15. 다음 글의 요지로 알맞은 것은?

At the beginning of the semester, a ceramics instructor decided to divide her class into two groups and announced that the students on the left side of the studio would be graded on the quantity of work they produced, while the students on the right side of the studio would be graded solely on the quality of their work. The "quantity" group was required to produce fifty pounds of pots to receive an "A," forty pounds for a "B," and so on. On the other hand, the "quality" group only needed to produce one perfect pot to receive an "A." When it came time to grade, the teacher was surprised to find that the highest quality work was produced by the "quantity" group. While this group was busy producing a large number of pots and learning from the process, the "quality" group spent their time theorizing about perfection and had little chance to refine their techniques through hands-on experience.

① More does not necessarily mean better.
② The process is not justified by external results.
③ Perfection demands a detailed planning process.
④ Learning from multiple attempts breeds excellence.

문 16. 밑줄 친 부분에 들어갈 말로 알맞은 것은?

Our kids have too much stuff, too many choices, and they're exposed to too much information. Their lives are busy, and this affects their ability to pay attention. Researchers conducted an experiment to streamline the lives of children with attention deficit disorder. They made changes to their environment by reducing the number of toys, extracurricular activities, and screen time. Instead, they encouraged more opportunities for free play and daydreaming. Remarkably, in only four months, 68 percent of the children reported their problems had disappeared. Their academic skills also increased by 37 percent. This shows that children must be provided with time, with freedom, so that they can connect themselves to the real world as well as with themselves. It's a matter of _____ their lives in order to create a qualitatively better experience for them.

① planning
② simplifying
③ overseeing
④ diversifying

문 17. 다음 글의 흐름상 어색한 문장은?

It's no secret that the Internet is saturated with all kinds of information, much of which is unverified and sometimes even harmful. ① Yet, in the blink of an eye, this information circulates without confirmation. ② It is all too easy to believe the latest gossip on Twitter or get lost in YouTube videos featuring false rumors. ③ What is most concerning is that some of this baseless online information could hurt certain individuals, companies, and even entire industries. ④ However, our lives are now so intertwined with the Internet that it has become an essential resource for daily information needs. Even if such information is corrected or disproved, chances are that the audience's attention has long shifted, the damage has already been done, and the original misinformation continues to float around online for future discovery.

문 18. 주어진 문장이 들어갈 위치로 알맞은 것은?

While such tendencies can also be seen in some financial circles in Europe, art lovers and most art collectors are more hesitant.

Over the past few years, the list of record prices paid at auctions has changed ever more rapidly. The enormous prices paid for some paintings create a widespread belief that the rate of return on investments in art is in general very high. (①) Especially in the United States, an increasing number of investors believe that purchasing art provides not only aesthetic pleasure but also financial benefits. (②) American banks, and recently also auction houses, strengthen the trend of viewing art as an investment by extending credit and by hiring "art investment counsellors" thus suggesting that it is financially rewarding to buy art. (③) They warn that art objects should not be treated as financial assets. (④) Their belief is that art should be owned for its intrinsic value rather than for financial purposes.

문 19. 주어진 글 다음에 이어질 글의 순서로 알맞은 것은?

A teenager joins a line of people boarding a spaceship. Once on board, he approaches a bed, crawls in, closes the lid and falls asleep.

(A) All of these stories have one thing in common: people enter an unconscious state in which they can survive for a long time. However, nothing like this is yet possible in the real world for any organism, let alone humans.

(B) It is employed in a lot of science fiction. There's Captain America, for instance, who survived nearly 70 years frozen in ice. And Han Solo was frozen in carbonite in Star Wars.

(C) His body is frozen for a trip to a planet several light-years from Earth. A few years later he wakes up, still the same age. This ability to put his life on pause while asleep is called "suspended animation."

① (A) — (C) — (B)
② (B) — (A) — (C)
③ (C) — (A) — (B)
④ (C) — (B) — (A)

문 20. 밑줄 친 부분에 들어갈 말로 알맞은 것은?

Our perceptions about our lives are the outcome of many forces that shape experience, each having an impact on whether we feel good or bad. Most of these forces are beyond control. There is not much we can do about our looks, our temperament, or our constitution. We cannot decide — at least so far — how tall we will grow, or how smart we will get. We can choose neither parents nor time of birth, and it is not in your power or mine to decide whether there will be a war or a depression. The instructions contained in our genes, the pull of gravity, the pollen in the air, the historical period into which we are born — these and countless other conditions determine what we see, what we hear, and how we feel. It is not surprising that we should believe that our lives are primarily determined by _____.

① outside factors
② collective efforts
③ voluntary choices
④ our way of thinking

※ 밑줄 친 부분에 들어갈 말로 알맞은 것을 고르시오. [문 10. ~ 문 11.]

문 10.
A: Hey, do you know why our storage room is locked?
B: It is? That's unusual.
A: I know. Who do you think might have the key?
B: Mr. Jenson, probably. _____?
A: My mouse suddenly stopped working, so I'm looking for a spare one.
B: Oh, I see. You should ask Mr. Jenson.

① Why do you think he locked it
② Do you know where I could find him
③ Are there any spare keys lying around
④ Is there something you need from there

문 11.
A: Hello, this is Riverview Hotel. How may I help you?
B: Hi, I'd like to know if I could book the Emerald Hall for a business seminar next Monday from 2 p.m. to 5 p.m.
A: I'm afraid the hall is already booked. The Diamond Hall is available though.
B: Oh, we're expecting around 100 attendees. Will the hall be large enough?
A: _____
B: I see. I'd like to book it then, please.

① Sorry, we don't accept overnight stays.
② Yes, it's the same size as the Emerald Hall.
③ No, the hall isn't suitable for a crowd that size.
④ Yes, the topic of the seminar is to be announced.

문 12. 두 사람의 대화 중 자연스럽지 않은 것은?

① A: Mom, we're out of cereal.
   B: Oh, that reminds me I need to go grocery shopping.
② A: It's freezing in our office.
   B: Tell me about it. My hands and feet are ice-cold.
③ A: My sister went behind my back.
   B: You're lucky to have someone who supports you.
④ A: I really like the novel you recommended to me.
   B: Speaking of which, the author just released a new one.

문 13. 다음 글의 제목으로 알맞은 것은?

One of the enduring truths about human beings is that we lie — frequently and often quite casually. In fact, according to the recent claims of many psychologists, the impulse to deceive resides deep within our genes. As one scholar of deception puts it, "Lying is not exceptional; it is normal, and more often spontaneous and unconscious than cynical and coldly analytical. Our minds and bodies produce deceit." Numerous studies confirm that few people can make it through a typical day without lying. In one, subjects asked to keep diaries of their conversations reported that they told lies anywhere from 30 percent to 50 percent of the time on topics including their feelings, their actions and their plans. Some 60 percent of newly introduced individuals lie to one another within minutes simply to create a favorable impression, and dating couples apparently lie to each other even more.

① How to Break the Habit of Lying
② Lying as a Necessary Evil to Protect Others
③ Lying: The Innate, Central Trait of Humanity
④ How Lying Has Contributed to Human Evolution

문 14. 다음 글의 주제로 알맞은 것은?

Your biological clock makes you the most alert during daylight hours and the most drowsy in the early morning hours. Consequently, most people do their best work during the day. Our society that operates non-stop, however, demands that some people work at night. Nearly one-quarter of all workers work shifts that are not during the daytime, and more than two-thirds of these workers have problems with sleepiness and/or difficulty sleeping. Because their work schedules are at odds with powerful sleep-regulating cues like sunlight, night shift workers often find themselves drowsy at work. In fact, the fatigue they experience can be dangerous. Major industrial accidents — such as the Three Mile Island and Chernobyl nuclear power plant accidents and the Exxon Valdez oil spill — have been caused, in part, by mistakes made by overly tired workers on a night shift.

① reasons night shifts are increasing
② the effects and risks of working overnight
③ negative impact of job stress on sleep quality
④ possible treatment for excessive daytime sleepiness

문 15. 다음 글의 요지로 알맞은 것은?

Ideas are the spark of creativity, the starting point of something great. But without execution, they are nothing more than fleeting thoughts. Invention requires action, and it requires bringing ideas to life through hard work, dedication and perseverance. Without the will to act, ideas remain dormant and unfulfilled, lost in the endless sea of possibilities that exist in the mind. Those who have truly impacted the world have done so through a combination of creativity and execution. They have taken their ideas and brought them to life, making them tangible and real. From the wheel to the Internet, every great invention began as a simple idea that someone decided to act upon.

① Cooperation is key in turning ideas into reality.
② Great inventors adapt to changing circumstances.
③ Ideas gain meaning when they are put into action.
④ Sometimes an accidental event leads to a great invention.

문 16. 밑줄 친 부분에 들어갈 말로 알맞은 것은?

In the 1998 film *Saving Private Ryan*, director Steven Spielberg took on the epic topic of the Normandy invasion of Europe in June 1944 on D-day. The first half hour provides one of the most powerful, horrible, realistic views of battle ever created or replicated on film. And yet, as moving and convincing as the scene is, _____ abound. The German Tiger tanks of a Panzer division used against American troops in the movie were not actually there on D-day. The battle against the Nazi Panzer division in Normandy was also a mistake — the division was nowhere near Normandy at the time. The P-51 fighter planes that were shown as "tank destroyers" were, in reality, mostly used to defend other aircraft during the war. The antitank aircraft used at Normandy were actually Hawker Typhoons which were British, not American.

① misdeeds
② imitations
③ inaccuracies
④ collaborations

문 17. 다음 글의 흐름상 어색한 문장은?

Some end-of-life materials retain so much value that there are markets for their collection, separation, and reprocessing. Among them is copper, the world's most reusable resource. ① Recycled copper retains 95 percent of its value because previous use and processing involves only minor contamination. ② Nearly three-quarters of copper used in new products comes from recycled copper. ③ As a key player in renewable energy, copper is essential for the production of solar panels and wind turbines. ④ Old copper is actually so valuable and easily recycled that thieves steal copper pipe and wire from vacant houses and power stations. In fact, the US Department of Energy estimates that copper theft causes nearly $1 billion in losses to US businesses every year.

문 18. 주어진 문장이 들어갈 위치로 알맞은 것은?

However, a careful look at the history of science reveals that basic knowledge has resulted in many remarkable applications of great value.

Some individuals may perceive applied science as "useful" and basic science as "useless" as the former solves real-world problems while the latter focuses on theoretical concepts. (①) A question these people might pose to a scientist who advocates basic science would be, "What for?" (②) They claim that it is time to move on from basic science in order to find solutions to actual problems. (③) This is why many scientists maintain that basic knowledge is necessary before researchers develop an application, and that applied science therefore relies on basic science. (④) While it is true that there are problems that demand immediate attention, scientists would find few solutions without the help of the wide foundation of knowledge that basic science generates.

문 19. 주어진 글 다음에 이어질 글의 순서로 가장 적절한 것은?

The fact that the two hemispheres of the brain have different strong suits doesn't mean that they are fundamentally alien to each other.

(A) The children whose left hemispheres have been removed through the surgery initially lose their language ability. But astonishingly, in time, the right hemisphere compensates for the loss and assumes most of the language functions, leading to their recovery.

(B) When medications fail to control the seizures, the children may need surgery to have the entire affected hemisphere removed.

(C) To the contrary, a remarkable phenomenon shows that the two hemispheres are cut from the same cloth. In the case of Rasmussen's syndrome, young children with this condition have severe seizures limited to one hemisphere.

① (B) — (A) — (C)
② (B) — (C) — (A)
③ (C) — (A) — (B)
④ (C) — (B) — (A)

문 20. 밑줄 친 부분에 들어갈 말로 알맞은 것은?

Some people tend to place a great deal of value on logic and discount the importance of emotion. You can't win a debate with an emotional argument, of course, but conversation is not debate and human beings are inherently illogical. We are emotional creatures. To remove, or attempt to remove, emotion from your conversation is to extract a great deal of meaning. Imagine your friend talking about his pending divorce, and you try to comfort him by saying, "Don't feel bad. Almost half of marriages end in divorce anyway." or "One psychologist says divorce can actually improve your kids' chances at a lasting healthy relationship." In this case, you use facts to respond to emotion. They may be true, but they're completely unhelpful to your friend who is in need of emotional support. A conversation is not a college lecture course. No matter how awkward it may feel to be on the listening end of someone's heartbreak, _____ is rarely the right response.

① escaping into logic
② doubting the given facts
③ breaking off a conversation
④ making sympathetic remarks

2024년도 9급 공무원 공개경쟁채용시험 필기시험 답안지

2024년도 9급 공무원 공개경쟁채용시험 필기시험 답안지

심슨영어연구소 카페 cafe.naver.com/shimson2000

WORK BOOK

2024
심우철

실전동형
모의고사

최근 2개년 공무원 영어 시험의
유형 및 난이도를 완벽히 재현한
봉투형 모의고사 8회분

Season 1

커넥츠 공단기
인터넷 강의
gong.conects.com

STEP 1
Word review 1

01
- 001 manufacturer
- 002 urgent
- 003 identify
- 004 pressing
- 005 selective
- 006 extensive
- 007 mandatory

02
- 008 eligible
- 009 injured
- 010 qualified
- 011 disciplined
- 012 established
- 013 grant

03
- 014 let on
- 015 alter
- 016 conceal
- 017 exclude
- 018 disclose

04
- 019 yield to
- 020 proceed with
- 021 ignore
- 022 uphold
- 023 represent

- 024 surrender

05
- 025 lead up to
- 026 practically

06
- 027 available

07
- 028 design
- 029 affect

08
- 030 discrimination
- 031 segregate
- 032 devotion

09
- 033 intermittent
- 034 fast
- 035 alternate

10
- 036 spare

11
- 037 suitable

12
- 038 be out of
- 039 go behind one's back

13
- 040 impulse
- 041 deceive
- 042 spontaneous
- 043 subject
- 044 favorable

14
- 045 alert
- 046 shift

	047 ☐☐☐	fatigue	
15	048 ☐☐☐	execution	
	049 ☐☐☐	nothing more than	
	050 ☐☐☐	fleeting	
	051 ☐☐☐	dedication	
	052 ☐☐☐	tangible	
16	053 ☐☐☐	invasion	
	054 ☐☐☐	replicate	
17	055 ☐☐☐	retain	
	056 ☐☐☐	separation	
	057 ☐☐☐	vacant	
18	058 ☐☐☐	reveal	
	059 ☐☐☐	application	
19	060 ☐☐☐	alien to	
	061 ☐☐☐	astonishingly	
	062 ☐☐☐	compensate for	
	063 ☐☐☐	assume	
	064 ☐☐☐	phenomenon	
20	065 ☐☐☐	discount	
	066 ☐☐☐	inherently	
	067 ☐☐☐	extract	
	068 ☐☐☐	awkward	
	069 ☐☐☐	sympathetic	

ANSWER

01	001 제조사		11	037 적합한
	002 긴급한		12	038 ~이 다 떨어지다
	003 확인하다			039 ~을 배신하다
	004 긴급한		13	040 충동
	005 선별적인			041 속이다
	006 광범위한			042 즉흥적인
	007 의무적인			043 피실험자
02	008 자격을 갖춘			044 호의적인
	009 다친		14	045 초롱초롱한
	010 자격을 갖춘			046 교대
	011 훈련된			047 피로
	012 확립된, 저명한		15	048 실행
	013 보조금			049 ~에 지나지 않는
03	014 누설하다			050 잠깐의
	015 바꾸다			051 헌신
	016 숨기다			052 분명히 실재하는
	017 배제하다		16	053 침공
	018 누설하다			054 재현하다, 복제하다
04	019 ~에 굴복하다		17	055 유지하다, 보유하다
	020 ~을 진행하다			056 분리
	021 무시하다			057 비어 있는
	022 지지하다		18	058 드러내다
	023 대표하다			059 응용, 적용
	024 굴복하다		19	060 ~와 다른, 이질적인
05	025 ~에 이르다			061 놀랍게도
	026 사실상			062 ~을 보완[보상]하다
06	027 이용 가능한			063 (역할을) 맡다, 담당하다
07	028 설계하다			064 현상
	029 영향을 미치다		20	065 경시하다
08	030 차별			066 본질적으로
	031 인종 차별을 하다, 분리하다			067 빼내다, 추출하다
	032 헌신			068 어색한
09	033 간헐적인			069 공감하는, 연민의
	034 단식하다			
	035 번갈아 일어나는			
10	036 여분의			

STEP 1
Word review 2

01
- 001 abandon
- 002 deliberately
- 003 cease
- 004 resist
- 005 adopt
- 006 invert

02
- 007 perpetual
- 008 formal
- 009 lasting
- 010 inclusive
- 011 definitive

03
- 012 take up
- 013 master
- 014 instruct
- 015 undertake
- 016 appreciate

04
- 017 iron out
- 018 settle
- 019 exploit
- 020 identify
- 021 reproduce

05
- 022 alteration
- 023 collective

- 024 emerge

06
- 025 complain
- 026 defect

07
- 027 submit

08
- 028 prestigious
- 029 initially
- 030 split

09
- 031 wholesale
- 032 stock

10
- 033 field
- 034 responsible

11
- 035 give it a shot
- 036 in vain

12
- 037 pack

13
- 038 detect
- 039 administer
- 040 innocent

14
- 041 ultimately
- 042 decorate
- 043 holistic

15
- 044 solely
- 045 theorize

16
- 046 streamline

학습일 _____   맞은 개수 _____

047 ☐☐☐	deficit	
048 ☐☐☐	disorder	
049 ☐☐☐	oversee	
17 050 ☐☐☐	be saturated with	
051 ☐☐☐	correct	
052 ☐☐☐	disprove	
18 053 ☐☐☐	tendency	
054 ☐☐☐	hesitant	
055 ☐☐☐	aesthetic	
056 ☐☐☐	intrinsic	
19 057 ☐☐☐	crawl	
058 ☐☐☐	unconscious	
059 ☐☐☐	suspend	
20 060 ☐☐☐	perception	
061 ☐☐☐	temperament	
062 ☐☐☐	countless	

ANSWER

01	001 그만두다		12	037 짐을 싸다
	002 의도적으로		13	038 탐지하다
	003 그만두다			039 실시하다
	004 반대하다			040 무고한
	005 채택하다		14	041 궁극적으로
	006 뒤집다			042 장식하다
02	007 영구적인			043 전인적인
	008 정식의		15	044 오로지
	009 영구적인			045 이론화하다
	010 포괄적인		16	046 단순화하다
	011 확정적인			047 결핍
03	012 시작하다			048 장애
	013 숙달하다			049 감독하다
	014 가르치다		17	050 ~으로 가득 차 있다
	015 시작하다			051 정정[수정]하다
	016 인정하다			052 반박하다
04	017 해결하다		18	053 경향
	018 해결하다			054 망설이는
	019 이용하다			055 미적인
	020 식별하다			056 내재적인
	021 복제하다		19	057 기어가다
05	022 변화			058 무의식적인
	023 총체적인			059 일시중지하다
	024 떠오르다		20	060 인식, 지각
06	025 불평하다			061 기질, 성질
	026 결함			062 무수한
07	027 제출하다			
08	028 명성이 있는, 권위 있는			
	029 처음에			
	030 나누다			
09	031 도매의			
	032 갖추다			
10	033 분야			
	034 책임감 있는			
11	035 한 번 해보다			
	036 헛된			

STEP 1
Word review 3

#			
01	001	insufficient	
	002	short	
	003	abundant	
	004	exhausted	
	005	distribute	
02	006	initiative	
	007	pledge	
	008	scheme	
	009	objection	
	010	investigation	
03	011	turn down	
	012	fulfill	
	013	review	
	014	refuse	
	015	manage	
04	016	stand in for	
	017	assist	
	018	imitate	
	019	substitute	
	020	acknowledge	
05	021	distortion	
	022	corruption	
	023	alternative	

	024	commitment
06	025	fatal
	026	deadly
	027	challenging
	028	accidental
07	029	potential
08	030	tense
09	031	handle
10	032	(just) around the corner
11	033	run one's business
	034	file a complaint
12	035	relative
	036	fortune
	037	outrage
	038	prosper
13	039	chronic
	040	misuse
	041	addiction
	042	prescribe
14	043	mitigate
	044	dwell on
15	045	native
	046	adorned with

	047 ☐☐☐	distinct
	048 ☐☐☐	extinct
	049 ☐☐☐	endangered
16	050 ☐☐☐	preference
	051 ☐☐☐	infancy
	052 ☐☐☐	peak
	053 ☐☐☐	adolescence
17	054 ☐☐☐	plagiarize
	055 ☐☐☐	compelling
18	056 ☐☐☐	surplus
	057 ☐☐☐	nomadic
	058 ☐☐☐	identical
	059 ☐☐☐	bring about
19	060 ☐☐☐	differentiate
20	061 ☐☐☐	vocation
	062 ☐☐☐	mediocre

ANSWER

01	001	부족한		037	분노하게 만들다
	002	부족한		038	번영하다
	003	풍부한	13	039	만성의
	004	고갈된		040	남용하다; 남용
	005	분배하다		041	중독
02	006	계획		042	(약을) 처방하다
	007	약속	14	043	완화하다
	008	계획		044	~을 오래 끌다, 숙고하다
	009	반대	15	045	토종인
	010	조사		046	~으로 치장된
03	011	거절하다		047	뚜렷한
	012	이행하다		048	멸종된
	013	검토하다		049	멸종 위기에 처한
	014	거절하다	16	050	선호
	015	감당하다		051	유아기
04	016	대신하다		052	정점에 이르다
	017	돕다		053	청소년기, 사춘기
	018	모방하다, 본받다	17	054	표절하다
	019	대신하다		055	강렬한
	020	인정하다	18	056	잉여
05	021	왜곡		057	유목의
	022	부패		058	동일한
	023	대안		059	~을 초래하다
	024	헌신	19	060	구별하다
06	025	치명적인	20	061	직업, 천직
	026	치명적인		062	보통의, 평범한
	027	힘든			
	028	우발적인			
07	029	잠재적인			
08	030	긴장된			
09	031	대처하다			
10	032	아주 가까운			
11	033	사업을 운영하다			
	034	항의를 제기하다			
12	035	친척			
	036	재산			

STEP 1
Word review 4

01	001 ☐☐☐	myth
	002 ☐☐☐	prevalent
	003 ☐☐☐	sincere
	004 ☐☐☐	absolute
	005 ☐☐☐	constant
	006 ☐☐☐	widespread
02	007 ☐☐☐	admiration
	008 ☐☐☐	esteem
	009 ☐☐☐	hostility
	010 ☐☐☐	gratitude
	011 ☐☐☐	sympathy
03	012 ☐☐☐	lay aside
	013 ☐☐☐	sustain
	014 ☐☐☐	dismiss
	015 ☐☐☐	tolerate
	016 ☐☐☐	confront
04	017 ☐☐☐	give rise to
	018 ☐☐☐	contradict
	019 ☐☐☐	intensify
	020 ☐☐☐	confirm
	021 ☐☐☐	trigger
05	022 ☐☐☐	respective
	023 ☐☐☐	considerate
	024 ☐☐☐	respectable
	025 ☐☐☐	considerable
06	026 ☐☐☐	refer to
	027 ☐☐☐	stereotype
	028 ☐☐☐	regarding
07	029 ☐☐☐	cutting-edge
08	030 ☐☐☐	navigate
	031 ☐☐☐	resilient
09	032 ☐☐☐	take a day off
	033 ☐☐☐	be caught up
10	034 ☐☐☐	stock
	035 ☐☐☐	a portion of
11	036 ☐☐☐	slip one's mind
	037 ☐☐☐	give sb some slack
12	038 ☐☐☐	bond
	039 ☐☐☐	nurture
	040 ☐☐☐	attachment
	041 ☐☐☐	polarize
13	042 ☐☐☐	cope with
	043 ☐☐☐	shortcut
	044 ☐☐☐	classify
	045 ☐☐☐	employ
	046 ☐☐☐	make sense of

14	047	ongoing
	048	concern
	049	escalating
	050	regardless of
15	051	monumental
	052	prominent
16	053	make use of
17	054	welfare
18	055	pessimistic
	056	optimist
	057	inclination
19	058	intentionally
	059	attraction
20	060	respiratory
	061	exhale
	062	stale

ANSWER

01	001 미신		037 ~을 봐주다	
	002 널리 퍼져있는	12	038 유대	
	003 진실한		039 양육하다	
	004 절대적인		040 애착	
	005 변함없는		041 양극화하다	
	006 널리 퍼진	13	042 ~에 대처하다	
02	007 존경		043 지름길	
	008 존경		044 분류하다	
	009 적대감		045 이용[사용]하다	
	010 고마움		046 ~을 이해하다	
	011 공감	14	047 계속 진행되는	
03	012 제쳐두다		048 우려, 걱정	
	013 지속시키다		049 상승하는	
	014 떨쳐내다		050 ~에 상관없이	
	015 견디다	15	051 기념비적인	
	016 맞서다		052 눈에 띄는	
04	017 불러일으키다	16	053 ~을 이용하다	
	018 모순되다	17	054 복지	
	019 강화하다	18	055 비관적인	
	020 확인하다		056 낙관론자	
	021 촉발하다		057 의향	
05	022 각자의	19	058 일부러	
	023 사려 깊은		059 매력, 끌림	
	024 존경할 만한	20	060 호흡계의	
	025 상당한		061 내쉬다	
06	026 ~을 언급하다		062 신선하지 않은, 오래된	
	027 고정관념			
	028 ~에 관하여			
07	029 최첨단의			
08	030 길을 찾다			
	031 회복력 있는			
09	032 하루 휴가를 얻다			
	033 ~에 사로잡히다			
10	034 주식			
	035 ~의 부분			
11	036 깜빡하다			

STEP 1
Word review 5

01
- 001 ingenious
- 002 striking
- 003 intricate
- 004 inventive
- 005 convenient

02
- 006 curtail
- 007 diminish
- 008 threaten
- 009 sacrifice
- 010 devastate

03
- 011 come to light
- 012 trivial

04
- 013 abuse
- 014 scarcity
- 015 isolation
- 016 complexity
- 017 combat

05
- 018 break off
- 019 look after
- 020 fall behind
- 021 play up to

06
- 022 reliable
- 023 turning point

07
- 024 imperative
- 025 provoke
- 026 inhabit

08
- 027 fossil
- 028 mammal

09
- 029 challenge
- 030 cast doubt on
- 031 scrutinize

10
- 032 life expectancy
- 033 vulnerability
- 034 elevate

11
- 035 stink

12
- 036 transfer

13
- 037 upcoming

14
- 038 budget proposal
- 039 conduct

15
- 040 fieldwork
- 041 demanding

16
- 042 separate

17
- 043 addiction
- 044 criminalize
- 045 offense
- 046 imprisonment

18	047	in terms of
	048	competence
	049	completion
	050	improvable
19	051	indecision
	052	prioritize
	053	paralysis
20	054	witness
	055	operational
	056	transparency
	057	psychological
	058	instantaneous

ANSWER

01	001	독창적인	13	037	다가오는
	002	인상적인	14	038	예산안
	003	복잡한		039	수행하다
	004	독창적인	15	040	현장 조사
	005	편리한		041	까다로운
02	006	줄이다	16	042	구분하다
	007	줄이다	17	043	중독
	008	위협하다		044	불법화하다
	009	희생하다		045	범죄, 위반
	010	완전히 파괴하다		046	수감
03	011	밝혀지다	18	047	~의 관점에서
	012	사소한, 하찮은		048	능력, 역량
04	013	오용		049	완수
	014	부족		050	개선 가능한
	015	고립	19	051	우유부단함
	016	복잡성		052	우선순위를 정하다
	017	싸우다, 방지하다		053	마비
05	018	분리시키다	20	054	목격하다, 보다
	019	보살피다		055	운영의
	020	뒤쳐지다		056	투명성
	021	아첨하다		057	심리[정신]적인
06	022	믿을 만한		058	즉각적인
	023	전환점			
07	024	필수의, 긴급한			
	025	자극하다			
	026	서식하다			
08	027	화석			
	028	포유동물			
09	029	이의를 제기하다			
	030	~을 의심하다			
	031	세밀히 조사하다			
10	032	기대 수명			
	033	취약성			
	034	높이다			
11	035	악취가 나다			
12	036	옮기다			

STEP 1
Word review 6

01	001	subordinate
	002	secondary
	003	appropriate
	004	independent
	005	sophisticated
02	006	heritage
	007	ritual
	008	legacy
	009	integrity
	010	commodity
03	011	take into account
04	012	layoff
	013	precise
	014	inevitable
	015	distinctive
	016	confidential
05	017	hold on
	018	hold by
	019	keep up with
	020	keep away from
06	021	statistical
	022	credible
07	023	run for
	024	measure
	025	notable
	026	tackle
08	027	withdraw
	028	infamous
	029	massacre
09	030	guarantee
	031	confidence
10	032	propel
	033	economical
	034	in synchrony with
11	035	put sb on the list
12	036	reunion
	037	mingle
	038	be on the fence
13	039	masterpiece
	040	contribution
14	041	reputable
15	042	exponential
	043	lifespan
	044	straightforward
	045	obesity
16	046	groundbreaking

학습일 _____ 맞은 개수 _____

	047 ☐☐☐	obedience
	048 ☐☐☐	distress
	049 ☐☐☐	disturb
	050 ☐☐☐	conscience
17	051 ☐☐☐	billion
	052 ☐☐☐	insurance
18	053 ☐☐☐	imitate
	054 ☐☐☐	mimic
19	055 ☐☐☐	defensive
	056 ☐☐☐	willingness to
20	057 ☐☐☐	get fired
	058 ☐☐☐	automation
	059 ☐☐☐	replace
	060 ☐☐☐	displace

ANSWER

01	001	부차적인	037	(사람들과) 어울리다
	002	부차적인	038	고민 중인, 결정하지 못한
	003	적절한	13 039	걸작
	004	독자적인	040	기여, 공로
	005	정교한	14 041	평판이 좋은
02	006	유산	15 042	기하급수적인
	007	의식	043	수명
	008	유산	044	직접의, 정직한
	009	정직, 온전함	045	비만
	010	상품	16 046	획기적인
03	011	고려하다	047	순응
04	012	해고	048	고통
	013	정확한	049	불안하게 하다
	014	불가피한	050	양심
	015	독특한	17 051	10억
	016	비밀의	052	보험
05	017	붙잡다; 기다리다	18 053	모방하다, 흉내 내다
	018	고수하다	054	모방하다
	019	따라가다	19 055	방어적인
	020	멀리하다	056	기꺼이 ~하려는 마음
06	021	통계의	20 057	해고되다
	022	믿을 만한	058	자동화
07	023	~에 출마하다	059	대체하다
	024	조치	060	대체하다, 쫓아내다
	025	유명한, 눈에 띄는		
	026	해결하다		
08	027	철수하다		
	028	악명 높은		
	029	대학살		
09	030	보증하다, 보장하다		
	031	신용, 신뢰		
10	032	나아가게 하다		
	033	경제적인, 잘 아끼는		
	034	~에 맞춰, ~와 동시에		
11	035	~을 명단에 올리다		
12	036	동창회		

STEP 1
Word review 7

#			
01	001	confine
	002	reflect
	003	remove
	004	restrict
	005	embrace
02	006	adverse
	007	inferior
	008	advantageous
	009	opposed
	010	corresponding
03	011	on the verge of
	012	owing to
	013	at the point of
	014	relating to
	015	in the event of
04	016	use up
	017	stand by
	018	stick to
	019	make out
05	020	iconic
06	021	elderly
	022	pandemic
07	023	display
	024	organize
08	025	now and then
09	026	come in handy
	027	in charge of
10	028	crash
	029	recover
11	030	conquer
	031	doomed
	032	expedition
	033	succeed in
12	034	determinant
	035	undermine
13	036	maltreatment
	037	medieval
	038	property
	039	humane
	040	parental
14	041	latitude
	042	acidic
15	043	owe A to B
	044	projection
	045	premature
16	046	forager

학습일 _____ 맞은 개수 _____

047 profitable

048 sip

17 049 intelligence

050 exceptional

051 quality

18 052 classic

053 sensory

054 extraordinary

055 strain

19 056 in the interest of

057 burden

058 companion

20 059 in the face of

060 tremendous

061 lineage

062 grasp

063 compromise

ANSWER

01	001 제한하다	037 중세의
	002 반영하다	038 재산
	003 제거하다	039 인도적인
	004 제한하다	040 부모의
	005 수용하다	**14** 041 위도
02	006 반대의	042 산성의
	007 열등한	**15** 043 A는 B 덕분이다
	008 이로운	044 예상
	009 반대의	045 미숙한
	010 상응하는	**16** 046 먹이를 구하는 사람, 사냥꾼
03	011 ~의 직전에	047 얻을 것이 많은, 수익성이 좋은
	012 ~때문에	048 홀짝 마심, 한 모금
	013 ~의 직전에	**17** 049 지능
	014 ~에 관해	050 아주 뛰어난
	015 ~의 경우에	051 자질
04	016 다 쓰다	**18** 052 전형적인
	017 지지하다; 대기하다	053 감각의
	018 고수하다	054 특별한
	019 이해하다	055 긴장
05	020 상징적인	**19** 056 ~(의 이익)을 위하여
06	021 나이 든	057 부담을 지우다
	022 전 세계적 유행병	058 동반자
07	023 보여주다	**20** 059 ~에도 불구하고
	024 준비하다	060 엄청난
08	025 가끔	061 계보
09	026 효과[쓸모]가 있다	062 잡다, 쥐다
	027 ~을 담당하는	063 타협
10	028 고장 나다	
	029 복구하다, 되찾다	
11	030 정복하다	
	031 불운한	
	032 원정, 탐험	
	033 ~에 성공하다	
12	034 결정 요인	
	035 약화시키다	
13	036 학대	

STEP 1
Word review 8

01	001	coherent
	002	novel
	003	central
	004	consistent
	005	compelling
02	006	nurture
	007	rear
	008	exhibit
	009	classify
	010	protect
03	011	on the grounds of
	012	in spite of
	013	in place of
	014	in virtue of
	015	in search of
04	016	carry out
	017	depend on
	018	look down on
	019	come down to
05	020	instinct
	021	take advantage of
06	022	acclaim
07	023	drown
	024	insight
	025	influential
08	026	touch
	027	cry out
09	028	pick on
	029	take a rain check
10	030	cram
	031	break (a) habit
11	032	self-imposed
	033	rid A of B
	034	withstand
	035	injection
12	036	circuit
	037	celestial
	038	insist
13	039	legal
	040	trial
	041	be accused of
14	042	alliance
	043	predominant
	044	means
15	045	recruit
	046	historic

16	047	criminal
	048	brutality
	049	perpetrator
	050	offender
	051	viable
17	052	scarce
	053	conflict
	054	address
18	055	commercialize
	056	resistance
	057	physically
19	058	entitle
	059	scarcity
	060	at the cost of
	061	peripheral
20	062	eternal
	063	mourn
	064	nonexistence

ANSWER

01	001	일관성 있는		037	천체의
	002	새로운		038	주장하다
	003	중심의	**13**	039	법률의
	004	일관된		040	재판
	005	설득력 있는		041	~의 혐의를 받다
02	006	기르다	**14**	042	제휴
	007	기르다		043	지배적인
	008	전시하다		044	수단
	009	분류하다	**15**	045	모집하다
	010	보호하다		046	역사적으로 중요한
03	011	~의 이유로	**16**	047	범죄자
	012	~에도 불구하고		048	잔인성
	013	~대신에		049	가해자
	014	~때문에		050	범죄자
	015	~을 찾아서		051	실행 가능한
04	016	수행하다	**17**	052	희소한
	017	의존하다		053	갈등
	018	얕보다		054	다루다
	019	결국 ~이 되다	**18**	055	상용화하다
05	020	본능		056	저항성
	021	~을 이용하다		057	물리적으로
06	022	찬사, 호평	**19**	058	제목을 붙이다
07	023	물에 빠지다		059	희소성
	024	통찰, 이해		060	~을 희생하여
	025	영향력이 큰		061	주변(부)의
08	026	감동시키다	**20**	062	영원한
	027	~을 외치다		063	애도하다
09	028	~을 괴롭히다		064	비존재
	029	다음을 기약하다			
10	030	벼락치기 공부하다			
	031	습관을 고치다			
11	032	스스로 부과한			
	033	A에게서 B를 없애다			
	034	견디어 내다			
	035	주사			
12	036	회로			

STEP 2
Syntax review

01 This sparked the Montgomery bus boycott by 17,000 Black citizens that led to a U.S. Supreme Court decision declaring that segregation on buses was illegal.

02 Other types include alternate-day fasting where you fast every other day, and the eat-stop-eat method which involves choosing two days of the week on which you don't eat for a full 24-hour period.

03 While it is true that there are problems that demand immediate attention, scientists would find few solutions without the help of the wide foundation of knowledge that basic science generates.

04 Initially limited to writers from the Commonwealth, Ireland, and Zimbabwe, it was later expanded in 2013 to include authors from any nationality, provided their work is originally written in English and published in the UK or Ireland.

05 American banks, and recently also auction houses, strengthen the trend of viewing art as an investment by extending credit and by hiring "art investment counsellors" thus suggesting that it is financially rewarding to buy art.

06 In Brian De Palma's gangster film The Untouchables, there is a scene on the steps of a train station in which, during a shoot-out, a stroller containing a baby rolls down the steps coming dangerously close to the bullets.

07 Almost every child takes a pencil and tries to draw, yet there are many parents who spend thousands of dollars in trying to make great artists of children who have only the most mediocre artistic ability.

08 Just because a child finds it more amusing to idle the hours away with a pencil or a brush than to go into the harvest field or into the kitchen doesn't mean that this preference is an indication of either talent or genius.

09 The Director-General of the Food and Agriculture Organization of the United Nations has urged governments to continue their support for developing countries in need of external assistance due to crop failures, civil unrest, insecurity or escalating food costs.

10 Also, the fact that unemployment periods tend to be longer in middle-aged adults than younger groups adds to the problem because a person's inclination and ability to find a job decrease the longer the person has been unemployed.

11 Much survey work, however, doesn't need to meet these demanding standards as it is typically done on a one-time basis by organizations that want quick snapshots of particular groups of people, such as employees or local residents.

12 In addition, in a state of information overload, we struggle to process and retain all the information we receive, making it difficult to prioritize information and determine what is truly relevant to our decision-making process.

13 The ability, for example, to leave the den to hunt or explore with confidence that the community would protect your family until you returned was one of the most important factors in the survival of our species.

14 But this slow rate of economic growth turned out to owe less to Hindu culture than to imported British socialist economic planning.

15 That India has an emerging middle class of several hundred million, and that English is an official language spoken by some 50-100 million people position India to play a major role in global markets.

16 Even the best moms — those gracious, calm magicians, perfectly dressed, bringing home-baked brownies and clean-faced toddlers to their older child's school events in between their jobs — have feelings of regret about some aspects of their mothering.

17 To ensure he'd withstand these side effects and go through with the treatment, Ariely, a movie lover, allowed himself to watch an unlimited number of movies on the days of his injections, only after he had taken the dose.

18 And there may come a day late in my life in which I will return to my first belief and insist to my grandchildren that Pluto is a planet.

19 One contributing factor to the rising brutality is the involvement of a significant proportion of young offenders in substance abuse, which often acts as a pathway to further criminal behavior.

20 In an effort to only give full consideration to that which is in the tunnel — and therefore to what appears to be the most pressing concern — they no longer attend to other, broader factors.

01

[1회 8번]

This sparked the Montgomery bus boycott (by 17,000 Black citizens) [that led to a U.S. Supreme Court decision [declaring that segregation on buses was illegal]].

구문 해설
첫 번째 that은 the Montgomery bus boycott를 선행사로 받는 주격 관계대명사이고, 두 번째 that은 명사절을 이끌어 declaring의 목적어 역할을 하고 있다. declaring 이하는 a U.S. Supreme Court decision을 수식하는 현재분사구이다.

문장 해석
이것은 17,000명의 흑인 시민들에 의한 Montgomery 버스 보이콧을 촉발했고, 이는 버스 내 인종 차별을 불법으로 선언하는 미국 대법원의 판결로 이어졌다.

02

[1회 9번]

Other types include alternate-day fasting [where you fast (every other day)], and the eat-stop-eat method [which involves choosing two days of the week [on which you don't eat (for a full 24-hour period)]].

구문 해설
alternate-day fasting과 the eat-stop-eat method가 등위접속사 and로 병렬되어 문장의 동사 include의 목적어 역할을 하고 있다. where는 alternate-day fasting을 선행사로 받는 관계부사로, 뒤에 완전한 문장이 나오고 있다. 첫 번째 which는 the eat-stop-eat method를 선행사로 받는 주격 관계대명사이다. '전치사 + 관계대명사' 형태인 on which 뒤에 완전한 문장이 나왔고, which의 선행사는 choosing의 목적어인 two days of the week이다.

문장 해석
다른 유형에는 이틀에 한 번 단식하는 격일 단식과 일주일 중 2일을 선택하여 24시간 내내 음식을 먹지 않는 eat-stop-eat 방식이 있다.

03

While it is true that there are problems [that demand immediate attention], scientists would find few solutions (without the help (of the wide foundation (of knowledge [that basic science generates]))).

구문 해설
while은 대조를 나타내는 접속사로 쓰였으며, while이 이끄는 부사절에서 가주어(it)-진주어(that절) 구문이 쓰이고 있다. 첫 번째 that은 problems를 선행사로 받는 주격 관계대명사이고, 두 번째 that은 knowledge를 선행사로 받는 목적격 관계대명사이다.

문장 해석
즉각적인 관심이 필요한 문제들이 있는 것은 사실이지만, 과학자들은 기초 과학이 만들어 내는 광범위한 지식 기반의 도움 없이는 해결책을 거의 찾지 못할 것이다.

04

Initially limited to writers (from the Commonwealth, Ireland, and Zimbabwe), it was (later) expanded (in 2013) to include authors (from any nationality), provided (that) their work is (originally) written (in English) and (is) published (in the UK or Ireland).

구문 해설
Initially limited ~ Zimbabwe는 분사구문이며, 전치사 from의 목적어로 명사 3개가 'A, B, and C' 형태로 병렬되어 있다. to include는 목적을 나타내는 to 부정사의 부사적 용법으로 쓰였다. provided는 조건을 나타내는 분사형 접속사로 뒤에 that이 생략되어 있으며, that절 내에서 동사 2개가 등위접속사 and로 병렬되었다.

문장 해석
처음에 영연방, 아일랜드, 짐바브웨의 작가로 제한되었지만, 이후 2013년에 그것은 작품이 최초에 영어로 쓰이고 영국이나 아일랜드에서 출판되는 전제하에 모든 국적의 작가를 포함하도록 확대되었다.

05

American banks, and (recently also) auction houses, strengthen the trend (of viewing art (as an investment)) (by extending credit) and (by hiring "art investment counsellors") thus suggesting that it is (financially) rewarding to buy art.

구문 해설
명사구 2개가 등위접속사 and로 병렬되어 문장의 주어 역할을 하고 있다. by가 이끄는 전치사구 2개가 등위접속사 and로 병렬되어 문장의 동사 strengthen을 수식하고 있다. thus suggesting 이하는 분사구문이며, 명사절을 이끄는 접속사 that이 suggesting의 목적어 역할을 하고 있다. that절 내에서 가주어(it)-진주어(to buy) 구문이 쓰이고 있다.

문장 해석
미국 은행들은 물론 최근에는 경매 회사들도 신용 대출을 확대하고 '미술품 투자 상담사'를 고용함으로써 미술품 구매가 금전적으로 보상이 된다는 것을 시사하여 미술품을 투자물로 보는 경향을 강화한다.

06

(In Brian De Palma's gangster film *The Untouchables*), there is a scene (on the steps of a train station) [in which, (during a shoot-out), a stroller [containing a baby] rolls down the steps coming dangerously close to the bullets].

구문 해설
'전치사 + 관계대명사' 형태인 in which 뒤에 완전한 문장이 나왔고, which의 선행사는 문장의 주어인 a scene이다. containing a baby는 a stroller를 수식하는 현재분사구이며, coming 이하는 분사구문이다.

문장 해석
Brian De Palma의 갱스터 영화 〈The Untouchables〉에는 총격전이 벌어지는 동안 아기를 태운 유모차가 계단을 굴러 내려가 총알에 아슬아슬하게 가까이 다가가는 기차역 계단 장면이 있다.

07

Almost every child takes a pencil and tries to draw, yet there are many parents [who spend thousands of dollars in trying to make great artists (of children [who have (only) the most mediocre artistic ability])].

구문 해설
두 개의 절이 등위접속사 yet으로 병렬된 구조이다. 앞의 절에서는 동사 2개가 등위접속사 and로 병렬되어 있다. 첫 번째 who는 many parents를 선행사로 받는 주격 관계대명사이고, 두 번째 who는 children을 선행사로 받는 주격 관계대명사이다. 'spend + 시간 + in RVing'는 '~하는 데 시간을 쓰다'라는 의미의 준동사 관용표현이다. 'make A (out) of B'는 'B에서 A를 만들다'라는 의미의 표현이다.

문장 해석
거의 모든 아이들이 연필을 들고 그림을 그리려 하지만, 그저 몹시 평범한 예술적 능력을 지녔을 뿐인 아이를 위대한 예술가로 만들고자 수천 달러를 쓰는 부모들이 많다.

08

Just because a child finds it more amusing to idle the hours away (with a pencil or a brush) than to go (into the harvest field or into the kitchen) doesn't mean that this preference is an indication (of either talent or genius).

구문 해설
'Just because A doesn't mean B'는 'A하다고 해서 B하는 것은 아니다'라는 의미의 구문으로, A와 B에는 각각 절이 위치한다. because절 내에서는 5형식 동사로 쓰인 find가 to 부정사를 목적어로 취하면서 가목적어(it)-진목적어(to idle) 구문이 쓰였다. to 부정사구 두 개가 비교급 구문 'more ~ than'으로 비교되고 있으며, 각 부정사구 내에서 'A or B' 구문이 전치사의 목적어 역할을 하고 있다. that은 명사절을 이끌어 mean의 목적어 역할을 한다. of가 이끄는 전치사구에서 'A 또는 B'라는 의미의 상관접속사 구문 'either A or B'가 쓰여 명사 2개가 짝을 이루고 있다.

문장 해석
단지 아이가 추수밭이나 부엌에 들어가기보다는 연필이나 붓을 들고 하릴없이 시간 보내기를 더 즐거워한다고 해서, 이러한 선호가 재능이나 천재성의 표시를 의미하는 것은 아니다.

09

The Director-General (of the Food and Agriculture Organization (of the United Nations)) has urged
S   V
governments to continue their support (for developing countries (in need of external assistance (due to
O   OC
crop failures, civil unrest, insecurity or escalating food costs))).
    A   B   C   D

구문 해설
문장의 주어는 of가 이끄는 전치사구가 이중으로 명사를 수식하는 형태를 띠고 있다. 5형식 동사로 쓰인 urge가 to 부정사 to continue를 목적격 보어로 취하고 있다. 전치사 for가 이끄는 전치사구가 their support를, in이 이끄는 전치사구가 developing countries를, due to가 이끄는 전치사구가 need of external assistance를 수식하는 삼중 구조이다. (동)명사 4개가 'A, B, C or D' 형태로 병렬되어 전치사 due to의 목적어 역할을 하고 있다.

문장 해석
유엔 식량농업기구 사무총장은 정부에 흉작, 내전, 치안 불안, 또는 식량 비용 상승 때문에 외부 지원이 필요한 개발도상국에 대한 지원을 계속할 것을 촉구했다.

10

Also, the fact [that unemployment periods tend to be longer (in middle-aged adults) than (in) younger
       S   S'1   V'1
groups] adds to the problem because a person's inclination and ability to find a job decrease the longer
         V   O   S'2   V'2
the person has been unemployed.
    S''   V''

구문 해설
that은 the fact와 동격을 이루는 접속사이다. that절에서 비교급 표현 longer와 그 짝을 이루는 상관접속사 than이 쓰여 두 개의 전치사구가 비교되고 있다. to find는 ability를 수식하는 to 부정사의 형용사적 용법으로 쓰였다. the longer는 '~하면 할수록'이라는 뜻의 'the 비교급'으로, 조건을 나타내는 절을 이끄는 접속사 역할을 하고 있다.

문장 해석
또한 실업 기간이 젊은 층보다 중년층에서 더 긴 경향이 있다는 사실은 문제를 더욱 악화시키는데, 이는 한 사람이 실직한 상태가 길어질수록 구직할 의향과 능력이 감소하기 때문이다.

11

Much survey work, (however), doesn't need to meet these demanding standards as it is (typically) done (on a one-time basis) (by organizations [that want quick snapshots (of particular groups of people, (such as employees or local residents))]).

구문 해설
as는 이유를 나타내는 접속사로 쓰였다. 'on a(n) + 형용사 + basis'는 '~을 기준으로'라는 의미의 표현이다. that은 organizations를 선행사로 받는 주격 관계대명사이다.

문장 해석
그러나, 대부분의 설문 조사 작업은 일반적으로 직원이나 지역 주민과 같은 특정 집단 사람들에 대한 빠른 짤막한 정보를 원하는 조직에서 일회성으로 수행하기 때문에 이러한 까다로운 기준을 충족할 필요가 없다.

12

In addition, (in a state of information overload), we struggle to process and retain all the information [(that) we receive], making it difficult to prioritize information and (to) determine what is (truly) relevant (to our decision-making process).

구문 해설
문장의 동사구에서 struggle의 목적어로 to 부정사 2개가 등위접속사 and로 병렬되었다. all the information을 선행사로 받는 목적격 관계대명사 that[which]이 information과 we 사이에 생략되어 있다. making 이하는 분사구문이며, 5형식 동사로 쓰인 make가 to 부정사를 목적어로 취하면서 가목적어(it)-진목적어(to prioritize/to determine) 구문이 쓰였다. 두 개의 to 부정사구가 등위접속사 and로 병렬되어 진목적어 역할을 하고 있다. what은 명사절을 이끄는 관계대명사로 determine의 목적어와 is의 주어 역할을 동시에 하고 있다.

문장 해석
게다가, 정보 과부하 상태에서 우리는 우리가 받는 모든 정보를 처리하고 기억하는 데 애를 써서, 정보의 우선순위를 정하고 의사결정 과정에 진정으로 관련 있는 것을 결정하기가 어렵게 된다.

13

The ability, (for example), to leave the den to hunt or (to) explore (with confidence [that the community would protect your family until you returned]) was one of the most important factors (in the survival of our species).

구문 해설
to leave는 ability를 수식하는 to 부정사의 형용사적 용법으로 쓰였고, 등위접속사 or로 병렬된 to hunt와 (to) explore는 목적을 나타내는 to 부정사의 부사적 용법으로 쓰였다. that은 confidence와 동격을 이루는 접속사이다. until은 시간을 나타내는 접속사로 쓰였다.

문장 해석
예를 들어, 당신이 돌아올 때까지 공동체가 당신의 가족을 보호해 줄 것이라는 확신을 가지고 사냥을 하거나 탐험을 하기 위해 굴을 떠날 수 있었던 힘은 우리 종의 생존에 있어서 가장 중요한 요소 중 하나였다.

14

But this slow rate of economic growth turned out to owe less (to Hindu culture) than (to imported British socialist economic planning).

구문 해설
문장의 동사구에서 2형식 동사로 쓰인 turn out이 to 부정사 to owe를 보어로 취하고 있다. 'owe A to B'는 'A를 B에 신세지다'라는 의미의 표현이며, 전치사 to가 이끄는 두 개의 구가 비교급 구문 'less ~ than'으로 비교되고 있다.

문장 해석
그러나 이러한 느린 경제 성장률은 힌두 문화보다는 영국의 사회주의 경제 계획의 도입에서 비롯된 것으로 밝혀졌다.

15

That India has an emerging middle class of several hundred million, and that English is an official language [spoken (by some 50-100 million people)] position India to play a major role (in global markets).

구문 해설
명사절을 이끄는 접속사 that 2개가 등위접속사 and로 병렬되어 문장의 주어 역할을 하고 있다. spoken by some 50-100 million people은 an official language를 수식하는 과거분사구이다. to play는 목적을 나타내는 to 부정사의 부사적 용법으로 쓰였다.

문장 해설
인도에는 수억 명의 신흥 중산층이 있다는 점과 영어가 약 5천만 명에서 1억 명의 인구가 사용하는 공식 언어라는 점은 세계 시장에서 인도가 중요한 역할을 하도록 자리매김 해준다.

16

(Even) the best moms — those gracious, calm magicians, [[(perfectly) dressed], [bringing home-baked brownies and clean-faced toddlers (to their older child's school events) (in between their jobs)]] — have feelings of regret (about some aspects of their mothering).

구문 해설
the best moms와 동격인 긴 명사구가 대시(—)로 삽입된 구조이다. perfectly dressed와 bringing ~ jobs는 각각 those gracious, calm magicians를 수식하는 과거분사구와 현재분사구이다.

문장 해설
심지어 최고의 엄마들, 즉 완벽하게 옷을 입고, 집에서 구운 브라우니를 들고 얼굴이 깨끗한 어린 아기를 데리고 일이 비는 시간에 더 큰 아이의 학교 행사에 오는, 우아하고 침착한 그 마술사들조차 자신의 엄마 노릇의 일부 측면에 대해 후회의 감정을 지니고 있다.

17

To ensure (that) he'd withstand these side effects and go through with the treatment, Ariely, a movie lover, allowed himself to watch an unlimited number of movies (on the days of his injections), only after he had taken the dose.

구문 해설
To ensure는 목적을 나타내는 to 부정사의 부사적 용법으로 쓰였다. ensure와 he 사이에 명사절 접속사 that이 생략되어 있으며, that절 내에서 동사 withstand와 go through with가 등위접속사 and로 병렬되었다. 문장의 주어 Ariely와 동격인 명사구 a movie lover가 쉼표로 삽입되었으며, 5형식 동사로 쓰인 allow가 to 부정사 to watch를 목적격 보어로 취하고 있다. only after는 '~하고 나서야'라는 의미의 시간 접속사이다.

문장 해석
이러한 부작용을 견디고 치료를 완수할 것을 확실히 하기 위해서, 영화광인 Ariely는 주사를 맞는 날에는 스스로 영화를 무제한으로 볼 수 있도록 했는데, 오로지 그 용량을 맞고 난 후에만 그렇게 했다.

18

And there may come a day (late in my life) [in which I will return (to my first belief) and insist (to my grandchildren) that Pluto is a planet]].

구문 해설
'전치사 + 관계대명사' 형태인 in which 뒤에 완전한 문장이 나왔고, which의 선행사는 문장의 주어인 a day이다. 관계사절 내에서 동사 2개가 등위접속사 and로 병렬되어 있다. that은 명사절을 이끌어 insist의 목적어 역할을 하고 있다.

문장 해석
그리고 말년에는 내 첫 믿음으로 돌아가 내 손자들에게 명왕성이 행성이라고 주장할 날이 올지도 모른다.

19

One contributing factor (to the rising brutality) is the involvement (of a significant proportion of young offenders) (in substance abuse), [which (often) acts (as a pathway (to further criminal behavior))].

구문 해설
주어와 주격 보어가 긴 전치사구로 수식된 명사구의 형태를 띠고 있는데, 주격 보어에서 전치사 of가 이끄는 구와 in이 이끄는 구는 각각 the involvement를 수식한다. which는 substance abuse를 선행사로 받는 주격 관계대명사이다. as가 이끄는 전치사구가 관계사절의 동사 acts를 수식하고 있다.

문장 해석
증가하는 잔인성에 기여하는 요인 중 하나는 상당수의 청소년 범죄자가, 종종 추가 범죄 행위로 이어지는 경로로 작용하는 약물 남용에 연루되어 있다는 것이다.

20

(In an effort to only give full consideration (to that [which is (in the tunnel)]) — and therefore (to what appears to be the most pressing concern —)) they (no longer) attend (to other, broader factors).

구문 해설
'in an effort to RV'는 '~해보려는 노력으로'라는 의미의 표현이다. which는 that을 선행사로 받는 주격 관계대명사이다. 대시(—) 사이의 구는 앞에 나온 전치사구 to that which is in the tunnel을 부연 설명한다. what은 명사절을 이끄는 관계대명사로 전치사 to의 목적어와 appears의 주어 역할을 동시에 하고 있다. what절 내에서 2형식 동사로 쓰인 appear가 to 부정사 to be를 보어로 취하고 있다.

문장 해석
터널 안에 있는 것, 즉 그러므로 가장 시급한 관심사로 보이는 것만 온전히 고려하려는 노력에서, 그들은 더 이상 다른 더 광범위한 요소에는 관심을 기울이지 않는다.

STEP 3
Grammar review 1

01 The days leading up to Christmas are practically a celebration in their own right, <u>offer</u> various ways to savor the holiday season.   O / X

02 There is a sense of goodwill which takes root in the soil of childhood memories and <u>blossom</u> annually.   O / X

03 It's a kind of magic too powerful <u>to be limited</u> to just one day.   O / X

04 I would rather go for a hike than spending the day indoors.   O / X

05 We will see if the weather improves before planning the picnic.   O / X

06 The master key believed to have lost was finally found by them.   O / X

07 A number of books on social philosophy are available at the library.   O / X

08 그 놀이터는 과거에 훨씬 더 조용했었다. O / X
→ The playground was used to be much quieter in the past.

09 그녀가 집을 나서자마자 비가 오기 시작했다. O / X
→ No sooner she had left the house than it started raining.

10 그 소프트웨어는 모든 장치에 쉽게 설치할 수 있게 설계되었다. O / X
→ The software is designed to be easy to install it on any device.

11 물을 마시면 갈증이 경기력에 영향을 미치지 않게 할 수 있다. O / X
→ Drinking water can keep thirst affecting your performance.

ANSWER

01 X, offer → offering	**05** X, improves → will improve	**09** X, she had left → had she left
02 X, blossom → blossoms	**06** X, have lost → have been lost	**10** X, install it → install
03 O	**07** O	**11** X, affecting → from affecting
04 X, spending → spend	**08** X, was used → used	

STEP 3
Grammar review 2

01   Climate change is a broad topic <u>what</u> includes periodic alterations in Earth's climate.   O / X

02   It's caused by natural forces <u>combined</u> with the effects of various human activities.   O / X

03   Over the last 100 years, the collective weight of human activities <u>emerged</u> as an important factor.   O / X

04   The child asked his parents that he could have a pet.   O / X

05   It is of no use to complain without proposing solutions.   O / X

06   A student who put a bandage on her finger has just had it take off.   O / X

07   The customer demanded that the product replaced due to a structural defect.   O / X

08 그는 아무 일도 없었다는 듯이 나를 향해 미소를 지었다. O / X
→ He smiled at me as if nothing had happened.

09 보고서를 제시간에 제출할 것을 기억하는 것이 중요하다. O / X
→ It's important to remember submitting the report on time.

10 집을 나서기 전에 창문이 모두 닫혀 있는지 확인해라. O / X
→ Make sure that all windows are closed before you will leave the house.

11 그녀의 재능은 노래보다는 악기 연주에 있다. O / X
→ Her talent is not so much in playing musical instruments as in singing.

ANSWER

01 X, what → that 또는 which	05 O	09 X, submitting → to submit
02 O	06 X, take → taken	10 X, you will leave → you leave 또는 leaving
03 X, emerged → has emerged	07 X, replaced → (should) be replaced	11 X, in playing musical instruments as in singing → in singing as in playing musical instruments
04 X, that → if 또는 whether	08 O	

STEP 3
Grammar review 3

01 Only a few of the 70-80 species of poisonous mushrooms are fatal when <u>ingesting</u>.   O / X

02 Many of these deadly fungi <u>bear</u> a particularly deceptive resemblance to edible species.   O / X

03 This makes identification challenging and <u>increasing</u> the risk of accidental ingestion.   O / X

04 The sale prices will be valid <u>until the end of the week</u>.   O / X

05 After hearing the arguments, she <u>convinced of</u> their logic.   O / X

06 They <u>were living</u> in the city since they graduated from college.   O / X

07 I <u>look forward to discuss</u> potential partnerships with your company.   O / X

08 당신의 주말 계획이 어떻게 되는지 알려주세요. O / X
→ Let me know what your plans are for the weekend.

09 어떤 이유로도 중요한 마감일을 놓쳐서는 안 된다. O / X
→ On no account important deadlines should be missed.

10 그곳의 분위기는 긴장되어 있어 모두가 눈을 마주치길 피하는 것 같다. O / X
→ The atmosphere there seems tense, with everyone avoiding eye contact.

11 그 소설은 내가 최근에 읽은 그 어떤 책보다 더 흥미진진하다. O / X
→ The novel is more fascinating than any other books I have read recently.

ANSWER

01 X, ingesting → ingested	05 X, convinced → was convinced	09 X, important deadlines should → should important deadlines
02 O	06 X, were → have been	
03 X, increasing → increases	07 X, discuss → discussing	10 O
04 O	08 O	11 X, books → book

STEP 3
Grammar review 4

01 The word *nerd* first appeared in the book *If I Ran the Zoo*, <u>where</u> one of the zoo creatures was called a "nerd."   O / X

02 A 1951 Newsweek article also used the word *nerd* to refer to "a drip or a square," <u>that</u> is closer to modern stereotypes regarding nerds.   O / X

03 We <u>should have booked</u> our tickets earlier to get better seats.   O / X

04 I learned about cutting-edge technology <u>while attended the conference</u>.   O / X

05 By the time <u>we reach at the summit</u>, we will have hiked for several hours.   O / X

06 The achievement of the team is something you <u>cannot help but applauding</u>.   O / X

07 어떤 이들은 그가 예술계에서 경력을 쌓았다는 것에 놀라워한다. O / X
→ Some find it surprised that he pursued a career in art.

08 이번 주말에 같이 요가 수업을 받는 게 어때? O / X
→ What do you say to getting a yoga class together this weekend?

09 가이드북은 여행객들이 그 도시의 길을 쉽게 찾도록 돕기 위해 설계되었다. O / X
→ The guidebook is designed to help travelers navigating the city easily.

10 운동을 통해 다져진 그녀의 몸은 스트레스에 더욱 회복력 있게 되었다. O / X
→ Strengthened through exercise, her body became more resilient to stress.

ANSWER

01 O
02 X, that → which
03 O
04 X, attended → attending 또는 I attended
05 X, reach at → reach
06 X, applauding → applaud
07 X, surprised → surprising
08 O
09 X, navigating → (to) navigate
10 O

STEP 3
Grammar review 5

01 How busy I am, don't hesitate to ask for assistance. ○/×

02 The couple are having trouble to find a reliable babysitter. ○/×

03 The black cat chasing a bird was seen climb the tall tree. ○/×

04 He told me the Battle of Gettysburg had brought a turning point in the Civil War. ○/×

05 The first dinosaur fossils with structures that could be considered as feathers were found in the 1990s. ○/×

06 Despite the first dinosaurs being thought to have emerged some 245 million years ago, dinosaurs with feathers have been dated to only 180 million years ago. ○/×

07 이제 우리가 다가오는 행사 계획을 세우기 시작할 때이다. ○/×
→ It is about time we start planning for the upcoming event.

08 현재 상황을 고려하면, 그 계획은 재고되는 것이 당연하다. ○/×
→ Given the current circumstances, the plan may well reconsider.

09 John은 시험 결과에 만족하지 못했고, 그의 부모님도 마찬가지였다. ○/×
→ John wasn't satisfied with the exam results, and neither was his parents.

10 새는 날개를 엄청 빠르게 움직여 공중에 떠 있을 수 있다. O / X
→ The bird moves its wings incredibly fast, allowing itself to float in the air.

11 학생의 3분의 1은 도서관에서 공부하는 것을 선호한다. O / X
→ One third of the students prefers studying in the library.

12 예산안이 부결된 이유를 제게 설명해 주실 수 있나요? O / X
→ Can you explain me why the budget proposal was rejected?

13 베개에 머리를 대고 누우면 수면의 질이 향상될 수도 있다. O / X
→ Lying with your head placing on a pillow may improve sleep quality.

14 직무 능력 평가는 4개월마다 시행된다. O / X
→ Employee performance evaluations are conducted every four month.

ANSWER

01 X, How → However	06 O	11 X, prefers → prefer
02 X, to find → (in) finding	07 X, start → started 또는 should start	12 X, me → to me
03 X, climb → to climb	08 X, reconsider → be reconsidered	13 X, placing → placed
04 X, had brought → brought	09 X, was → were	14 X, month → months
05 O	10 O	

STEP 3
Grammar review 6

01 His speech is often thought as a powerful message of inspiration. O / X

02 The more goals you set, the more motivated you'll be to achieve them. O / X

03 The theory requiring vast statistical analyses are likely to be proven credible. O / X

04 The director encouraged the actors to raise their voices while the performance. O / X

05 Among the most infamous events were the attack on the Arab village on April 9, 1948. O / X

06 The news of a massacre there spread widely and inspired both panic and revenge. O / X

07 Days later, Arab forces attacked a Jewish convoy approached a hospital, killing 78. O / X

08 당신의 부주의가 하마터면 재앙을 불러올 뻔했다. O / X
→ Your carelessness came near to cause a disaster.

09 그 팀은 소프트웨어 개발 프로젝트를 완수하려고 노력했다. O / X
→ The team tried to get the software development project completed.

10 이 걸작들을 그린 예술가가 전시회를 열고 있다. O / X
→ The artist whose painted these masterpieces is holding an exhibition.

11 그 회사는 확장되었을 뿐만 아니라, 공로로 상을 타기도 했다. O / X
→ Not only has the firm expanded, but it has also awarded for its contribution.

12 한 소년이 던진 공이 호수에 떨어졌다. O / X
→ The ball thrown by a boy landed in the lake.

13 내가 정보를 찾은 웹 사이트는 평판이 좋다. O / X
→ The website which I found the information is reputable.

14 만약 내가 결과를 알았다면 그런 위험을 감수하지 않았을 것이다. O / X
→ If I had known the results, I wouldn't take such a risk.

15 그들이 인터넷에서 보는 모든 것을 믿는 것은 어리석은 짓이다. O / X
→ It's stupid for them to believe everything they look at on the internet.

ANSWER

01 X, thought → thought of	06 O	11 X, awarded → been awarded
02 O	07 X, approached → approaching	12 O
03 X, are → is	08 X, cause → causing	13 X, which → on which 또는 where
04 X, while → during	09 O	14 X, take → have taken
05 X, were → was	10 X, whose → who	15 X, for → of

STEP 3
Grammar review 7

01 The city has widely known for its iconic landmarks. O / X

02 Scarcely had he entered the hall when everyone got silently. O / X

03 Each of the volunteers are expected to follow the guidelines. O / X

04 The streets crowded with visitors during the annual festival are lively. O / X

05 She found joy in that others perceived as a boring job. O / X

06 The program aims to provide the elderly with social activities. O / X

07 So shocked were they by the news that they couldn't believe it. O / X

08 Predicting when a pandemic will end requires constant analysis. O / X

09 그들이 결혼한 지 10년이 되었다. O / X
→ It was ten years since they got married.

10 그는 오류가 생기지 않도록 계산을 두 번 확인했다. O / X
→ He checked the calculations twice lest there should not be an error.

11 나는 그 웹 사이트에서 보여주는 업데이트된 메뉴를 자주 확인한다. O / X
→ I frequently check the updated menu displaying on the website.

12 우리는 행사를 준비한 후, 손님들이 도착하기를 기다렸다. O / X
→ Having organized the event, we waited the arrival of the guests.

13 적절한 안전 조치를 시행하는 것이 필수적이다. O / X
→ It is essential that proper safety measures be implemented.

14 그 선수는 팬들의 관심을 유지하기 위해 때때로 그들과 대화를 나눈다. O / X
→ The player talks to the fans now and then to keep them engaged.

15 갑작스러운 사태 전환으로 인해 나는 신중하게 세운 계획을 변경해야 했다. O / X
→ The sudden turn of events made me to change my carefully laid plans.

16 그곳은 다양한 액티비티를 제공했는데, 그중 대부분이 패키지에 포함되어 있었다. O / X
→ It offered various activities, most of them were included in the package.

ANSWER

01 X, has → has been	07 O	13 O
02 X, silently → silent	08 O	14 O
03 X, are → is	09 X, was → is 또는 has been	15 X, to change → change
04 O	10 X, should not be → (should) be	16 X, them → which
05 X, that → what	11 X, displaying → displayed	
06 O	12 X, waited → awaited 또는 waited for	

STEP 3
Grammar review 8

01 My parents have gone to Europe, so I'm alone now. O / X

02 Should she study abroad, she could gain valuable experiences. O / X

03 The cake he baked is more delicious as the one from the bakery. O / X

04 Trust your instincts to avoid taking advantage of in any situation. O / X

05 He finally noticed the small note left on his desk. O / X

06 It takes me three hours to get to work every day. O / X

07 The film received acclaim for its intense, humor, and sensitivity. O / X

08 Participating in a coding class, we practiced developing applications. O / X

09 협업에 있어서 성공은 정직함에 달려있다.
    → Success relies on honesty when it comes to collaborate. O / X

10 그녀는 수영 초보자임에도 불구하고 물에 빠진 아이를 구했다.
    → A beginner swimmer as she was, she saved a drowning child. O / X

11 나는 지난주에 들었던 강의에서 얻은 통찰을 공유할 것이다. O / X
→ I'm going to share insights from the lecture I listened to last week.

12 토론을 유발하는 소설을 쓴 그 작가의 영향력이 커졌다. O / X
→ The writer whose novels spark discussions have become influential.

13 그들은 높은 수준에서 경쟁할 수 있을 정도로 열심히 훈련했다. O / X
→ They trained enough hard to compete at a high level.

14 그는 계속 정보를 얻도록 업계 뉴스를 읽는 것을 원칙으로 삼는다. O / X
→ He makes a point of reading industry news to stay informing.

15 두 후보 모두 경험이 부족하다는 비판을 받았다. O / X
→ Either of the candidates was criticized for their lack of experience.

16 그녀의 공연에 감동한 관객들은 앙코르를 외쳤다. O / X
→ Touching by her performance, the audience cried out for an encore.

ANSWER

01 O	07 X, intense → intensity	13 X, enough hard → hard enough
02 O	08 O	14 X, informing → informed
03 X, more → as 또는 as the → than the	09 X, collaborate → collaborating	15 X, Either → Both / was → were
04 X, taking → being taken	10 X, A beginner → Beginner	16 X, Touching → Touched
05 O	11 O	
06 O	12 X, have → has	

Staff

Writer	심우철
Director	정규리
Researcher	강다비다 / 장은영
Design	강현구
Manufacture	김승훈
Marketing	윤대규 / 한은지 / 장승재 / 유경철

발행일   2024년 2월 19일 (2쇄)

Copyright ⓒ 2024
by Shimson English Lab.

All rights reserved. No part of this publication may be reproduced, stored in a retrieval system or transmitted in any form or by any means, electronic, mechanical, photocopying, recording or otherwise, without any prior written permission of the copyright owner.

본 교재의 독창적인 내용에 대한 일체의 무단 전재 · 모방은 법률로 금지되어 있습니다.
파본은 교환해 드립니다.

내용문의 http://cafe.naver.com/shimson2000

정답 및 해설

2024
심우철

실전동형
모의고사

최근 2개년 공무원 영어 시험의
유형 및 난이도를 완벽히 재현한
봉투형 모의고사 8회분

Season 1

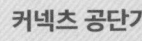

심우철 교수

약력
연세대학교 졸업, 연세대 국제학 대학원 졸업
現) 공단기 영어 대표강사
現) (주)심슨영어사 대표이사, 심슨북스 대표이사
前) 이투스 영어영역 대표강사
前) 메가스터디 영어영역 대표 강사
前) 노량진 메가스터디학원 최다 수강생 보유

저서
심슨 보카
심슨 구문/문법/독해
심슨 구문/문법/독해 500제
문법 풀이 전략서
이것만은 알고 가자
심우철 하프 모의고사
심우철 실전동형 모의고사

**영어가 쉬워지는
새로운 전환점을 만나다!**

교재 미리보기
Preview

최소시간 X 최대효과 = 초고효율 심우철 합격영어

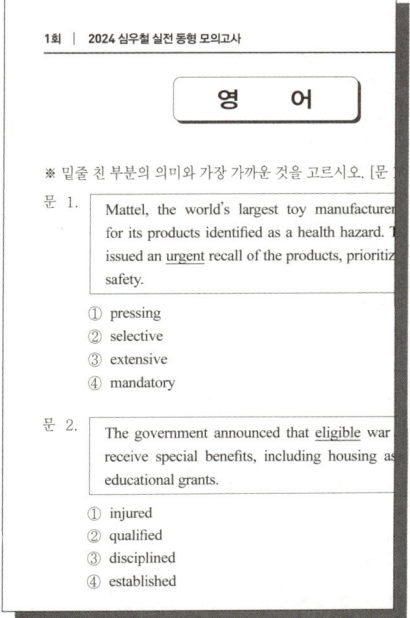

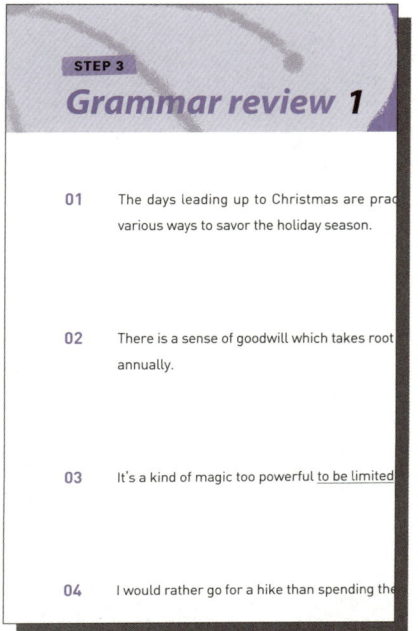

최근 2개년 8회분 시험 완벽 반영

2022년부터 2023년까지 최근 2개년의 국가직·지방직 기출을 완벽하게 재현했습니다. 각 문항에 실제 시험과 동일한 유형을 배치하고, 최근 기출의 난이도를 고려하여 문제를 제작하였습니다. 지문의 길이와 문항의 난도 또한 실제 시험과 최대한 동일하게 구성된, 심우철 실전 동형 모의고사가 시험장에서 여러분의 자신감이 되어줄 것입니다.

모의고사에 수록된 어휘, 구문, 문법 복습용 워크북 제공

모의고사에 출제된 문항을 이용해 어휘, 구문, 문법 세 가지 요소를 모두 복습할 수 있도록 워크북을 제공합니다. 어휘 테스트지를 제공하여 실전 동형 모의고사에 수록된 핵심 어휘를 복습할 수 있도록 구성하였습니다. 핵심 구문 패턴을 학습할 수 있도록 구문 분석을 제공합니다. 문법 문항 선택지의 정오를 복습하고, 어려운 문법 포인트를 학습할 수 있도록 변형 문제를 제공합니다. 실전 동형 모의고사 한 권으로 문제 풀이와 더불어 어휘, 구문, 문법까지 모두 학습할 수 있습니다.

풍부하고 상세한 해설지 제공

최소시간 x 최대효과의 모토를 해설지에도 담았습니다. 수험생들의 번거로움을 덜고자 해설지에 지문을 수록하여 복습을 용이하게 하였고, 빠른 정답을 제공하여 정답 확인 시간을 최소화할 수 있도록 하였습니다. 또한, 혼자서도 학습할 수 있도록 상세한 해설을 수록하였습니다. 특히 정답뿐만 아니라 오답 보기에 대한 해설까지 자세하게 풀이하여 최대효과를 누릴 수 있도록 하였습니다.

교재 미리보기
Contents

심우철 실전 동형 모의고사 해설 **1**회 · 6쪽

심우철 실전 동형 모의고사 해설 **2**회 · 14쪽

심우철 실전 동형 모의고사 해설 **3**회 · 22쪽

심우철 실전 동형 모의고사 해설 **4**회 · 30쪽

심우철 실전 동형 모의고사 해설 **5**회 · 38쪽

심우철 실전 동형 모의고사 해설 **6**회 · 47쪽

심우철 실전 동형 모의고사 해설 **7**회 · 56쪽

심우철 실전 동형 모의고사 해설 **8**회 · 64쪽

Answer
빠른 정답표

최소시간 X 최대효과 = 초고효율 심우철 합격영어

1회차

01	02	03	04	05
①	②	④	④	③
06	07	08	09	10
③	③	④	③	④
11	12	13	14	15
②	③	③	②	③
16	17	18	19	20
③	③	③	④	①

2회차

01	02	03	04	05
①	②	③	①	④
06	07	08	09	10
④	②	④	③	④
11	12	13	14	15
②	②	②	②	④
16	17	18	19	20
②	④	③	④	①

3회차

01	02	03	04	05
①	②	③	③	④
06	07	08	09	10
②	②	④	③	②
11	12	13	14	15
②	①	①	②	④
16	17	18	19	20
③	③	④	③	②

4회차

01	02	03	04	05
④	①	②	④	①
06	07	08	09	10
④	④	①	④	①
11	12	13	14	15
④	④	①	②	④
16	17	18	19	20
④	④	③	③	②

5회차

01	02	03	04	05
③	②	④	①	②
06	07	08	09	10
③	②	③	①	④
11	12	13	14	15
②	③	①	③	②
16	17	18	19	20
④	③	③	①	③

6회차

01	02	03	04	05
①	②	④	②	④
06	07	08	09	10
②	①	②	④	③
11	12	13	14	15
③	②	④	④	②
16	17	18	19	20
③	②	②	①	②

7회차

01	02	03	04	05
③	③	②	①	①
06	07	08	09	10
①	③	④	②	④
11	12	13	14	15
④	④	④	③	②
16	17	18	19	20
③	②	①	②	③

8회차

01	02	03	04	05
③	①	③	③	④
06	07	08	09	10
③	④	①	①	③
11	12	13	14	15
④	③	④	②	②
16	17	18	19	20
④	②	①	③	③

회차 1
Answer

01	02	03	04	05
①	②	④	④	③
06	07	08	09	10
③	③	④	③	④
11	12	13	14	15
②	③	③	②	③
16	17	18	19	20
③	③	③	④	①

01 밑줄 친 부분의 의미와 가장 가까운 것은? [어휘]

Mattel, the world's largest toy manufacturer, apologized for its products identified as a health hazard. The company issued an urgent recall of the products, prioritizing customer safety.

① pressing ② selective
③ extensive ④ mandatory

[해설] urgent는 '긴급한'이라는 뜻으로, 이와 의미가 가장 가까운 것은 ① 'pressing (긴급한)'이다.
② 선별적인 ③ 광범위한 ④ 의무적인
[해석] 세계에서 가장 큰 장난감 제조사인 Mattel은 건강상 위험한 것으로 확인된 자사 제품들에 대해 사과했다. 그 회사는 고객의 안전을 우선시하면서, 그 제품들에 대한 긴급한 리콜을 했다.
[어휘] manufacturer 제조사 identify 확인하다 hazard 위험 (요소) issue a recall 리콜하다 prioritize 우선시하다

[정답] ①

02 밑줄 친 부분의 의미와 가장 가까운 것은? [어휘]

The government announced that eligible war veterans can receive special benefits, including housing assistance and educational grants.

① injured ② qualified
③ disciplined ④ established

[해설] eligible은 '자격을 갖춘'이라는 뜻으로, 이와 의미가 가장 가까운 것은 ② 'qualified(자격을 갖춘)'이다.
① 다친 ③ 훈련된 ④ 확립된, 저명한
[해석] 정부는 자격을 갖춘 참전 용사들이 주거지원과 교육보조금을 포함한 특별한 혜택들을 받을 수 있다고 발표했다.
[어휘] announce 발표하다 war veteran 참전 용사 assistance 지원 grant 보조금

[정답] ②

03 밑줄 친 부분의 의미와 가장 가까운 것은? [이어동사]

It is important for actors not to let on any details about the thrilling plot twist before the release of the movie.

① alter ② conceal
③ exclude ④ disclose

[해설] let on은 '누설하다'라는 뜻으로, 이와 의미가 가장 가까운 것은 ④ 'disclose(누설하다)'이다.
① 바꾸다 ② 숨기다 ③ 배제하다
[해석] 배우들이 영화 개봉 전 스릴 넘치는 줄거리 반전에 대해 어떤 세부 사항도 누설하지 않는 것은 중요하다.
[어휘] thrilling 스릴 넘치는, 소름 끼치는 plot 줄거리 twist 반전

[정답] ④

04 밑줄 친 부분의 의미와 가장 가까운 것은? [이어동사]

After a lengthy debate, the committee had to yield to the majority opinion and proceed with the proposed plan.

① ignore ② uphold
③ represent ④ surrender

[해설] yield to는 '~에 굴복하다'라는 뜻으로, 이와 의미가 가장 가까운 것은 ④ 'surrender(굴복하다)'이다.
① 무시하다 ② 지지하다 ③ 대표하다
[해석] 위원회는 오랜 논의 끝에 다수 의견에 굴복하여 제안된 계획을 진행해야 했다.
[어휘] lengthy 긴 committee 위원회 majority 다수 proceed with ~을 진행하다

[정답] ④

05 밑줄 친 부분 중 어법상 옳지 않은 것은? [문법]

The days leading up to Christmas are practically a celebration in their own right, ① offering various ways to savor the holiday season. Trees are decorated, carols are sung, and gingerbread houses rise and fall. There is a sense of goodwill ② which takes root in the soil of childhood memories and ③ blossom annually — a kind of magic too powerful ④ to be limited to just one day.

[해설] (blossom → blossoms) 관계사절 내의 동사는 문맥상 등위접속사 and로 병렬된 takes와 blossom이다. 이때 주어는 which가 수식하는 단수 명사 a sense of goodwill이므로, 그에 수일치하여 단수 동사 blossoms가 되어야 한다.
① 타동사 offer 뒤에 목적어인 various ways가 있고, 문맥상 분사구문의 의미상 주어인 The days가 다양한 방법을 '제공하는' 것이므로 능동의 현재분사 offering은 적절하게 쓰였다.
② which는 a sense of goodwill을 선행사로 받는 주격 관계대명사로, 뒤에 주어가 없는 불완전한 절이 오고 있는 것은 적절하다.
④ '너무 ~해서 ~할 수 없다'라는 의미의 'too ~ to RV' 구문이 쓰이고 있다. 또한 a kind of magic이 단 하루로 '한정하는' 것이 아니라 '한정되는' 것이므로 수동형으로 적절하게 쓰였다.

[해석] 크리스마스에 이르는 날들은 사실상 그 자체만으로도 기념행사이며, 그 연휴를 만끽할 수 있는 다양한 방법들을 제공한다. 트리가 장식되고, 캐럴이 불리고, 진저브레드 하우스가 오르내린다. 어린 시절 추억의 흙에 뿌리를 내리고 매년 꽃을 피우는 온정감이 있는데, 이는 너무 강력해서 단 하루로 한정될 수 없는 일종의 마법이다.

[어휘] lead up to ~에 이르다 practically 사실상 celebration 기념행사 in one's own right 자기만으로도 savor 만끽하다 goodwill 온정 blossom 꽃 피우다 annually 매년

[정답] ③

06 어법상 옳지 않은 것은? [문법]

① I would rather go for a hike than spend the day indoors.
② We will have our picnic if the weather improves tomorrow.
③ The master key believed to have lost was finally found by them.
④ A number of books on social philosophy are available at the library.

[해설] (have lost → have been lost) believed to have lost는 The master key를 수식하는 분사구인데, 마스터키가 '분실한' 것이 아니라 '분실된' 것이므로 수동태인 have been lost로 쓰여야 한다. 참고로 분실된 것으로 '믿어진' 것이므로 수동의 과거분사 believed는 적절하게 쓰였고, 그렇게 추정된 시점이 키가 발견된 시점(과거)보다 앞서므로 완료부정사의 쓰임도 옳다. 또한 키가 '발견된' 것이므로 was found의 쓰임은 적절하다.
① 'would rather A than B'는 'B하기보다는 차라리 A하는 것이 낫다'라는 뜻으로 A와 B에는 동사원형이 온다. 따라서 go와 spend는 적절하게 쓰였다. 참고로 indoors는 '실내에서'라는 뜻의 부사이다.
② if가 이끄는 조건 부사절에서는 현재시제가 미래시제를 대신하므로 improves는 적절하게 쓰였다.
④ '많은'이라는 뜻의 a number of 뒤에는 '복수 명사 + 복수 동사'가 와야 하므로, books와 are는 적절하게 쓰였다.

[해석] ① 나는 실내에서 하루를 보내기보다 차라리 하이킹을 가고 싶다.
② 우리는 내일 날씨가 좋아지면 소풍을 갈 것이다.
③ 분실된 것으로 추정된 마스터키가 마침내 그들에게 발견되었다.
④ 그 도서관에는 사회 철학에 관한 많은 책이 구비되어 있다.

[어휘] philosophy 철학 available 이용 가능한

[정답] ③

07 우리말을 영어로 잘못 옮긴 것은? [문법]

① 그 놀이터는 과거에 훨씬 더 조용했었다.
→ The playground used to be much quieter in the past.
② 그녀가 집을 나서자마자 비가 오기 시작했다.
→ No sooner had she left the house than it started raining.
③ 그 소프트웨어는 모든 장치에 쉽게 설치할 수 있게 설계되었다.
→ The software is designed to be easy to install it on any device.
④ 물을 마시면 갈증이 경기력에 영향을 미치지 않게 할 수 있다.
→ Drinking water can keep thirst from affecting your performance.

[해설] (install it → install) easy가 포함된 난이형용사 구문이 쓰이고 있는데, to 부정사의 목적어가 주어로 오는 경우 중복을 피해 to 부정사의 목적어 자리는 비어 있어야 한다. 따라서 to install 뒤의 it을 삭제해야 한다. 참고로 소프트웨어가 '설계된' 것이므로 수동태 is designed는 적절하게 쓰였다.
① 'used to RV'는 '~하곤 했다'라는 뜻의 구문으로 주어진 우리말에 맞게 쓰였다. '~하기 위해 사용되다'라는 뜻인 'be used to RV'와 '~하는 데 익숙하다'라는 뜻인 'be used to RVing'와의 구분에 유의해야 한다. 비교급 강조 부사로 much가 쓰인 것도 적절하다.
② '~하자마자 ~했다'라는 의미의 'No sooner + had + S + p.p. ~ than + S + 과거동사' 구문이 적절하게 쓰였다.
④ 'keep + O + from RVing'는 'O가 ~하지 못하게 하다'라는 뜻의 구문으로 주어진 우리말에 맞게 쓰였다. 'O가 계속 ~하게 하다'라는 뜻인 'keep + O + RVing'와의 구분에 유의해야 한다. 또한 affect는 전치사 없이 목적어를 바로 받는 완전타동사이다.

[어휘] design 설계하다 install 설치하다 device 장치 thirst 갈증 affect 영향을 미치다

[정답] ③

08 다음 글의 내용과 일치하지 않는 것은? [불일치]

Rosa Parks was born in 1913 in Tuskegee, Alabama. Early in life, she experienced racial discrimination and attended a segregated school. Though she had to leave school at 16, she returned to high school to obtain a diploma after her marriage to Raymond Parks. Her defining moment came on December 1, 1955, when she rejected the bus driver's order to give up her bus seat to a white passenger. For this, she was arrested and fined under Montgomery's segregation laws. This sparked the Montgomery bus boycott by 17,000 Black citizens that led to a U.S. Supreme Court decision declaring that segregation on buses was illegal. Even before her brave act on the bus, she was active in the civil rights movement, supporting Black voting rights despite many obstacles. Her devotion to racial equality earned her the title of "Mother of the Civil Rights Movement."

① Rosa got married before she earned a high school diploma.
② Rosa was arrested for not offering her seat to a white person.
③ Due to the bus boycott, segregation on buses became illegal.
④ Rosa began fighting for Black voting rights after the bus boycott.

[해설] 마지막 2번째 문장에서 Rosa는 좌석 양보를 거부한 행동을 하기 전부터 흑인 투표권을 지지하며 민권 운동에 참여했다는 것을 알 수 있으므로, 글의 내용과 일치하지 않는 것은 ④ '버스 보이콧 이후에 Rosa는 흑인 투표권을 위해 싸우기 시작했다.'이다.
① Rosa는 고등학교 졸업장을 얻기 전에 결혼했다. → 3번째 문장에서 언급된 내용이다.
② Rosa는 백인에게 자리를 양보하지 않았다는 이유로 체포되었다. → 4, 5번째 문장에서 언급된 내용이다.
③ 버스 보이콧으로 인해 버스 내 인종 차별은 불법이 되었다. → 마지막 3번째 문장에서 언급된 내용이다.

[해석] Rosa Parks는 1913년 앨라배마주 Tuskegee에서 태어났다. 어린 시절 그녀는 인종 차별을 경험했고 (인종으로) 분리된 학교에 다녔다. 비록 그녀가 16세에 학교를 떠나야 했지만, 그녀는 Raymond Parks와의 결혼 이후에 졸업장을 따기 위해 고등학교로 돌아갔다. 그녀의 결정적인 순간은 백인 승객에게 버스 좌석을 양보하라는 버스 기사의 지시를 거부했던 1955년 12월 1일에 찾아왔다. 이로 인해 그녀는 Montgomery의 인종 차별법에 따라 체포되어 벌금을 물게 되었다. 이것은 17,000명의 흑인 시민들에 의한 Montgomery 버스 보이콧을 촉발했고, 이는 버스 내 인종 차별을 불법으로 선언하는 미국 대법원의 판결로 이어졌다. 버스에서 그녀가 한 용감한 행동 이전에도 그녀는 많은 장애물에도 불구하고 흑인 투표권을 지지하며 민권 운동에 적극적으로 참여했다. 인종 평등에 대한 그녀의 헌신은 그녀에게 '시민권 운동의 어머니'라는 이름을 안겨주었다.

[어휘] discrimination 차별 segregate 인종 차별을 하다, 분리하다 diploma 졸업장 defining 결정적인 fine 벌금을 물리다 spark 촉발하다 boycott 보이콧, 불매 운동 Supreme Court 대법원 civil rights movement 시민 평등권 운동(특히 1950~1960년대의 미국 흑인 평등권 요구 운동) obstacle 장애물 devotion 헌신

[정답] ④

09 다음 글의 내용과 일치하는 것은? [일치]

Intermittent fasting is a type of eating pattern that involves cycling between periods of fasting and eating. The most common type of intermittent fasting is the 16/8 method, where individuals fast for 16 hours and eat within an 8-hour period for 3 or 4 days a week. Other types include alternate-day fasting where you fast every other day, and the eat-stop-eat method which involves choosing two days of the week on which you don't eat for a full 24-hour period. You can consume beverages during fasting as long as they don't contain sugar, like unsweetened tea or black coffee. Intermittent fasting has been shown to have many health benefits. But it is important to note that it may not be suitable for everyone, especially those with certain medical conditions or who are pregnant or breastfeeding.

① The 16/8 method requires fasting for 16 hours every day.
② You fast every other day for the eat-stop-eat method.
③ Drinking black coffee is allowed during the fasting period.
④ Breastfeeding moms particularly benefit from intermittent fasting.

[해설] 4번째 문장에서 단식 중에도 블랙커피처럼 설탕이 들어 있지 않은 음료는 섭취할 수 있다고 언급되므로, 글의 내용과 일치하는 것은 ③ '단식 기간에 블랙커피를 마시는 것이 허용된다.'이다.
① 16/8 방식은 매일 16시간 동안 금식하는 것을 요한다. → 2번째 문장에서 16/8 방식은 일주일에 3일 또는 4일을 16시간 동안 금식하는 것이라고 언급되므로 옳지 않다.
② eat-stop-eat 방식으로 이틀에 한 번 단식한다. → 3번째 문장에서 eat-stop-eat 방식은 일주일 중 2일을 24시간 동안 금식하는 것이라고 언급되며, 이틀에 한 번 단식하는 것은 격일 단식 방식임을 알 수 있으므로 옳지 않다.
④ 모유 수유 중인 산모에게는 간헐적 단식이 특히 도움 된다. → 마지막 문장에서 간헐적 단식은 모유 수유 중인 사람에게는 적합하지 않을 수 있다고 언급되므로 옳지 않다.

[해석] 간헐적 단식은 금식과 식사 사이를 주기적으로 오가는 것을 수반하는 식습관의 일종이다. 간헐적 단식의 가장 일반적인 유형은 16/8 방식으로, 이 경우 사람들은 일주일에 3일 또는 4일을 16시간 동안 금식하고 8시간 이내에서 식사한다. 다른 유형에는 이틀에 한 번 단식하는 격일 단식과 일주일 중 2일을 선택하여 24시간 내내 음식을 먹지 않는 eat-stop-eat 방식이 있다. 단식 중에도 무가당 차나 블랙커피처럼 설탕이 들어 있지 않은 음료는 섭취할 수 있다. 간헐적 단식은 많은 건강상 이점이 있는 것으로 밝혀졌다. 그러나 이것이 모두에게, 특히 특정 질병이 있거나 임신 또는 모유 수유 중인 사람에게는 적합하지 않을 수도 있다는 점에 유의해야 한다.

[어휘] intermittent 간헐적인, 간간이 일어나는 fast 단식하다 alternate 번갈아 일어나는 every other day 이틀에 한 번 beverage 음료 note 유의하다 suitable 적합한 medical condition 질병 pregnant 임신 중인 breastfeed 모유를 먹이다

[정답] ③

10 밑줄 친 부분에 들어갈 말로 가장 적절한 것은? [생활영어]

A: Hey, do you know why our storage room is locked?
B: It is? That's unusual.
A: I know. Who do you think might have the key?
B: Mr. Jenson, probably. _____?
A: My mouse suddenly stopped working, so I'm looking for a spare one.
B: Oh, I see. You should ask Mr. Jenson.

① Why do you think he locked it
② Do you know where I could find him
③ Are there any spare keys lying around
④ Is there something you need from there

[해설] A가 여분의 마우스를 찾고 있는 와중에 창고가 잠겨있는 것을 발견한 것에 관해 대화를 나누고 있다. B가 빈칸 내용을 묻자 A는 자신의 마우스가 고장 나서 여분의 마우스를 찾고 있다면서 자신이 창고에 들어가려 한 이유를 설명하고 있다. 따라서 빈칸에 들어갈 말로 가장 적절한 것은 ④ '거기에서 필요한 게 있어'이다.
① 그가 왜 그것을 잠갔을까
② 그를 어디에서 찾을 수 있는지 알아
③ 굴러다니는 여분의 열쇠가 있나

[해석] A: 저기, 우리 창고가 왜 잠겼는지 알아?
B: 그래? 이상하네.
A: 그러니까. 누가 열쇠를 가지고 있을 것 같아?
B: 아마 Jenson 씨일 거야. 거기에서 필요한 게 있어?
A: 내 마우스가 갑자기 작동을 멈춰서 여분의 마우스를 찾고 있어.
B: 아, 그렇구나. Jenson 씨에게 여쭤보는 게 좋겠어.

[어휘] storage room 창고 lie around 놓여 있다, 굴러다니다 spare 여분의

[정답] ④

11 밑줄 친 부분에 들어갈 말로 가장 적절한 것은? [생활영어]

A: Hello, this is Riverview Hotel. How may I help you?
B: Hi, I'd like to know if I could book the Emerald Hall for a business seminar next Monday from 2 p.m. to 5 p.m.
A: I'm afraid the hall is already booked. The Diamond Hall is available though.
B: Oh, we're expecting around 100 attendees. Will the hall be large enough?
A: _____
B: I see. I'd like to book it then, please.

① Sorry, we don't accept overnight stays.
② Yes, it's the same size as the Emerald Hall.
③ No, the hall isn't suitable for a crowd that size.
④ Yes, the topic of the seminar is to be announced.

[해설] 비즈니스 세미나를 위해 호텔 홀을 예약하려는 상황이다. B가 다이아몬드 홀의 크기가 충분할지 묻자 A가 빈칸 내용을 언급하였고, 이에 B가 그럼 그 홀을 예약하겠다고 했으므로, 빈칸에 들어갈 말로 가장 적절한 것은 ② '네, 그곳은 에메랄드 홀과 같은 크기입니다.'이다.
① 죄송합니다만, 숙박은 받지 않습니다.
③ 아니요, 그 홀은 그 정도 인원에는 적합하지 않습니다.
④ 네, 세미나 주제는 곧 발표될 예정입니다.

[해석] A: 안녕하세요, Riverview 호텔입니다. 어떻게 도와드릴까요?
B: 안녕하세요, 다음 주 월요일 오후 2시부터 5시까지 비즈니스 세미나를 위해 에메랄드 홀을 예약할 수 있는지 알고 싶습니다.
A: 죄송하지만 그 홀은 이미 예약이 찼습니다. 그렇지만 다이아몬드 홀은 사용 가능합니다.
B: 아, 저희는 약 100명의 참석자를 예상하고 있어요. 홀이 충분히 클까요?
A: 네, 그곳은 에메랄드 홀과 같은 크기입니다.
B: 그렇군요. 그럼 그곳으로 예약하겠습니다.

[어휘] book 예약하다 attendee 참석자 overnight 숙박 suitable 적합한

[정답] ②

12 두 사람의 대화 중 자연스럽지 않은 것은? [생활영어]

① A: Mom, we're out of cereal.
B: Oh, that reminds me I need to go grocery shopping.
② A: It's freezing in our office.
B: Tell me about it. My hands and feet are ice-cold.
③ A: My sister went behind my back.
B: You're lucky to have someone who supports you.
④ A: I really like the novel you recommended to me.
B: Speaking of which, the author just released a new one.

[해설] 여동생이 자신을 배신했다는 A의 말에, 지지해 주는 사람이 있다는 건 행운이라는 B의 응답은 모순된다. 따라서 대화 중 자연스럽지 않은 것은 ③이다.

[해석] ① A: 엄마, 시리얼이 다 떨어졌어요.
B: 아, 그 말을 들으니 장 보러 가야 한다는 게 생각나네.
② A: 우리 사무실 너무 추워.
B: 그러게 말이야. 내 손과 발이 얼음처럼 차가워.
③ A: 내 여동생이 나를 배신했어.
B: 너를 지지해 주는 사람이 있다는 건 행운이야.
④ A: 네가 추천해 준 소설 정말 좋다.
B: 말이 나와서 말인데, 그 작가가 얼마 전에 신작을 냈어.

[어휘] be out of ~이 다 떨어지다 ice-cold 얼음처럼 차가운 go behind one's back ~을 배신하다 speaking of which 말이 나와서 말인데 release 출시하다

[정답] ③

13. 다음 글의 제목으로 알맞은 것은?

One of the enduring truths about human beings is that we lie — frequently and often quite casually. In fact, according to the recent claims of many psychologists, the impulse to deceive resides deep within our genes. As one scholar of deception puts it, "Lying is not exceptional; it is normal, and more often spontaneous and unconscious than cynical and coldly analytical. Our minds and bodies produce deceit." Numerous studies confirm that few people can make it through a typical day without lying. In one, subjects asked to keep diaries of their conversations reported that they told lies anywhere from 30 percent to 50 percent of the time on topics including their feelings, their actions and their plans. Some 60 percent of newly introduced individuals lie to one another within minutes simply to create a favorable impression, and dating couples apparently lie to each other even more.

① How to Break the Habit of Lying
② Lying as a Necessary Evil to Protect Others
③ Lying: The Innate, Central Trait of Humanity
④ How Lying Has Contributed to Human Evolution

14. 다음 글의 주제로 알맞은 것은?

Your biological clock makes you the most alert during daylight hours and the most drowsy in the early morning hours. Consequently, most people do their best work during the day. Our society that operates non-stop, however, demands that some people work at night. Nearly one-quarter of all workers work shifts that are not during the daytime, and more than two-thirds of these workers have problems with sleepiness and/or difficulty sleeping. Because their work schedules are at odds with powerful sleep-regulating cues like sunlight, night shift workers often find themselves drowsy at work. In fact, the fatigue they experience can be dangerous. Major industrial accidents — such as the Three Mile Island and Chernobyl nuclear power plant accidents and the Exxon Valdez oil spill — have been caused, in part, by mistakes made by overly tired workers on a night shift.

① reasons night shifts are increasing
② the effects and risks of working overnight
③ negative impact of job stress on sleep quality
④ possible treatment for excessive daytime sleepiness

15 다음 글의 요지로 알맞은 것은? [요지]

Ideas are the spark of creativity, the starting point of something great. But without execution, they are nothing more than fleeting thoughts. Invention requires action, and it requires bringing ideas to life through hard work, dedication and perseverance. Without the will to act, ideas remain dormant and unfulfilled, lost in the endless sea of possibilities that exist in the mind. Those who have truly impacted the world have done so through a combination of creativity and execution. They have taken their ideas and brought them to life, making them tangible and real. From the wheel to the Internet, every great invention began as a simple idea that someone decided to act upon.

① Cooperation is key in turning ideas into reality.
② Great inventors adapt to changing circumstances.
③ Ideas gain meaning when they are put into action.
④ Sometimes an accidental event leads to a great invention.

[해설] 아이디어를 실행에 옮기지 않으면 그것은 아무 쓸모가 없으며 위대한 발명은 아이디어를 실현함으로써 시작되었다는 내용의 글이다. 따라서 글의 요지로 가장 적절한 것은 ③ '아이디어는 행동으로 옮겨질 때 의미를 얻는다.'이다.
① 아이디어를 현실로 만드는 데는 협력이 핵심이다. → 아이디어를 현실화하는 데 있어 협력이 중요하다는 내용은 언급된 바 없다.
② 위대한 발명가는 변화하는 환경에 적응한다. → 변하는 환경에 적응하는 능력의 중요성을 강조하는 글이 아니다.
④ 때로는 우연한 사건이 위대한 발명으로 이어지기도 한다. → 의도치 않은 사건이 위대한 발명으로 이어지기도 한다는 내용의 글이 아니다.

[해석] 아이디어는 창의력의 불꽃이자 위대한 무언가의 출발점이다. 그러나 실행이 없다면 그것은 한순간의 생각에 지나지 않는다. 발명에는 행동이 필요하며, 그것은 고된 일과 헌신, 인내를 통해 아이디어를 현실화하는 것을 요한다. 행동하려는 의지가 없다면, 아이디어는 마음속에 존재하는 끝없는 가능성의 바다에서 길을 잃은 채 휴면 상태로 실현되지 못한 채 남게 된다. 세상에 진정한 영향을 끼친 사람들은 창의성과 실행력을 결합하여 그렇게 했다. 그들은 자신의 아이디어를 가지고 그것을 살려내어, 실재하고 현실인 것으로 만들었다. 바퀴에서 인터넷에 이르기까지, 모든 위대한 발명은 누군가가 실행에 옮기기로 결심한 단순한 아이디어에서 시작되었다.

[어휘] spark 불꽃 execution 실행 nothing more than ~에 지나지 않는 fleeting 잠깐의 bring sth to life ~을 현실화시키다 dedication 헌신 perseverance 인내 will 의지 dormant 성장[활동]을 중단한, 휴면기의 unfulfilled 실현되지 않은 endless 끝없는 possibility 가능성 combination 결합, 조합 tangible 분명히 실재하는 act upon ~에 따라 행동하다

[정답] ③

16 밑줄 친 부분에 들어갈 말로 알맞은 것은? [빈칸완성]

In the 1998 film *Saving Private Ryan*, director Steven Spielberg took on the epic topic of the Normandy invasion of Europe in June 1944 on D-day. The first half hour provides one of the most powerful, horrible, realistic views of battle ever created or replicated on film. And yet, as moving and convincing as the scene is, _____ abound. The German Tiger tanks of a Panzer division used against American troops in the movie were not actually there on D-day. The battle against the Nazi Panzer division in Normandy was also a mistake — the division was nowhere near Normandy at the time. The P-51 fighter planes that were shown as "tank destroyers" were, in reality, mostly used to defend other aircraft during the war. The antitank aircraft used at Normandy were actually Hawker Typhoons which were British, not American.

① misdeeds   ② imitations
③ inaccuracies ④ collaborations

[해설] 영화 <라이언 일병 구하기>는 전투 장면들을 훌륭하게 연출했지만 그 장면들은 실제 사실과는 다르다는 내용의 글이다. 빈칸 뒤에서 그 영화에서 나타난 오류들에 관해 설명하고 있으므로, 빈칸에 들어갈 말로 가장 적절한 것은 ③ '오류'이다.
① 악행 → 영화에 많은 오류들이 있었다는 사실만을 논할 뿐, 그것의 부도덕성을 지적하는 글이 아니므로 적절하지 않다.
② 모방 → 영화가 유럽의 Normandy 상륙작전을 재현하려 했던 것은 맞지만, 정확히 재현하지 못했다는 것이 핵심이므로 적절하지 않다. 정답이 '모방'이기 위해서는 오히려 현실을 최대한 따라하려 했다는 내용이 주를 이뤄야 할 것이다.
④ 협업 → 빈칸 뒤의 내용이 전투 중에 이뤄진 협업을 강조하는 내용은 아니므로 적절하지 않다.

[해석] 1998년 영화 <라이언 일병 구하기>에서 Steven Spielberg 감독은 1944년 6월 디데이(공격 개시일)를 맞아 유럽의 노르망디 상륙작전이라는 장대한 주제를 떠맡았다. 영화 초반 30분은 지금까지 영화로 제작되거나 재현된 전투 장면 중 가장 강렬하고 끔찍하며 사실적인 장면들 중 하나를 선사한다. 그러나 그 장면이 감동적이고 설득력이 있긴 하지만, 오류가 가득하다. 영화에서 미군에 대항하는 데 사용되었던 독일군 Panzer 사단의 Tiger 탱크는 디데이에 실제로 거기에 있지 않았다. 나치 Panzer 사단과 노르망디에서 대항했던 전투 역시 오류였는데, 당시 그 사단은 노르망디 근처의 어디에도 없었기 때문이다. '탱크 파괴자'로 묘사된 P-51 전투기는 실제로 전쟁 중 다른 항공기를 방어하는 데 주로 사용되었다. 노르망디에서 사용된 대전차 전투기는 실제로 미국제가 아닌 영국제 Hawker Typhoons였다.

[어휘] epic 장대한, 서사시적인 invasion 침공 D-day 공격 개시일 replicate 재현하다, 복제하다 convincing 설득력 있는 abound 아주 많다 division (육군의) 사단 troop 군대, 부대 defend 방어하다 antitank aircraft 전차 공격용 비행기

[정답] ③

17 다음 글의 흐름상 어색한 문장은?

Some end-of-life materials retain so much value that there are markets for their collection, separation, and reprocessing. Among them is copper, the world's most reusable resource. ① Recycled copper retains 95 percent of its value because previous use and processing involves only minor contamination. ② Nearly three-quarters of copper used in new products comes from recycled copper. ③ As a key player in renewable energy, copper is essential for the production of solar panels and wind turbines. ④ Old copper is actually so valuable and easily recycled that thieves steal copper pipe and wire from vacant houses and power stations. In fact, the US Department of Energy estimates that copper theft causes nearly $1 billion in losses to US businesses every year.

18 주어진 문장이 들어갈 위치로 알맞은 것은?

However, a careful look at the history of science reveals that basic knowledge has resulted in many remarkable applications of great value.

Some individuals may perceive applied science as "useful" and basic science as "useless" as the former solves real-world problems while the latter focuses on theoretical concepts. (①) A question these people might pose to a scientist who advocates basic science would be, "What for?" (②) They claim that it is time to move on from basic science in order to find solutions to actual problems. (③) This is why many scientists maintain that basic knowledge is necessary before researchers develop an application, and that applied science therefore relies on basic science. (④) While it is true that there are problems that demand immediate attention, scientists would find few solutions without the help of the wide foundation of knowledge that basic science generates.

19 주어진 글 다음에 이어질 글의 순서로 가장 적절한 것은? [순서배열]

The fact that the two hemispheres of the brain have different strong suits doesn't mean that they are fundamentally alien to each other.

(A) The children whose left hemispheres have been removed through the surgery initially lose their language ability. But astonishingly, in time, the right hemisphere compensates for the loss and assumes most of the language functions, leading to their recovery.

(B) When medications fail to control the seizures, the children may need surgery to have the entire affected hemisphere removed.

(C) To the contrary, a remarkable phenomenon shows that the two hemispheres are cut from the same cloth. In the case of Rasmussen's syndrome, young children with this condition have severe seizures limited to one hemisphere.

① (B) - (A) - (C)   ② (B) - (C) - (A)
③ (C) - (A) - (B)   ④ (C) - (B) - (A)

[해설] 주어진 글은 뇌의 두 반구가 서로 다른 강점이 있다고 해서 서로 완전히 다른 것은 아니라는 내용으로, 뒤에는 이를 To the contrary로 이어, 두 반구는 같은 부류라는 것을 보여주는 한 놀라운 현상이 있다며 그 사례를 소개하는 내용의 (C)가 오는 것이 자연스럽다. 그다음으로, (C)에서 언급된 severe seizures를 the seizures로 받아, 그 발작이 약물로 억제가 되지 않을 경우에 반구 전체를 제거하는 수술이 필요할 수도 있다는 내용의 (B)가 와야 한다. 마지막으로, 그 수술을 통해 왼쪽 반구를 제거한 아이들은 처음에 언어 능력을 상실하지만, 시간이 지나면서 오른쪽 반구가 그 기능을 담당하게 되어 언어 능력이 회복된다는 내용의 (A)로 글이 마무리되어야 한다. 따라서 글의 순서로 가장 적절한 것은 ④ '(C) - (B) - (A)'이다.

[해석] 뇌의 두 반구가 서로 다른 강점을 지니고 있다고 해서 서로 근본적으로 이질적이라는 뜻은 아니다. (C) 그와는 반대로, 한 놀라운 현상에 따르면 두 반구는 같은 부류이다. 라스무센 증후군의 경우, 이 질환을 가진 어린 아이들은 한쪽 반구에 국한된 심각한 발작을 일으킨다. (B) 약물이 발작을 억제하지 못하는 경우, 그 아이들은 병에 걸린 반구 전체를 제거하는 수술이 필요할 수도 있다. (A) 그 수술을 통해 왼쪽 반구를 제거한 아이들은 처음에 언어 능력을 잃게 된다. 그러나 놀랍게도 시간이 지나면 오른쪽 반구가 그 손실을 보완하여 언어 기능의 대부분을 담당하게 되고, 이는 그것(언어 기능)의 회복으로 이어진다.

[어휘] hemisphere (지구·뇌의) 반구 fundamentally 근본적으로 alien to ~와 다른, 이질적인 astonishingly 놀랍게도 compensate for ~을 보완[보상]하다 assume (역할을) 맡다, 담당하다 medication 약물 seizure 발작 remarkable 두드러지는 phenomenon 현상 cut from the same cloth 비슷한, 같은 부류인 limited to ~에 한정되어 Rasmussen's syndrome 라스무센 증후군

[정답] ④

20 밑줄 친 부분에 들어갈 말로 알맞은 것은? [빈칸완성]

Some people tend to place a great deal of value on logic and discount the importance of emotion. You can't win a debate with an emotional argument, of course, but conversation is not debate and human beings are inherently illogical. We are emotional creatures. To remove, or attempt to remove, emotion from your conversation is to extract a great deal of meaning. Imagine your friend talking about his pending divorce, and you try to comfort him by saying, "Don't feel bad. Almost half of marriages end in divorce anyway." or "One psychologist says divorce can actually improve your kids' chances at a lasting healthy relationship." In this case, you use facts to respond to emotion. They may be true, but they're completely unhelpful to your friend who is in need of emotional support. A conversation is not a college lecture course. No matter how awkward it may feel to be on the listening end of someone's heartbreak, _____ is rarely the right response.

① escaping into logic
② doubting the given facts
③ breaking off a conversation
④ making sympathetic remarks

[해설] 이 글은 대화에 있어 감정의 중요성을 강조하고 있다. 정서적 지지가 필요한 친구에게 사실적인 근거를 들어 위로하려는 사례가 나오는데, 이런 식으로 사실이나 논리에 기대어 조언하는 것은 쓸모가 없다는 것을 알 수 있다. 따라서 빈칸에 들어갈 말로 가장 적절한 것은 ① '논리로 도피하는 것'이다.

② 주어진 사실을 의심하는 것 → 사례에서 위로를 해주려 하는 사람은 상대방의 이혼이 진행 중인 사실을 의심하고 있는 것이 아니다.
③ 대화를 끊는 것
④ 공감하는 말을 하는 것 → 오히려 공감하는 말을 하는 것이 중요하다는 글이므로 반대된다.

[해석] 몇몇 사람들은 논리에 큰 가치를 두고 감정의 중요성을 경시하는 경향이 있다. 물론 당신은 감정적인 논쟁으로 토론에서 이길 수는 없지만, 대화는 토론이 아니며, 인간은 본질적으로 비논리적이다. 우리는 감정적인 생물이다. 대화에서 감정을 없애거나 없애려고 시도하는 것은 많은 의미를 없애버리는 것이다. 당신의 친구가 진행 중인 이혼에 관해 이야기하는데, 당신이 이렇게 그를 위로한다고 상상해보자. "낙담하지 마. 어차피 결혼의 거의 절반이 이혼으로 끝나는걸." 혹은 "어떤 심리학자가 그러는데, (부모의) 이혼은 실제로 아이들이 오래 가는 건전한 관계를 가질 가능성을 높여줄 수 있다." 이 경우, 당신은 사실을 이용해서 감정에 반응한 것이다. 그것들은 사실일 수도 있지만, 정서적 지지가 필요한 친구에게는 전혀 도움이 되지 않는다. 대화는 대학 강의가 아니다. 누군가의 상심을 듣는 입장에 있는 것이 아무리 어색하게 느껴질지라도, 논리로 도피하는 것은 거의 올바른 반응이 아니다.

[어휘] a great deal of 아주 많은 logic 논리 discount 경시하다 argument 주장, 논쟁 inherently 본질적으로 attempt to ~하려고 시도하다 extract 빼내다, 추출하다 pending 진행 중인 divorce 이혼 awkward 어색한 heartbreak 상심 doubt 의심하다 break off ~을 끊다 sympathetic 공감하는, 연민의

[정답] ①

회차 2
Answer

01	02	03	04	05
①	②	③	①	④
06	07	08	09	10
④	②	④	③	④
11	12	13	14	15
②	②	②	②	④
16	17	18	19	20
②	④	③	④	①

01 밑줄 친 부분의 의미와 가장 가까운 것은? 어휘

Departing from convention, the artist deliberately abandoned traditional methods. She made use of avant-garde techniques and created a groundbreaking masterpiece after several experiments.

① ceased   ② resisted
③ adopted ④ inverted

[해설] abandon은 '그만두다'라는 뜻으로, 이와 의미가 가장 가까운 것은 ① 'ceased (그만두다)'이다.
② 반대하다 ③ 채택하다 ④ 뒤집다
[해석] 그 예술가는 관습에서 벗어나 의도적으로 전통적인 방식을 그만두었다. 그녀는 아방가르드 기법을 사용했고 수차례의 실험 끝에 획기적인 걸작을 창조했다.
[어휘] depart from ~에서 벗어나다 deliberately 의도적으로 avant-garde 아방가르드(예술에서의 전위적인 사상) groundbreaking 획기적인

[정답] ①

02 밑줄 친 부분의 의미와 가장 가까운 것은? 어휘

Following successful negotiations, the nations signed a perpetual treaty aimed at peaceful relations and closer cooperation in various domains.

① formal   ② lasting
③ inclusive ④ definitive

[해설] perpetual은 '영구적인'이라는 뜻으로, 이와 의미가 가장 가까운 것은 ② 'lasting(영구적인)'이다.
① 정식의 ③ 포괄적인 ④ 확정적인
[해석] 성공적인 협상 끝에, 그 국가들은 평화적 관계와 다양한 영역에서의 더 긴밀한 협력을 목표로 하는 영구적인 조약에 서명했다.
[어휘] negotiation 협상 treaty 조약 cooperation 협력 domain 영역

[정답] ②

03 밑줄 친 부분의 의미와 가장 가까운 것은? 이어동사

Despite her fear of violence, Julia surprised herself by taking up boxing, drawn to the sport's mental challenges.

① mastering   ② instructing
③ undertaking ④ appreciating

[해설] take up은 '시작하다'라는 뜻으로, 이와 의미가 가장 가까운 것은 ③ 'undertaking (시작하다)'이다.
① 숙달하다 ② 가르치다 ④ 인정하다
[해석] 폭력에 대한 두려움에도 불구하고, Julia는 권투의 정신적 도전에 이끌려 스스로 놀랍게도 그 스포츠를 시작했다.
[어휘] violence 폭력

[정답] ③

04 밑줄 친 부분의 의미와 가장 가까운 것은? 이어동사

The developers were able to iron out bugs in the new software through continuous testing.

① settle   ② exploit
③ identify ④ reproduce

[해설] iron out은 '해결하다'라는 뜻으로, 이와 의미가 가장 가까운 것은 ① 'settle(해결하다)'이다.
② 이용하다 ③ 식별하다 ④ 복제하다
[해석] 그 개발자들은 지속적인 테스트를 통해 새로운 소프트웨어의 버그를 해결할 수 있었다.

[정답] ①

05 밑줄 친 부분 중 어법상 옳지 않은 것은? [문법]

Climate change is a broad topic ① that includes periodic alterations in Earth's climate caused by natural forces — biological, chemical, ② geologic and meteorological factors — ③ combined with the effects of various human activities. Over the last 100 years, however, the collective weight of human activities ④ emerged as an important factor in guiding the trajectory of global climates.

[해설] (emerged → has emerged) Over the last 100 years라는 기간을 나타내는 부사구가 나왔으므로 현재완료시제가 함께 쓰여야 한다. 이때 주어가 단수 명사인 the collective weight이므로 단수를 이용해 has emerged가 되어야 한다.
① that은 a broad topic을 선행사로 받는 주격 관계대명사로 쓰였으며, 뒤에 주어가 없는 불완전한 절이 오고 있는 것은 적절하다.
② 4개의 형용사가 등위접속사 and를 기준으로 병렬된 구조이다. biological, chemical, meteorological과 함께 형용사 geologic이 쓰인 것은 적절하다.
③ 문맥상 분사가 수식하고 있는 것은 natural forces이며, 자연적인 힘이 다양한 인간 활동의 영향과 '결합된' 것이므로 수동의 과거분사 combined는 적절하게 쓰였다.

[해석] 기후 변화는 다양한 인간 활동의 영향과 결합된 생물학적, 화학적, 지질학적, 기상학적 요인과 같은 자연적인 힘에 의한 지구 기후의 주기적인 변화를 포함하는 폭넓은 주제이다. 그러나 지난 100년 동안은 인간 활동의 총체적 비중이 지구 기후의 궤적을 이끄는 중요한 요소로 떠오르고 있다.

[어휘] periodic 주기적인 alteration 변화 geologic 지질학의 meteorological 기상학의 collective 총체적인 emerge 떠오르다 trajectory 궤적

[정답] ④

06 어법상 옳지 않은 것은? [문법]

① The child asked his parents if he could have a pet.
② It is of no use to complain without proposing solutions.
③ A student who put a bandage on her finger has just had it taken off.
④ The customer demanded that the product replaced due to a structural defect.

[해설] (replaced → (should) be replaced) demand와 같은 주·요·명·제·충·결 동사의 목적어로 쓰인 that절에는 '(should) + RV'가 온다. 여기서는 the product가 '교체되는' 것이므로 수동태인 (should) be replaced가 쓰여야 한다. 참고로 전치사구인 due to 뒤에 명사구 a structural defect가 온 것은 적절하다.
① ask가 4형식 동사로 쓰여, if절을 직접목적어로 취하고 있다. if가 명사절을 이끌 경우 타동사의 목적어로 쓰일 수 있으므로 적절하게 쓰였다.
② 'It is of no use to RV'는 '~해도 소용없다'라는 뜻을 갖는 관용표현이므로 to complain은 적절하게 쓰였으며, 전치사 without 뒤에 동명사 proposing이 온 것도 적절하다.
③ A student를 선행사로 받는 주격 관계대명사가 불완전한 절을 이끌고 있다. 한편 사역동사 have는 목적어와 목적격 보어의 관계가 능동이면 RV를, 수동이면 p.p.를 목적격 보어로 취한다. 여기서는 it이 가리키는 것이 a bandage이고, 붕대는 '벗겨지는' 것이므로 과거분사 taken off의 쓰임은 적절하다.

[해석] ① 그 아이는 부모에게 반려동물을 키워도 되는지 물었다.
② 해결책을 제시하지 않고 불평하는 것은 아무런 소용이 없다.
③ 손가락에 붕대를 감고 있던 한 학생이 방금 그것을 벗겨냈다.
④ 그 고객은 구조적 결함 때문에 제품 교체를 요구했다.

[어휘] complain 불평하다 bandage 붕대 structural 구조적인 defect 결함

[정답] ④

07 우리말을 영어로 잘못 옮긴 것은? [문법]

① 그는 아무 일도 없었다는 듯이 나를 향해 미소를 지었다.
→ He smiled at me as if nothing had happened.
② 보고서를 제시간에 제출할 것을 기억하는 것이 중요하다.
→ It's important to remember submitting the report on time.
③ 집을 나서기 전에 창문이 모두 닫혀 있는지 확인해라.
→ Make sure that all windows are closed before leaving the house.
④ 그녀의 재능은 노래보다는 악기 연주에 있다.
→ Her talent is not so much in singing as in playing musical instruments.

[해설] (submitting → to submit) 가주어(It)-진주어(to remember) 구문이 쓰인 문장이다. 그런데 'remember RVing'는 '~한 것을 기억하다'라는 의미이고, 'remember to RV'는 '~할 것을 기억하다'라는 의미이다. 주어진 우리말에 따르면 '제출할 것을 기억하는' 것이기 때문에 to submit가 쓰여야 한다.
① 주어진 우리말에 따라 '마치 ~이었던 것처럼'이란 뜻의 as if 가정법 과거완료가 쓰여, 종속절에 had happened가 쓰인 것은 적절하다.
③ 접속사 that이 명사절을 이끌고 있다. 형용사로 쓰인 all 뒤에 복수 명사 windows가 오고, 창문이 '닫히는' 것이므로 수동태 복수 동사 are closed가 쓰인 것은 적절하다. 또한 before 이하의 분사구문에서 의미상 주어가 청자인 you이며, you가 집을 '떠나는' 것이므로 능동의 현재분사 leaving은 적절하게 쓰였다.
④ 'not so much A as B'는 'A라기보다는 B인'이라는 뜻을 지닌 표현이므로, 주어진 우리말에 따라 A와 B의 위치가 적절하게 놓여 있다.

[어휘] submit 제출하다

[정답] ②

08 다음 글의 내용과 일치하지 않는 것은? [불일치]

The Booker Prize, formerly known as the Man Booker Prize, is one of the most prestigious literary awards in the world. Established in 1969, the prize aims to recognize outstanding works of fiction written in the English language. Initially limited to writers from the Commonwealth, Ireland, and Zimbabwe, it was later expanded in 2013 to include authors from any nationality, provided their work is originally written in English and published in the UK or Ireland. The influence of the prize is such that the winner will almost certainly see the sales increase significantly, besides the £50,000 that comes with the prize. A sister prize, the International Booker Prize, is awarded for a book translated into English and published in the UK or Ireland. For this award, the £50,000 prize money is split evenly between the author and the translator of the winning novel.

① The Booker Prize awards remarkable works of fiction.
② To win the Booker Prize, novels must be written in English.
③ The scope of authors eligible for the Booker Prize widened in 2013.
④ The winning author of the International Booker Prize receives £50,000.

[해설] 마지막 문장에서 국제 부커상의 상금 5만 파운드는 수상 소설의 작가와 번역가에게 균등하게 나눈다고 언급되므로, 글의 내용과 일치하지 않는 것은 ④ '국제 부커상의 수상 작가는 5만 파운드를 받는다.'이다.
① 부커상은 주목할 만한 소설 작품을 수여한다. → 2번째 문장에서 언급된 내용이다.
② 부커상을 타기 위해서는 소설이 영어로 쓰여야 한다. → 2, 3번째 문장에서 언급된 내용이다.
③ 2013년에 부커상을 탈 자격이 있는 작가의 범위가 넓어졌다. → 3번째 문장에서 언급된 내용이다.

[해석] 이전에 맨부커상으로 알려졌던 부커상은 세계에서 가장 권위 있는 문학상 중 하나이다. 1969년에 제정된 이 상은 영어로 쓰인 뛰어난 소설 작품을 선정하는 것을 목표로 한다. 처음에 영연방, 아일랜드, 짐바브웨의 작가로 제한되었지만, 이후 2013년에 그것은 작품이 최초에 영어로 쓰이고 영국이나 아일랜드에서 출판되는 전제하에 모든 국적의 작가를 포함하도록 확대되었다. 수상자는 이 상과 함께 주어지는 5만 파운드 외에 판매량이 크게 증가하는 것을 목격할 것이 거의 확실할 정도로 이 상은 영향력이 있다. 자매 상인 국제 부커상은 영어로 번역되어 영국 또는 아일랜드에서 출판된 책에 수여된다. 이 상은 5만 파운드의 상금이 수상 소설의 작가와 번역가에게 균등하게 나뉜다.

[어휘] prestigious 명성이 있는, 권위 있는 literary 문학의 establish 설립하다 fiction 소설 initially 처음에 nationality 국적 originally 처음에 split 나누다 eligible 자격이 있는

[정답] ④

09 다음 글의 내용과 일치하는 것은? [일치]

A rack jobber is a vendor who rents space in a retail store or supermarket to display and sell products. Some rack jobbers are distributors, bringing in products from larger wholesale companies to sell in local stores. Others actually make or manufacture their own items and contract with store owners to use their floor space. Before contracting with a retailer, a rack jobber conducts market research to try to predict if the store's regular customers will be interested in his or her goods. The jobber determines what quantities of items to stock and what percentage of profits should be given to the retailer. As the job title implies, a rack jobber usually brings his or her own rack to display goods.

① Rack jobbers don't manufacture their own products.
② Market research is conducted after contracting with a retailer.
③ Rack jobbers decide how much of the profit goes to the retailer.
④ Rack jobbers generally use the store's rack to display their items.

[해설] 마지막 2번째 문장에서 진열 도매상은 수익의 몇 퍼센트를 소매업자에게 제공해야 하는지를 결정한다고 했으므로, 글의 내용과 일치하는 것은 ③ '진열 도매상은 수익의 얼마가 소매업체에 갈지를 결정한다.'이다.
① 진열 도매상은 자신의 상품을 제조하지 않는다. → 3번째 문장에서 일부 진열 도매상은 실제로 직접 상품을 만들거나 제조한다고 언급되므로 옳지 않다.
② 소매업체와 계약한 후에 시장 조사가 수행된다. → 4번째 문장에서 진열 도매상은 소매점과 계약하기 전에 시장 조사를 수행한다고 언급되므로 적절하지 않다.
④ 진열 도매상은 일반적으로 상점의 선반을 이용하여 상품을 진열한다. → 마지막 문장에서 진열 도매상은 일반적으로 자신의 선반을 가져와 물품을 진열한다고 언급되므로 적절하지 않다.

[해석] 진열 도매상은 소매점이나 슈퍼마켓의 공간을 임대하여 제품을 진열하고 판매하는 상인이다. 일부 진열 도매상은 유통업자로, 대형 도매업체에서 제품을 가져와 지역 매장에서 판매한다. 다른 이들은 실제로 직접 상품을 만들거나 제조하고 매장 공간을 사용하기 위해 점주와 계약한다. 소매점과 계약하기 전에, 진열 도매상은 시장 조사를 수행하여 매장의 단골손님이 자신의 상품에 관심을 가질지 예측하려고 한다. 도매상은 어느 정도 양의 물품을 갖춰야 하는지, 수익의 몇 퍼센트를 소매업자에게 제공해야 하는지 결정한다. 직책명에서 알 수 있듯이, 진열 도매상은 일반적으로 자신의 선반을 가져와 물품을 진열한다.

[어휘] rack jobber 진열 도매상 vendor (행)상인, 노점상 retail store 소매점 display 진열하다 distributor 유통업체 wholesale 도매의 manufacture 제조하다 contract with ~과 계약하다 regular customer 단골 goods 제품 stock 갖추다 profit 수익

[정답] ③

10 밑줄 친 부분에 들어갈 말로 가장 적절한 것은?

A: I heard someone came in for an interview yesterday.
B: Yes, I interviewed her for the senior manager position.
A: Oh, how was she?
B: She has a lot of experience in the field, and she seemed very responsible. She's definitely a candidate.
A: _____
B: Yes, I need to choose between three people. It's a very hard decision to make.

① Do you think you'll get the job?
② Who else interviewed her with you?
③ Is she the only candidate for the position?
④ Are there others you're considering as well?

[해설] 시니어 매니저로 채용할 사람을 면접 본 것에 관해 대화를 나누는 상황이다. 빈칸 내용에 대한 응답으로 B가 그렇다고 하며, 세 명 중에 선택해야 한다고 말하고 있으므로, 빈칸에 들어갈 말로 가장 적절한 것은 ④ '네가 고려하고 있는 다른 사람들도 있어?'이다.
① 네가 그 일자리를 얻을 것 같아?
② 누가 너와 함께 그녀를 면접 봤어?
③ 그 직책에 있어 그녀가 유일한 후보야?

[해석] A: 어제 면접을 보러 온 사람이 있다고 들었어.
B: 응, 시니어 매니저 자리를 놓고 면접을 봤어.
A: 아, 그녀는 어땠어?
B: 그녀는 그 분야에서 경험이 많고 책임감이 강해 보였어. 확실히 그녀는 후보야.
A: 네가 고려하고 있는 다른 사람들도 있어?
B: 응, 세 명 중에 선택해야 해. 정말 어려운 결정이야.

[어휘] field 분야 responsible 책임감 있는 candidate 후보

[정답] ④

11 밑줄 친 부분에 들어갈 말로 가장 적절한 것은?

A: Did you apply for the audition for the play Macbeth?
B: No, and I don't plan to either.
A: Why not? You've been preparing so hard for it.
B: Well, I've failed at every audition I've had so far. I must be horrible at acting. There's no chance I'll make it anyway.
A: Oh, come on. _____ You need to leave the past behind. Things might turn out differently this time.

① I second that.
② Snap out of it.
③ Don't give it a shot.
④ The audition will be in vain.

[해설] 오디션에 매번 떨어져 다른 오디션에도 지원하지 않으려 하는 B를 A가 격려하는 상황이다. 낙담하고 있는 B에게 A는 따뜻한 말을 전하거나 따끔한 충고를 할 것을 유추할 수 있으므로, 빈칸에 들어갈 말로 가장 적절한 것은 ② '정신 차려.'이다.
① 동감이야.
③ 그거 시도하지 마.
④ 그 오디션은 헛수고가 될 거야.

[해석] A: Macbeth 연극 오디션에 지원했어?
B: 아니, 그리고 그럴 계획도 없어.
A: 왜? 너 그걸 위해서 정말 열심히 준비했잖아.
B: 음, 난 지금까지 한 모든 오디션에서 탈락했어. 난 연기를 정말 못하는 게 분명해. 어차피 합격할 가능성도 없어.
A: 아, 왜 그래. 정신 차려. 과거는 잊어버려야 해. 이번에는 상황이 달라질지도 모르잖아.

[어휘] turn out (일·결과가 어떤 방식으로) 되다 give it a shot 한 번 해보다 in vain 헛된

[정답] ②

12 두 사람의 대화 중 자연스럽지 않은 것은?

① A: Is the date for the conference set?
   B: I'll check right now and get back to you.
② A: May I ask what you do for a living?
   B: I live just a few streets down from here.
③ A: I'm meeting up with Wendy tomorrow.
   B: Oh, you are? Tell her I say hi.
④ A: When are you going to start packing your luggage?
   B: I'll get to it eventually. There's no need to rush.

[해설] 어떤 일을 하는지 물어보는 A에게 자신이 어디에 사는지를 설명하는 B의 응답은 적절하지 않다. 따라서 대화 중 자연스럽지 않은 것은 ②이다.

[해석] ① A: 회의 날짜가 정해졌나요?
B: 지금 확인해서 다시 알려드리겠습니다.
② A: 어떤 일을 하시는지 여쭤봐도 될까요?
B: 저는 여기에서 조금 떨어진 곳에 살고 있어요.
③ A: 나 내일 Wendy와 만나기로 했어.
B: 아, 그래? 그녀에게 안부 전해줘.
④ A: 언제부터 짐을 싸기 시작할 거니?
B: 언젠가는 할 거예요. 서두를 필요 없어요.

[어휘] conference 회의 pack 짐을 싸다 rush 서두르다

[정답] ②

13 다음 글의 제목으로 알맞은 것은?

Over the years, scientists have developed a variety of technologies and techniques for detecting lies. Topping the list are polygraph machines, often called lie detectors, which relate changes in heart rate, blood pressure and electro-dermal reactivity to a subject's truthfulness. Widely used by law enforcement agencies and businesses, however, lie detectors have increasingly come under critical scrutiny. In 2002, a National Academy of Sciences panel reviewed data from several decades of polygraphs and concluded that there was "little basis for the expectation that a polygraph test could have extremely high accuracy." In fact, the panel estimated that if polygraphs were administered to a group of 10,000 people that included 10 spies, nearly 1,600 innocent people would fail the test — and two of the spies would pass.

① Polygraphs Make Lying Powerless
② Polygraph Machines: Highly Controversial
③ Ways to Improve the Lie Detector's Accuracy
④ Characteristics of People Prone to Lie Detection

해설 이 글은 거짓말 탐지기가 널리 사용됨에도 불구하고, 그것의 정확도에 대한 근거가 거의 없다는 연구 결과를 제시하고 있다. 따라서 글의 제목으로 가장 적절한 것은 ② '거짓말 탐지기: 논란의 여지가 매우 많은'이다.
① 거짓말 탐지기는 거짓말을 무력하게 만든다 → 거짓말 탐지기가 거짓말을 무력하게 만드는 것이 아니라, 오히려 거짓말을 해도 거짓말 탐지기는 이를 잘 걸러내지 못한다는 점을 주장하는 글이다.
③ 거짓말 탐지기의 정확도를 향상하는 방법 → 거짓말 탐지기의 정확도를 어떻게 개선할 수 있는지를 설명하는 글이 아니다.
④ 거짓말 감지를 쉽게 당하는 사람들의 특징 → 거짓말 탐지기에 잘 감지되는 사람들이 어떤 특징을 가지고 있는지는 언급되지 않았다.

해석 수년에 걸쳐, 과학자들은 거짓말을 탐지하기 위한 다양한 기술과 기법을 개발해 왔다. 그중에서도 거짓말 탐지기(lie detector)라고도 불리는 거짓말 탐지기(polygraph)는 심박수, 혈압, 전기 피부 반응성의 변화를 피실험자의 진실성과 연관시킨다. 그러나 법 집행 기관과 기업에서 널리 사용되는 거짓말 탐지기는 점점 더 비판적인 정밀 검토를 받고 있다. 2002년, 미국 국립과학원의 한 패널은 수십 년 동안의 거짓말 탐지기의 데이터를 검토하고, "거짓말 탐지기 검사가 매우 높은 정확도를 가질 수 있다는 기대에 대한 근거가 거의 없다"라고 결론지었다. 실제로, 그 패널은 10명의 스파이가 포함된 10,000명의 집단에 거짓말 탐지기 검사를 실시할 경우, 약 1,600명의 무고한 사람들이 검사에 불합격하고 스파이 중 두 명은 통과할 것으로 추정했다.

어휘 a variety of 다양한 detect 탐지하다 top the list 목록의 꼭대기에 있다 polygraph 거짓말 탐지기 relate A to B A를 B에 연결시키다 electro-dermal 전기 피부의 reactivity 반응성 subject 피실험자 truthfulness 진실성 law enforcement agency 법 집행 기관 under scrutiny 정밀 조사를 받는 accuracy 정확성 estimate 추정하다 administer 실시하다 innocent 무고한

정답 ②

14 다음 글의 주제로 알맞은 것은?

The medical community is beginning to realize how important the hospital environment is to patient recovery. Specifically, art can create a calming and positive environment in the hospital, which can reduce stress and anxiety, ultimately promoting faster healing and better overall well-being. To make hospitals more welcoming, famous artists are being asked to decorate old hospitals and modernize new ones. About 100 of the National Health Service's 2,500 hospitals have acquired collections of modern art to display in corridors and treatment rooms. The effect has been amazing, as patients have reported a noticeable improvement in their overall mood and reduction in stress levels. Incorporating art into the hospital environment has become a widely accepted method of enhancing the holistic health and well-being of patients.

① doubts about the healing power of art
② positive effects of bringing art into hospitals
③ absolute necessity of building more hospitals
④ various attempts to find places to display art

해설 미술 작품을 병원 내에 전시하는 것이 긍정적인 분위기를 조성하여 환자들의 회복에 좋은 영향을 미친다는 내용의 글이다. 따라서 글의 주제로 가장 적절한 것은 ② '병원에 미술을 도입하는 것의 긍정적인 효과'이다.
① 미술의 치유력에 대한 의구심 → 미술의 치유력을 긍정하는 글이므로 반대된다.
③ 더 많은 병원을 지을 절대적 필요성 → 병원의 수가 부족하다는 점을 지적하는 글이 아니다.
④ 미술을 전시하기 위한 장소를 찾기 위한 다양한 시도들 → 병원 외에 다른 장소는 언급되지 않았으므로 '장소'는 너무 포괄적이며, 미술을 전시할 장소를 찾기 위한 여러 시도들에 관해 설명하는 글이 아니므로 적절하지 않다.

해석 의료계는 병원 환경이 환자 회복에 얼마나 중요한지 깨닫기 시작하고 있다. 특히, 미술은 병원에 차분하고 긍정적인 환경을 조성하는데, 그것은 스트레스와 불안을 줄여 궁극적으로 더 빠른 치유와 더 나은 전반적인 복지를 촉진할 수 있다. 병원을 더욱 친근하게 만들기 위해, 유명 미술가들이 오래된 병원을 꾸미고 새 병원을 현대화해달라는 요청을 받고 있다. 국민건강서비스의 2,500개 병원 중 약 100개 병원이 복도와 치료실에 전시할 현대 미술 컬렉션을 구입해왔다. 환자들이 전반적인 기분에 있어 눈에 띄는 개선과 스트레스 수준의 감소를 보고한 것과 같이 그 효과는 놀라웠다. 병원 환경에 미술을 접목하는 것은 환자의 전반적인 행복과 복지를 향상하는 방법으로 널리 인정받아왔다.

어휘 recovery 회복 specifically 특히, 구체적으로 ultimately 궁극적으로 promote 촉진하다 healing 치료 overall 전반적인 well-being 복지, 행복 decorate 장식하다 modernize 현대화하다 corridor 복도 treatment 치료 noticeable 눈에 띄는 reduction 감소 incorporate 포함하다 enhance 향상하다 holistic 전인적인

정답 ②

15 다음 글의 요지로 알맞은 것은? [요지]

At the beginning of the semester, a ceramics instructor decided to divide her class into two groups and announced that the students on the left side of the studio would be graded on the quantity of work they produced, while the students on the right side of the studio would be graded solely on the quality of their work. The "quantity" group was required to produce fifty pounds of pots to receive an "A," forty pounds for a "B," and so on. On the other hand, the "quality" group only needed to produce one perfect pot to receive an "A." When it came time to grade, the teacher was surprised to find that the highest quality work was produced by the "quantity" group. While this group was busy producing a large number of pots and learning from the process, the "quality" group spent their time theorizing about perfection and had little chance to refine their techniques through hands-on experience.

① More does not necessarily mean better.
② The process is not justified by external results.
③ Perfection demands a detailed planning process.
④ Learning from multiple attempts breeds excellence.

[해설] 가장 훌륭한 도자기는 가장 높은 질의 도자기 하나를 만들어야 했던 집단이 아니라, 질에 상관없이 많은 양의 도자기를 만들어야 했던 집단에서 나왔다는 내용의 글이다. 이는 많은 시도를 통해 얻는 학습의 중요성을 역설하는 것이므로, 글의 요지로 알맞은 것은 ④ '여러 시도를 통한 학습이 우수성을 낳는다.'이다.
① 많은 것이 반드시 더 좋은 것은 아니다. → 오히려 많은 도자기를 만든 집단에서 가장 높은 질의 도자기가 나왔으므로 반대된다.
② 과정은 외부적인 결과로 정당화되지 않는다. → 좋은 결과가 그 과정까지 정당화하지는 않는다는 내용의 글이 아니다.
③ 완벽은 치밀한 계획 과정을 필요로 한다. → 오히려 치밀하게 계획하려고 했던 것이 결과에 악영향을 미친 것이므로 적절하지 않다.

[해석] 학기 초에 한 도예 강사는 자기 반을 두 집단으로 나누기로 결정하고, 스튜디오의 왼쪽에 있는 학생들은 만들어 낸 작품의 양으로 성적을 매기겠다고 한 반면, 스튜디오의 오른쪽에 있는 학생들은 작품의 질로만 성적을 매기겠다고 발표했다. '양' 집단은 'A'를 받기 위해서 50파운드의 도자기를, 'B'를 위해서 40파운드의 도자기를 만들어야 하는 식이었다. 반면에 '질' 집단은 'A'를 받기 위해서 완벽한 도자기 하나만 만들면 되었다. 성적을 매길 때가 되었을 때, 그 교사는 가장 높은 질의 작품이 '양' 집단에 의해 만들어졌다는 것을 알고 깜짝 놀랐다. 이 집단은 많은 수의 도자기를 생산하며 그 과정에서 배우는 데 바빴던 반면에, '질' 집단은 완벽함에 대한 이론을 세우는 데 시간을 보냈고 실제 경험을 통해 기술을 다듬을 기회가 거의 없었다.

[어휘] semester 학기 ceramics 도예 instructor 강사 announce 발표하다 solely 오로지 theorize 이론화하다 refine 다듬다

[정답] ④

16 밑줄 친 부분에 들어갈 말로 알맞은 것은? [빈칸완성]

Our kids have too much stuff, too many choices, and they're exposed to too much information. Their lives are busy, and this affects their ability to pay attention. Researchers conducted an experiment to streamline the lives of children with attention deficit disorder. They made changes to their environment by reducing the number of toys, extracurricular activities, and screen time. Instead, they encouraged more opportunities for free play and daydreaming. Remarkably, in only four months, 68 percent of the children reported their problems had disappeared. Their academic skills also increased by 37 percent. This shows that children must be provided with time, with freedom, so that they can connect themselves to the real world as well as with themselves. It's a matter of _____ their lives in order to create a qualitatively better experience for them.

① planning
② simplifying
③ overseeing
④ diversifying

[해설] 주의력 결핍 장애가 있는 아이들을 대상으로 환경을 단순화하여 더 많은 자유를 부여한 것의 효과를 관찰한 실험을 소개하는 글이다. 따라서 빈칸에 들어갈 말로 알맞은 것은 ② '단순화하는'이다.
① 계획하는 → 아이의 삶을 계획하는 것의 중요성을 주장하는 글이 아니다.
③ 감독하는 → 아이의 삶을 지켜보는 것이 그들에게 더 많은 자유를 부여하는 것은 아니므로 적절하지 않다.
④ 다양화하는 → 환경을 '다양화하는' 대신 오히려 '단순하게' 하는 것이 좋다는 내용의 글이므로 반대된다.

[해석] 우리 아이들은 너무 많은 물건과 너무 많은 선택지를 가졌으며, 너무 많은 정보에 노출된다. 그들의 삶은 바쁘며, 이것은 그들이 주의를 기울이는 능력에 영향을 미친다. 연구자들은 주의력 결핍 장애가 있는 아이들의 삶을 단순화하는 실험을 진행했다. 그들은 장난감 수와 교과 외 활동, 그리고 화면 사용 시간을 줄여 그들의 환경에 변화를 주었다. 대신에, 그들은 자유 놀이와 공상할 수 있는 더 많은 기회를 장려했다. 놀랍게도, 단 4개월 만에 68%의 아이들은 자신의 문제가 사라졌다고 보고했다. 그들의 학업 능력 또한 37% 증가했다. 이것은 아이들이 자기 자신뿐 아니라 현실 세계에 연결될 수 있도록 시간과 자유를 제공받아야 한다는 것을 보여준다. 그것은 그들에게 질적으로 더 나은 (삶의) 경험을 만들어 주고자 그들의 삶을 단순화하는 것의 문제이다.

[어휘] pay attention 주의를 기울이다 streamline 단순화하다 deficit 결핍 disorder 장애 extracurricular 교과 외의 screen time (컴퓨터, 스마트 기기 등) 화면 사용 시간 daydream 공상하다 qualitatively 질적으로

[정답] ②

17 다음 글의 흐름상 어색한 문장은?

It's no secret that the Internet is saturated with all kinds of information, much of which is unverified and sometimes even harmful. ① Yet, in the blink of an eye, this information circulates without confirmation. ② It is all too easy to believe the latest gossip on Twitter or get lost in YouTube videos featuring false rumors. ③ What is most concerning is that some of this baseless online information could hurt certain individuals, companies, and even entire industries. ④ However, our lives are now so intertwined with the Internet that it has become an essential resource for daily information needs. Even if such information is corrected or disproved, chances are that the audience's attention has long shifted, the damage has already been done, and the original misinformation continues to float around online for future discovery.

18 주어진 문장이 들어갈 위치로 알맞은 것은?

While such tendencies can also be seen in some financial circles in Europe, art lovers and most art collectors are more hesitant.

Over the past few years, the list of record prices paid at auctions has changed ever more rapidly. The enormous prices paid for some paintings create a widespread belief that the rate of return on investments in art is in general very high. (①) Especially in the United States, an increasing number of investors believe that purchasing art provides not only aesthetic pleasure but also financial benefits. (②) American banks, and recently also auction houses, strengthen the trend of viewing art as an investment by extending credit and by hiring "art investment counsellors" thus suggesting that it is financially rewarding to buy art. (③) They warn that art objects should not be treated as financial assets. (④) Their belief is that art should be owned for its intrinsic value rather than for financial purposes.

19 주어진 글 다음에 이어질 글의 순서로 알맞은 것은? [순서배열]

A teenager joins a line of people boarding a spaceship. Once on board, he approaches a bed, crawls in, closes the lid and falls asleep.

(A) All of these stories have one thing in common: people enter an unconscious state in which they can survive for a long time. However, nothing like this is yet possible in the real world for any organism, let alone humans.

(B) It is employed in a lot of science fiction. There's Captain America, for instance, who survived nearly 70 years frozen in ice. And Han Solo was frozen in carbonite in Star Wars.

(C) His body is frozen for a trip to a planet several light-years from Earth. A few years later he wakes up, still the same age. This ability to put his life on pause while asleep is called "suspended animation."

① (A) - (C) - (B) ② (B) - (A) - (C)
③ (C) - (A) - (B) ④ (C) - (B) - (A)

[해설] 주어진 글은 한 청소년이 우주선에 탑승한 뒤에 침대에 들어가 뚜껑을 닫고 잠이 든다는 내용으로, 뒤에는 그의 몸이 먼 행성으로 가기 위해 얼어 있는 것이라고 부연하는 내용의 (C)가 와야 한다. 그다음으로, (C)의 마지막 문장에서 소개된 '가사 상태'의 개념을 It으로 받아, 그것이 공상 과학 소설에 자주 쓰인다는 내용의 (B)가 오는 것이 적절하다. 마지막으로, (B)에서 소개된 예시들을 these stories로 받아, 그 공통점을 설명한 뒤에 현실 세계에서는 그것이 불가능하다며 글을 마무리하는 (A)가 오는 것이 자연스럽다. 따라서 글의 순서로 알맞은 것은 ④ '(C) - (B) - (A)'이다.

[해석] 한 청소년이 우주선에 탑승하는 사람들의 행렬에 합류한다. 탑승하고 난 뒤, 그는 한 침대에 다가가 기어들어 가서 뚜껑을 닫고 잠이 든다. (C) 그의 몸은 지구에서 몇 광년 떨어진 행성으로 여행 가기 위해 얼어 있다. 몇 년 뒤 그는 여전히 같은 나이로 깨어난다. 잠든 동안 그의 생명을 일시 정지시키는 이 능력을 '가사 상태'라고 부른다. (B) 이것은 많은 공상 과학 소설에 이용된다. 예를 들어, 얼음 속에서 거의 70년을 언 채로 생존한 Captain America가 있다. 스타워즈에서는 Han Solo가 카보나이트에서 얼어 있었다. (A) 이 모든 이야기는 한 가지의 공통점이 있는데, 그것은 사람들이 오랫동안 생존할 수 있는 무의식적인 상태로 들어간다는 것이다. 그러나 아직 현실 세계에서는 인간은 물론 어떤 생물체도 이와 같은 것이 가능하지는 않다.

[어휘] board 탑승하다 approach 접근하다 crawl 기어가다 unconscious 무의식적인 employ 이용하다 fiction 소설 survive 생존하다 carbonite 탄소 ability 능력 pause 중지, 중단 suspend 일시중지하다

[정답] ④

20 밑줄 친 부분에 들어갈 말로 알맞은 것은? [빈칸완성]

Our perceptions about our lives are the outcome of many forces that shape experience, each having an impact on whether we feel good or bad. Most of these forces are beyond control. There is not much we can do about our looks, our temperament, or our constitution. We cannot decide — at least so far — how tall we will grow, or how smart we will get. We can choose neither parents nor time of birth, and it is not in your power or mine to decide whether there will be a war or a depression. The instructions contained in our genes, the pull of gravity, the pollen in the air, the historical period into which we are born — these and countless other conditions determine what we see, what we hear, and how we feel. It is not surprising that we should believe that our lives are primarily determined by _____.

① outside factors
② collective efforts
③ voluntary choices
④ our way of thinking

[해설] 이 글은 우리의 경험을 형성하는 많은 요인은 우리의 통제를 벗어난 것이라고 말하며 그 예시들을 나열하고 있다. 이는 우리의 삶이 외부 요인들에 의해 큰 영향을 받는다는 점을 강조하는 것으로, 빈칸에 들어갈 말로 알맞은 것은 ① '외부 요인들'이다.
② 집단적 노력 → 함께 노력하는 것이 우리의 삶을 결정한다는 것을 주장하는 글이 아니다.
③ 자발적 선택 → 오히려 우리의 자발적 선택이 아닌 외부 요인들에 의해 삶이 결정되는 면을 강조하는 글이므로 반대된다.
④ 우리가 생각하는 방식 → 우리가 생각하는 방식이 우리의 삶을 결정한다는 내용의 글이 아니다.

[해석] 우리의 삶에 대한 우리의 인식은 경험을 형성하는 많은 힘의 결과인데 각각의 힘은 우리가 기분이 좋은지 나쁜지에 영향을 준다. 이런 힘들의 대부분은 우리의 통제력을 넘어선다. 우리의 외모, 기질, 또는 체질에 대해서 우리가 어떻게 해볼 수 있는 것이 많지 않다. 우리는 적어도 현재까지는 우리가 얼마나 자랄지, 또는 우리가 얼마나 똑똑해질지 결정할 수 없다. 우리는 부모도, 출생 시기도 선택할 수 없으며, 전쟁이나 불황이 일어날 것인지를 결정하는 것은 당신이나 나의 권한이 아니다. 우리의 유전자 안에 있는 명령, 중력의 작용, 공기 중의 꽃가루, 우리가 태어나는 역사적 시기 등 이런 것들과 수많은 다른 조건들이 우리가 보고, 듣고, 느끼는 것을 결정한다. 우리의 삶이 주로 외부 요인들에 의해 결정된다고 믿는 것은 놀라운 일이 아니다.

[어휘] perception 인식, 지각 looks 표정, 모양새 temperament 기질, 성질 constitution 체질, 체격 neither A nor B A도 아니고 B도 아닌 depression 불경기, 불황 gene 유전자 pull 잡아당기기, 당기는 힘 gravity 중력 pollen 꽃가루 countless 무수한 collective 집단적인

[정답] ①

Answer

회차 3

01	02	03	04	05
①	②	③	③	④
06	07	08	09	10
②	②	④	③	②
11	12	13	14	15
②	①	①	②	④
16	17	18	19	20
③	③	④	③	②

01 밑줄 친 부분의 의미와 가장 가까운 것은? 〔어휘〕

The company's resources were insufficient to handle the surge in demand for its products.

① short
② abundant
③ exhausted
④ distributed

[해설] insufficient는 '부족한'이라는 뜻으로, 이와 의미가 가장 가까운 것은 ① 'short (부족한)'이다.
② 풍부한 ③ 고갈된 ④ 분배된
[해석] 그 회사의 자원은 자사 제품에 대한 수요 급증을 감당하기에 부족했다.
[어휘] surge 급증 demand 수요

[정답] ①

02 밑줄 친 부분의 의미와 가장 가까운 것은? 〔어휘〕

In response to valuable customer feedback, the enterprise announced an initiative to introduce innovative features and significantly enhance the overall user experience.

① pledge
② scheme
③ objection
④ investigation

[해설] initiative는 '계획'이라는 뜻으로, 이와 의미가 가장 가까운 것은 ② 'scheme(계획)'이다.
① 약속 ③ 반대 ④ 조사
[해석] 소중한 고객 피드백에 답하여, 그 회사는 혁신적인 특색을 도입하고 전반적인 사용자 경험을 크게 향상하기 위한 계획을 발표했다.
[어휘] valuable 소중한 enterprise 기업 innovative 혁신적인 significantly 크게 enhance 향상하다

[정답] ②

03 밑줄 친 부분의 의미와 가장 가까운 것은? 〔이어동사〕

Mary had to turn down the request for additional information.

① fulfill
② review
③ refuse
④ manage

[해설] turn down은 '거절하다'라는 뜻으로, 이와 의미가 가장 가까운 것은 ③ 'refuse (거절하다)'이다.
① 이행하다 ② 검토하다 ④ 감당하다
[해석] Mary는 추가 정보에 대한 요청을 거절해야 했다.

[정답] ③

04 밑줄 친 부분의 의미와 가장 가까운 것은? 〔이어동사〕

Michael had to stand in for the manager in overseeing daily operations.

① assist
② imitate
③ substitute
④ acknowledge

[해설] stand in for는 '대신하다'라는 뜻으로, 이와 의미가 가장 가까운 것은 ③ 'substitute(대신하다)'이다.
① 돕다 ② 모방하다, 본받다 ④ 인정하다
[해석] Michael은 일상 업무를 감독하는 데 있어 매니저를 대신해야 했다.
[어휘] oversee 감독하다 operation 작업, 업무

[정답] ③

05 밑줄 친 부분에 들어갈 말로 가장 적절한 것은? 〔어휘〕

The politician has shown _____ to transparency in governance, consistently engaging in open communication with citizens in person.

① distortion
② corruption
③ alternative
④ commitment

[해설] 시민들과 공개 소통을 몸소 꾸준히 해왔다는 콤마 뒤 내용으로 보아, 그 정치인이 투명한 통치에 온 힘을 다하고 있음을 알 수 있다. 따라서 빈칸에 들어갈 말로 가장 적절한 것은 ④ 'commitment(헌신)'이다.
① 왜곡 ② 부패 ③ 대안
[해석] 그 정치인은 시민들과의 열린 소통에 직접 꾸준히 참여하면서 통치의 투명성에 대한 헌신을 보여 왔다.
[어휘] transparency 투명성 governance 통치 consistently 지속적으로 in person 직접

[정답] ④

06 밑줄 친 부분 중 어법상 옳지 않은 것은?

Although only ① a few of the 70-80 species of poisonous mushrooms are fatal when ② ingesting, many of these deadly fungi ③ bear a particularly deceptive resemblance to edible species, making identification ④ challenging and increasing the risk of accidental ingestion.

[해설] (ingesting → ingested) 분사구문 when ingesting의 의미상 주어는 only a few of the 70-80 species of poisonous mushrooms인데, 버섯은 '섭취되는' 것이므로 수동의 과거분사 ingested가 되어야 한다.
① 문맥상 70-80종의 독버섯 중 겨우 '조금'이라는 뜻이 되어야 하므로 a few는 적절하게 쓰였으며, 뒤에 복수 명사 the 70-80 species와 복수 동사가 are이 온 것도 적절하다.
③ 주어가 복수 명사인 many of these deadly fungi이므로, 그에 수일치한 복수 동사 bear의 쓰임은 적절하다.
④ 5형식 동사로 쓰인 make가 목적격 보어로 형용사 challenging을 취하고 있는 것은 적절하다.

[해석] 70-80종의 독버섯 중 일부만이 섭취 시 치명적이지만, 이러한 치명적인 균류 중 다수는 식용종과 특히 기만적인 유사성을 지니고 있어 식별을 어렵게 하고 우발적으로 섭취할 위험을 늘린다.

[어휘] poisonous 독이 있는 fatal 치명적인 ingest 섭취하다 deadly 치명적인 fungus 균류(pl. fungi) bear 지니다 deceptive 속이는, 기만적인 resemblance 유사성 edible 식용의 identification 식별 challenging 힘든 accidental 우발적인

[정답] ②

---

07 밑줄 친 부분이 어법상 옳지 않은 것은?

① The sale prices will be valid until the end of the week.
② After hearing the arguments, she convinced of their logic.
③ They have been living in the city since they graduated from college.
④ I look forward to discussing potential partnerships with your company.

[해설] (convinced → was convinced) convince는 '확신시키다'라는 의미로 'convince A of B'의 구조를 취할 수 있는데, 이를 수동태로 바꾸면 '~을 확신하다'라는 의미인 'A be convinced of B'의 구조가 된다. 여기서는 주어인 she가 '확신한' 것이므로, convinced를 was convinced로 고쳐야 한다. 참고로 분사구문의 의미상 주어인 she가 주장을 '듣는' 것이므로 능동의 현재분사 hearing은 적절하게 쓰였다.
① by는 동작의 완료, until은 동작의 지속을 나타내는 표현과 함께 사용된다. 여기서는 상태의 지속을 나타내는 be valid가 있으므로 until의 쓰임은 적절하다.
③ since절에는 과거시제 graduated가, 주절에는 현재완료진행시제 have been living이 적절하게 쓰였다. 또한 완전자동사 graduate는 목적어를 취할 때 전치사를 함께 사용해야 하므로 뒤에 from이 온 것도 적절하다.
④ 'look forward to RVing'는 '~을 고대하다'라는 뜻의 동명사 관용표현이다. 이때 to는 전치사이므로 뒤에 동명사 discussing이 온 것은 적절하다.

[해석] ① 그 판매 가격은 이번 주말까지 유효할 것이다.
② 그녀는 그 주장을 듣고 나서 그들의 논리를 확신했다.
③ 그들은 대학을 졸업한 후부터 도시에 살고 있다.
④ 저는 귀사와 잠재적인 동업에 대해 논의할 수 있기를 기대합니다.

[어휘] valid 유효한 logic 논리, 타당성 potential 잠재적인

[정답] ②

---

08 우리말을 영어로 잘못 옮긴 것은?

① 당신의 주말 계획이 어떻게 되는지 알려주세요.
→ Let me know what your plans are for the weekend.
② 어떤 이유로도 중요한 마감일을 놓쳐서는 안 된다.
→ On no account should important deadlines be missed.
③ 그곳의 분위기는 긴장되어 있어 모두가 눈을 마주치길 피하는 것 같다.
→ The atmosphere there seems tense, with everyone avoiding eye contact.
④ 그 소설은 내가 최근에 읽은 그 어떤 책보다 더 흥미진진하다.
→ The novel is more fascinating than any other books I have read recently.

[해설] (books → book) 비교급을 이용하여 최상급을 표현하는 경우, '비교급 ~ than + all the other + 복수 명사' 또는 '비교급 ~ than + any other + 단수 명사' 형태를 취한다. 여기서는 any other가 쓰였으므로 뒤에 단수 명사 book이 쓰여야 한다. 참고로 소설이 '흥미를 끄는' 것이므로 능동의 현재분사형 fascinating은 적절하게 쓰였고, book과 I 사이에는 목적격 관계대명사가 생략되어 있어 read 뒤 목적어 자리가 비어 있는 것도 적절하다.
① 선행사를 포함한 관계대명사 what이 적절하게 쓰였다. 여기서 what은 know의 목적어 역할과 are의 보어 역할을 동시에 하고 있다.
② '어떠한 경우에도 ~않다'라는 뜻의 on no account라는 부정어가 문두에 왔으므로, 주어와 동사가 의문문의 어순으로 적절히 도치되었다. 또한 마감일이 '놓치는' 것이 아니라 '놓쳐지는' 것이므로 수동태 be missed도 적절하게 쓰였다.
③ 2형식 동사로 쓰인 seem이 형용사 tense를 보어로 취하고 있는 것은 적절하다. 또한 부대 상황을 나타내는 'with + O + OC' 분사구문이 쓰이고 있는데, everyone이 눈 마주침을 '피하는' 것이므로 능동의 현재분사 avoiding도 적절하게 쓰였다.

[어휘] atmosphere 분위기 tense 긴장된

[정답] ④

09 밑줄 친 부분에 들어갈 말로 가장 적절한 것은? [생활영어]

A: Did you know that bedbugs were found in our neighborhood?
B: Oh no, you've got to be kidding me! What should we do if they get inside our homes?
A: In that case, it's best to call a pest control expert.
B: _____
A: Even so, getting help from an expert will be a lot better than trying to handle the situation by yourself.

① But I haven't found any in my house yet.
② How did the bedbugs get inside your house?
③ I heard even specialists have difficulties, though.
④ Do you know the specific location they were found?

[해설] 빈대가 동네에 퍼진 상황에 관한 대화를 나누고 있다. 빈대가 집 안에 있는 경우에 해충 방제 전문가를 부르는 것이 가장 좋다는 A의 말에 B는 빈칸 내용을 언급하였다. 이에 A는 그런다 할지라도 전문가를 부르는 것이 낫다고 했으므로, 빈칸에서 B는 전문가를 부르는 것과 관련된 걱정을 표현했으리라 유추할 수 있다. 따라서 빈칸에 들어갈 말로 가장 적절한 것은 ③ '근데 전문가도 어려움을 겪는다고 들었는데.'이다.
① 하지만 우리 집에서는 아직 빈대를 발견하지 못했는걸.
② 빈대가 어떻게 네 집 안으로 들어간 거야?
④ 그것들이 발견된 구체적인 위치를 알고 있어?

[해석] A: 우리 동네에서 빈대가 발견된 거 알고 있었어?
B: 아, 말도 안 돼! 빈대가 집 안에 들어오면 어떻게 해야 해?
A: 그 경우에는 해충 방제 전문가를 부르는 게 가장 좋아.
B: 근데 전문가도 어려움을 겪는다고 들었는데.
A: 그런다 할지라도 전문가의 도움을 받는 것이 혼자서 그 상황을 대처하려 하는 것 보다는 훨씬 낫지.

[어휘] bedbug 빈대 pest 해충 handle 대처하다

[정답] ③

10 밑줄 친 부분에 들어갈 말로 가장 적절한 것은? [생활영어]

A: What do you feel like having for lunch?
B: Hmm. I was thinking of pasta. How about you?
A: Funny you should say that. I was thinking the same. _____?
B: There's a nice one that I frequently visit just around the corner, actually.
A: Alright, let's go there then.

① Where did you have lunch today
② Which restaurant should we go to
③ What kind of pasta is your favorite
④ Who else is joining us at the restaurant

[해설] 점심 메뉴에 관한 대화를 나누는 상황이다. 자신도 파스타를 생각 중이었다는 A가 빈칸 내용을 이어 물어봤는데, 이에 B는 자신이 자주 가는 레스토랑이 근처에 있다고 말했다. 따라서 빈칸에서 A는 어느 곳으로 갈지 물어봤음을 알 수 있으므로, 빈칸에 들어갈 말로 가장 적절한 것은 ② '어느 레스토랑에 갈까'이다.
① 오늘 점심은 어디서 먹었어
③ 어떤 종류의 파스타를 제일 좋아해
④ 레스토랑에 우리랑 같이 갈 사람은 누구야

[해석] A: 오늘 점심에 뭐 먹고 싶어?
B: 흠. 난 파스타 생각 중이었어. 너는 어때?
A: 마침 네가 그 말을 하네. 나도 같은 걸 생각 중이었거든. 어느 레스토랑에 갈까?
B: 사실 이 근처에 내가 자주 가는 괜찮은 곳이 있어.
A: 그래, 그럼 거기로 가자.

[어휘] frequently 자주 (just) around the corner 아주 가까운

[정답] ②

11 두 사람의 대화 중 자연스럽지 않은 것은?

① A: May I use your computer for a second?
   B: Sure, go ahead. I don't mind.
② A: What is it like to run your own business?
   B: A pet shop I've been running for three years now.
③ A: Aren't we supposed to have a meeting today?
   B: It was postponed to tomorrow, remember?
④ A: One of the flight attendants on the plane was so rude.
   B: I know who you're talking about. I want to file a complaint.

[해설] 자신의 사업을 운영하는 것이 어떤 느낌인지 물어보는 A에게 3년째 운영하고 있는 반려동물용품점이라는 B의 응답은 어색하다. 따라서 대화 중 자연스럽지 않은 것은 ②이다.

[해석] ① A: 네 컴퓨터를 잠깐 사용해도 될까?
B: 응, 당연하지. 상관없어.
② A: 자신의 사업을 운영하는 건 어떤 느낌이에요?
B: 제가 3년째 운영하고 있는 반려동물용품점입니다.
③ A: 우리 오늘 회의하기로 하지 않았어?
B: 내일로 미뤄졌잖아, 기억나?
④ A: 비행기에서 승무원 중 한 명이 너무 무례했어.
B: 네가 누구를 얘기하는지 알아. 항의를 제기하고 싶어.

[어휘] run one's business 사업을 운영하다 be supposed to ~하기로 되어 있다 postpone 미루다 flight attendant 승무원 file a complaint 항의를 제기하다

[정답] ②

12 다음 글의 제목으로 가장 적절한 것은?

The American author H. L. Mencken wrote in his book that a man is satisfied so long as he is earning more than his brother-in-law. This is because relatives are the closest individuals with whom we can compare our fortunes. Relativity also explains why people become discontented when they learn that their colleagues earn a higher salary. Industrial disputes are less about wages and more about what others in the company are earning in comparison. When we discovered what the bankers were earning during the recent financial crisis, we were outraged. But the bankers could not see the problem with their high salaries and bonuses because they were comparing themselves to other bankers who were prospering.

① Contentment Is Based on Comparison
② Comparison Makes People Work Harder
③ Always Keep Your Negative Emotions in Check
④ Salary Increases and Promotions: Why We Work

[해설] 우리는 우리 주변에 있는 사람들과 비교하며 만족이나 불만을 느낀다는 내용의 글이다. 따라서 글의 제목으로 가장 적절한 것은 ① '만족감은 비교에 기반한다'이다.
② 비교는 사람들을 더 열심히 일하게 만든다 → 사람들은 남들과 비교를 하면서 만족이나 불만을 느낀다는 글의 내용이, 이를 통해 사람들이 더 열심히 일하게 된다는 내용으로까지 전개되지는 않았다.
③ 항상 부정적인 감정을 억제하라 → 부정적인 감정을 억제하라고 권고하는 글이 아니다.
④ 급여 인상과 승진: 우리가 일하는 이유 → 단순 급여 인상과 승진보다는 남들과 비교해서 우리가 얼마나 버는지가 중요한 것이며, 우리가 일하는 이유를 분석하는 글 또한 아니다.

[해석] 미국 작가 H. L. Mencken은 그의 저서에서 사람은 자신의 처남보다 더 많이 벌고 있는 한 만족한다고 썼다. 이는 친척이 우리의 재산을 비교할 수 있는 가장 가까운 사람이기 때문이다. 상대성은 또한 사람들이 자신의 동료가 더 높은 연봉을 받는다는 사실을 알게 될 때 불만을 품는 이유를 설명한다. 노사 분쟁은 임금에 관한 것보다는 회사 내 다른 사람들이 상대적으로 얼마나 버는지에서 비롯된다. 최근 금융위기 동안 은행원들이 얼마나 버는지 알게 되었을 때 우리는 분노했다. 하지만 은행원들은 번영을 누리고 있는 다른 은행원들과 자신을 비교하고 있었기 때문에 자신의 높은 연봉과 보너스에 대한 문제를 인식하지 못했다.

[어휘] earn (돈을) 벌다 brother-in-law 처남 relative 친척 fortune 재산 discontented 불만족한 comparison 비교 financial 금융의 crisis 위기 outrage 분노하게 만들다 prosper 번영하다 promotion 승진

[정답] ①

13 다음 글의 주제로 가장 적절한 것은?

Prescription and over-the-counter medicines have greatly improved the treatment of many health conditions. They help relieve pain, reduce inflammation, and manage chronic diseases. However, like any other substance, medicines can be dangerous and even deadly if misused. People often take more than the recommended dose or mix different types of medicines. This behavior can lead to serious health consequences, including addiction, overdose, and even death. The negative aspect of medication misuse is not limited to illegal drugs; even the most commonly used medications, such as pain relievers, can be dangerous if misused. This concern becomes a reality when we don't take medications as prescribed by a healthcare professional.

① dangers of drug abuse
② symptoms of drug overdose
③ widespread use of illegal drugs
④ ways to avoid misusing medication

14 다음 글의 요지로 가장 적절한 것은?

Defensive pessimism is a cognitive strategy used by some individuals to achieve positive outcomes by taking a seemingly negative approach. Such individuals anticipate and prepare for worst-case scenarios. By considering all possible negative outcomes, defensive pessimists create a plan to mitigate any potential damage. Defensive pessimists do not dwell on the negative thoughts; instead, they use them as a tool to prepare for any obstacles that may arise. While defensive pessimism may seem counterintuitive, it can be a valuable strategy for succeeding in challenging situations. With this mindset, people can develop effective coping mechanisms and perform better under pressure.

① Optimism can make people neglect their duties.
② Expecting the worst can lead to positive results.
③ Negative thoughts can reinforce negative emotions.
④ Challenging situations bring out one's true character.

15 다음 글의 내용과 일치하지 않는 것은? [불일치]

Black-footed ferrets are North America's only native ferret species. They measure 18 to 24 inches and weigh less than three pounds. Their coats are yellow-beige, adorned with distinct black markings that blend into their natural habitat. In the early 1900s, it was believed that there were up to 5 million black-footed ferrets in the United States. However, due to habitat fragmentation and the decline of prairie dogs which constitute 90% of their diet, they were considered extinct by the 1970s. Fortunately, the species was rediscovered in 1981, leading to concerted efforts by various partners to give black-footed ferrets a second chance at survival. Through initiatives such as captive breeding and habitat protection, their population has been restored to around 300 in the wild. Biologists estimate that successful recovery of this endangered species would require about 3,000 adult ferrets.

① 검은발족제비의 털은 자연 서식지 환경에 잘 녹아든다.
② 1970년대에는 검은발족제비가 멸종했다고 여겨졌다.
③ 검은발족제비는 1980년대 초에 다시 발견되었다.
④ 현재 야생에는 약 3천 마리의 검은발족제비가 있다.

[해설] 마지막 두 문장에서 검은발족제비는 현재 야생에서 약 300마리가 있으며, 3,000은 종이 성공적으로 회복되는 데 필요하다고 추정되는 성체 검은발족제비의 개체 수임을 알 수 있다. 따라서 글의 내용과 일치하지 않는 것은 ④ '현재 야생에는 약 3천 마리의 검은발족제비가 있다.'이다.
① 검은발족제비의 털은 자연 서식지 환경에 잘 녹아든다. → 3번째 문장에서 언급된 내용이다.
② 1970년대에는 검은발족제비가 멸종했다고 여겨졌다. → 5번째 문장에서 언급된 내용이다.
③ 검은발족제비는 1980년대 초에 다시 발견되었다. → 마지막 3번째 문장에서 언급된 내용이다.

[해석] 검은발족제비는 북아메리카 유일의 토종 페럿 종이다. 그들은 18~24인치로 측정되고, 무게는 3파운드 미만이다. 그들의 털은 뚜렷한 검은 반점이 새겨진 노란 베이지색인데, 이것은 그들의 자연 서식지에 잘 녹아든다. 1900년대 초반, 미국에는 최대 500만 마리의 검은발족제비가 있었다고 여겨진다. 하지만 서식지 단편화와 그들 식단의 90%를 차지하는 프레리도그의 감소로 인해, 그들은 1970년대 무렵 멸종된 것으로 간주되었다. 다행히도, 이 종은 1981년에 재발견되었고, 이것은 검은발족제비에게 다시 생존 기회를 주기 위한 다양한 협력자들의 합심된 노력으로 이어졌다. 포획 사육과 서식지 보호와 같은 계획을 통해, 그들의 개체 수는 야생에서 300마리 정도로 회복되었다. 생물학자들은 이 멸종 위기종이 성공적으로 회복하려면 야생에 사는 성체 페럿이 3,000마리 정도 필요할 것으로 추정한다.

[어휘] ferret 페럿, 담비 native 토종인 measure 치수가 ~이다 weigh 무게가 ~이다 adorned with ~으로 치장된 distinct 뚜렷한 blend into ~에 섞이다 habitat 서식지 fragmentation 파편화 constitute ~을 구성하다 extinct 멸종된 concerted 협심한 initiative 계획 captive breeding 포획 사육 population 개체 수, 인구 restore 복구하다 endangered 멸종 위기에 처한

[정답] ④

16 다음 글의 흐름상 어색한 문장은? [일관성]

Preferences for sweets are found during infancy and childhood and peak in early adolescence. One study found that more than 40 percent of calories eaten by children came from sugar and fat. ① This preference declines in later years, which reduces their significance in food choice. ② The opposite is true for bitterness, which is strongly disliked by most children. ③ Research shows that some compounds found in bitter foods can be toxic when consumed in large amounts. ④ The ability to detect bitterness decreases with age, however, and many adults consume foods with otherwise unpleasant taste. There are some who remain especially sensitive to certain bitter compounds, in which case this tendency does not apply.

[해설] 단것에 대한 선호는 어린 시절에 강하게 나타나며 나이가 들면서 줄어드는 반면에, 쓴맛은 그 반대 경향을 보인다는 내용을 서술하는 글이다. 따라서 글의 흐름상 가장 어색한 문장은 쓴맛이 나는 음식에 있는 일부 화합물이 다량으로 섭취할 경우에 독성을 일으킬 수 있다는, 나이에 따라 특정한 맛에 대한 선호도가 변하는 것과 관련 없는 내용의 ③이다.

[해석] 단것에 대한 선호는 유아기와 아동기에 나타나며 초기 청소년기에 정점에 이른다. 한 연구는 설탕과 지방에서 어린이들이 섭취하는 칼로리의 40% 이상이 나온다는 것을 밝혀냈다. 이러한 선호가 나중에는 감소하여 음식 선택에서 차지하는 비중이 줄어든다. 이 반대에 해당하는 것이 쓴맛인데, 이는 대부분의 어린이들이 몹시 싫어한다. (연구는 쓴맛이 나는 음식에서 발견되는 일부 화합물은 다량 섭취할 경우 독성을 일으킬 수 있다는 점을 보여준다.) 하지만 쓴맛을 감지하는 능력은 나이가 들수록 감소하며, 많은 성인은 그렇지(쓴맛을 감지하는 능력이 감소하지) 않았더라면 불쾌한 맛이 났을 음식을 섭취한다. 특정한 쓴맛 성분에 특히 민감하게 반응하는 사람들도 있는데, 이 경우에는 이러한 경향이 적용되지 않는다.

[어휘] preference 선호 infancy 유아기 peak 정점에 이르다 adolescence 청소년기, 사춘기 significance 중요성, 의미 opposite 정반대 bitterness 쓴맛 compound 화합물 toxic 유독한 detect 발견하다 sensitive 민감한 tendency 경향

[정답] ③

17. 주어진 글 다음에 이어질 글의 순서로 가장 적절한 것은?

Homages are not simply scenes that copy or plagiarize previous films. Rather, homages deliberately evoke another film in order to show respect to that film and its filmmaker.

(A) A scene strikingly similar to this where a baby's stroller rolls down the steps during a crossfire was originally famously filmed in 1925 by the influential Soviet filmmaker Sergei Eisenstein, in *Battleship Potemkin*.

(B) By recreating this famous scene, De Palma pays tribute to Eisenstein's extraordinary skill as a filmmaker capable of creating compelling images.

(C) In Brian De Palma's gangster film *The Untouchables*, there is a scene on the steps of a train station in which, during a shoot-out, a stroller containing a baby rolls down the steps coming dangerously close to the bullets.

① (B) - (A) - (C)
② (B) - (C) - (A)
③ (C) - (A) - (B)
④ (C) - (B) - (A)

해설 주어진 글은 오마주는 이전 영화의 제작자에 대한 경의를 표하기 위해 의도적으로 그 영화를 환기시킨다는 내용으로, 뒤에는 그러한 오마주의 예시를 소개하는 (C)가 오는 것이 자연스럽다. 그다음으로, (C)에 나온 장면을 this로 받아, 이와 놀라울 정도로 비슷한 장면이 원래는 Sergei Eisenstein에 의해 촬영된 것이라는 내용의 (A)가 와야 한다. 마지막으로, (A)에서 언급된 장면을 this famous scene으로 받아, 그 유명한 장면을 재현함으로써 De Palma는 Eisenstein에게 경의를 표했다는 내용의 (B)로 글이 마무리되어야 한다. 따라서 글의 순서로 가장 적절한 것은 ③ '(C) - (A) - (B)'이다.

해석 오마주는 단순히 이전 영화를 베끼거나 표절한 장면이 아니다. 오히려 오마주는 그 영화와 영화 제작자에 대한 경의를 표하기 위해 의도적으로 그 영화를 환기시킨다. (C) Brian De Palma의 갱스터 영화 <The Untouchables>에는 총격전이 벌어지는 동안 아기를 태운 유모차가 계단을 굴러 내려가 총알에 아슬아슬하게 가까이 다가가는 기차역 계단 장면이 있다. (A) 이것과 놀라울 정도로 비슷한, 아기의 유모차가 총격전 중 계단 아래로 굴러 내려가는 장면은 원래 1925년 소련의 영향력 있는 영화 제작자 Sergei Eisenstein이 <Battleship Potemkin>에서 촬영한 것으로 유명하다. (B) 이 유명한 장면을 재현하여, De Palma는 강렬한 영상들을 만들어낼 수 있었던 Eisenstein의 영화 제작자로서의 비범한 기량에 경의를 표한다.

어휘 plagiarize 표절하다 deliberately 의도적으로 evoke (이미지를) 환기시키다, (감정을) 불러일으키다 stroller 유모차 roll down 굴러 내려오다 crossfire 십자 포화 influential 영향력 있는 compelling 강렬한 shoot-out 총격전 bullet 총알

정답 ③

18. 주어진 문장이 들어갈 위치로 가장 적절한 것은?

As a result, specialization emerged; farmers started focusing on their strengths, growing only specific crops and trading surplus produce for other goods.

Humans have existed for 200,000 years. During the first 99% of our history, our activities mainly revolved around survival and reproduction. (①) This was largely a response to the challenging global climactic conditions, which eventually stabilized only about 10,000 years ago. (②) Subsequently, people discovered the benefits of farming and irrigation, abandoning their nomadic lifestyle to cultivate stable crops. (③) However, not all farmlands were identical; regional differences in sunlight, soil quality, and other factors meant that certain farmers excelled in growing onions, while others thrived in cultivating apples. (④) This shift to individual crop production and surplus generation brought about the development and expansion of marketplaces and trade.

해설 주어진 문장은 그 결과로 특화가 시작되었다는 내용으로, 앞에는 이에 대한 원인이 나와야 하며, 뒤에는 그러한 특화에 관한 부연이 이어지는 것이 자연스럽다. ④ 앞은 농지가 다 똑같지는 않았기에 잘 재배되는 작물이 농부마다 달랐다는 내용이므로, 이것이 주어진 문장에서 언급된 특화의 원인임을 알 수 있다. 또한 문맥상 ④ 뒤의 This shift는 주어진 문장 내용을 가리키는 것을 알 수 있으므로, 주어진 문장이 들어갈 위치로 가장 적절한 것은 ④이다.

해석 인간은 20만 년 동안 존재해 왔다. 우리 역사의 처음 99% 동안, 우리의 활동은 주로 생존과 번식을 중심으로 돌아갔다. 이것은 주로 힘든 세계 기후 조건에 대한 반응이었는데, 이것은 약 1만 년 전에야 안정화되었다. 이후 사람들은 농업과 관개의 이점을 발견하여, 유목 생활을 버리고 안정적인 작물을 재배하였다. 하지만 모든 농경지가 똑같은 것은 아니어서, 햇빛, 토질, 그리고 다른 요소들의 지역적 차이는 어떤 농부들은 양파를 재배하는 데 탁월하고, 반면 다른 농부들은 사과를 재배하는 데 성공한다는 것을 뜻했다. 그 결과 특화가 나타나, 농부들은 자기 강점에 집중하기 시작하여, 특정한 작물만 재배하고 잉여 농산물을 다른 재화와 거래했다. 이러한 개별 작물 생산과 잉여 생산으로의 전환은 시장과 무역의 발전과 확장을 초래했다.

어휘 specialization 특화 emerge 나타나다, 출현하다 specific 특정한 surplus 잉여 revolve around ~을 중심으로 돌다 reproduction 번식 challenging 힘든, 까다로운 stabilize 안정화하다 irrigation 관개, 물을 댐 nomadic 유목의 cultivate 경작하다 identical 동일한 thrive 번성하다, 성공하다 shift 전환, 변화 bring about ~을 초래하다

정답 ④

19 밑줄 친 부분에 들어갈 말로 가장 적절한 것은?

If you aim to transform a disagreement into an opportunity for connection, it's crucial to differentiate between the past, present, and future. When disagreements revolve around what happened in the past, it's easy to get caught up in a cycle of "you said this, I said that." Focusing on what did or didn't happen in the past, or what past events led to the current situation, usually increases tension and decreases connection. A critical first step is to shift the focus to "Where are we now?" and the most important turning point comes when we focus on the road ahead. What are we trying to accomplish for the future? What are our long-term goals? What are our desires for our family, team, faith community, or industry? This _____ thinking shifts blame to a joint understanding about a shared future that we want to create together.

① cyclical
② analytical
③ progressive
④ multidimensional

20 밑줄 친 부분에 들어갈 말로 가장 적절한 것은?

Parents often persuade their children to enter vocations upon the tiniest possible excuses. Almost every child takes a pencil and tries to draw, yet there are many parents who spend thousands of dollars in trying to make great artists of children who have only the most mediocre artistic ability. Mere purposeless drawing of faces and figures is an entirely different thing from the years of hard work necessary to become a great artist. The mere writing of little essays and stories is quite a different thing from the long, arduous training necessary to become a writer of any acceptability. Just because a child finds it more amusing to idle the hours away with a pencil or a brush than to go into the harvest field or into the kitchen doesn't mean that this preference _____.

① illustrates the parents' passion for art
② is an indication of either talent or genius
③ blocks the opportunities for physical activity
④ has little to do with the child's innate ability

회차 4
Answer

01	02	03	04	05
④	①	②	④	①
06	**07**	**08**	**09**	**10**
④	④	①	④	①
11	**12**	**13**	**14**	**15**
④	④	①	②	③
16	**17**	**18**	**19**	**20**
④	④	③	③	②

---

01 밑줄 친 부분의 의미와 가장 가까운 것은? [어휘]

In many cultures, the belief in certain myths is prevalent, shaping daily practices.

① sincere
② absolute
③ constant
④ widespread

[해설] prevalent는 '널리 퍼져있는'이라는 뜻으로, 이와 의미가 가장 가까운 것은 ④ 'widespread(널리 퍼진)'이다.
① 진실한 ② 절대적인 ③ 변함없는
[해석] 많은 문화권에서, 특정 미신에 대한 믿음은 널리 퍼져있어 일상적인 관습을 형성한다.
[어휘] myth 미신

[정답] ④

---

02 밑줄 친 부분의 의미와 가장 가까운 것은? [어휘]

The volunteers helping others without expecting anything in return inspired admiration. And this has led to more people getting involved in meaningful activities.

① esteem
② hostility
③ gratitude
④ sympathy

[해설] admiration은 '존경'이라는 뜻으로, 이와 의미가 가장 가까운 것은 ① 'esteem(존경)'이다.
② 적대감 ③ 고마움 ④ 공감
[해석] 아무 대가도 기대하지 않고 다른 사람들을 도운 그 자원봉사자들은 존경심을 자아냈다. 그리고 이는 더 많은 사람이 의미 있는 활동에 참여하도록 이끌었다.
[어휘] in return 답례로 inspire 불어넣다, 고취하다

[정답] ①

---

03 밑줄 친 부분의 의미와 가장 가까운 것은? [이어동사]

During the busy workweek, Jane makes time to lay aside stress.

① sustain
② dismiss
③ tolerate
④ confront

[해설] lay aside는 '제쳐두다'라는 뜻으로, 이와 의미가 가장 가까운 것은 ② 'dismiss (떨쳐내다)'이다.
① 지속시키다 ③ 견디다 ④ 맞서다
[해석] 바쁜 근무 주간에도 Jane은 스트레스를 제쳐두는 시간을 갖는다.

[정답] ②

---

04 밑줄 친 부분의 의미와 가장 가까운 것은? [이어동사]

The change in the system gave rise to much speculation within the organization.

① contradicted
② intensified
③ confirmed
④ triggered

[해설] give rise to는 '불러일으키다'라는 뜻으로, 이와 의미가 가장 가까운 것은 ④ 'triggered(촉발하다)'이다.
① 모순되다 ② 강화하다 ③ 확인하다
[해석] 그 시스템의 변화는 조직 내에서 많은 추측을 불러일으켰다.
[어휘] speculation 추측, 짐작

[정답] ④

---

05 밑줄 친 부분에 들어갈 말로 가장 적절한 것은? [어휘]

The collaborative project resulted in a fragmented final product as team members persisted in their _____ opinions.

① respective
② considerate
③ respectable
④ considerable

[해설] 협업 프로젝트의 최종 결과물이 분열된 상태라는 내용으로 보아, 팀원들이 서로 다른 자신의 의견만을 고집했을 것으로 유추할 수 있다. 따라서 빈칸에 들어갈 말로 가장 적절한 것은 ① 'respective(각자의)'이다.
② 사려 깊은 ③ 존경할 만한 ④ 상당한
[해석] 그 협업 프로젝트는 팀원들이 각자의 의견을 고집하면서 분열된 최종 산출물을 낳았다.
[어휘] collaborative 협력하는 fragmented 분열된, 해체된 persist 고집하다

[정답] ①

06 밑줄 친 부분 중 어법상 옳지 않은 것은? 〔문법〕

> The word *nerd* first ① appeared in the book *If I Ran the Zoo*, ② where one of the zoo creatures ③ was called a "nerd." A 1951 Newsweek article also used the word *nerd* to refer to "a drip or a square," ④ that is closer to modern stereotypes regarding nerds.

[해설] (that → which) 관계대명사 that은 ,(콤마) 다음에 계속적 용법으로 쓸 수 없으므로, 콤마 뒤에서도 사용할 수 있으면서 똑같이 불완전한 절을 이끄는 which가 와야 한다.
① appear는 수동태로 쓸 수 없는 완전자동사로 적절하게 쓰였다.
② 장소 명사 the book *If I Ran the Zoo*를 선행사로 받는 관계부사 where 뒤에 완전한 절이 오고 있으므로 적절하게 쓰였다.
③ one of 뒤에는 '복수 명사 + 단수 동사'가 와야 하며, 한 생물이 "nerd"라고 '불린' 것이므로 수동태 단수 동사 was called는 적절하게 쓰였다.
[해석] 'nerd'라는 단어는 동물원 생물 중 하나가 "nerd"라고 불린 『If I Ran the Zoo』라는 책에 처음 등장했다. 1951년 Newsweek의 한 기사에서도 괴짜에 대한 현대적인 고정관념에 더 가까운 "drip or square"를 언급하기 위해 'nerd'라는 단어를 사용했다.
[어휘] nerd 괴짜 refer to ~을 언급하다 stereotype 고정관념 regarding ~에 관하여

[정답] ④

07 밑줄 친 부분이 어법상 옳지 않은 것은? 〔문법〕

> ① We should have booked our tickets earlier to get better seats.
> ② I learned about cutting-edge technology while attending the conference.
> ③ By the time we reach the summit, we will have hiked for several hours.
> ④ The achievement of the team is something you cannot help but applauding.

[해설] (applauding → applaud) '~할 수밖에 없다'라는 뜻의 표현은 'cannot help but RV' 구문을 이용할 수 있다. 같은 뜻을 지닌 'cannot help RVing' 구문과의 구분에 유의해야 한다.
① 'should have p.p.'는 '~했어야 했는데 (안 했다)'라는 의미로, to get 이하의 아쉬움이 드러나는 내용을 보았을 때 문맥상 적절하게 쓰였다.
② while 이하의 분사구문에서 의미상 주어인 I가 학회를 '참석한' 것이므로 능동의 현재분사 attending의 쓰임은 적절하다. 또한 attend는 전치사 없이 목적어를 바로 취하는 완전타동사로 적절하게 쓰였다.
③ by the time이 이끄는 시간 부사절에서는 현재시제가 미래시제를 대신하므로 reach의 쓰임은 적절하다. 또한 reach는 전치사 없이 목적어를 바로 취하는 완전타동사로 적절하게 쓰였다.
[해석] ① 우리는 더 좋은 자리를 얻기 위해 표를 더 일찍 예약했어야 했다.
② 나는 그 학회에 참석하면서 최첨단 기술에 대해 알게 되었다.
③ 우리가 정상에 도착할 때쯤, 우리는 몇 시간째 등산해 온 것이 될 것이다.
④ 그 팀의 성과는 박수갈채를 보내지 않을 수 없는 것이다.
[어휘] cutting-edge 최첨단의 conference 학회 summit 정상 applaud 갈채를 보내다

[정답] ④

08 우리말을 영어로 잘못 옮긴 것은? 〔문법〕

① 어떤 이들은 그가 예술계에서 경력을 쌓았다는 것에 놀라워한다.
→ Some find it surprised that he pursued a career in art.
② 이번 주말에 같이 요가 수업을 받는 게 어때?
→ What do you say to getting a yoga class together this weekend?
③ 가이드북은 여행객들이 그 도시의 길을 쉽게 찾도록 돕기 위해 설계되었다.
→ The guidebook is designed to help travelers navigate the city easily.
④ 운동을 통해 다져진 그녀의 몸은 스트레스에 더욱 회복력 있게 되었다.
→ Strengthened through exercise, her body became more resilient to stress.

[해설] (surprised → surprising) find가 5형식 동사로 쓰여 that절을 목적어로 취할 땐 'find + 가목적어 it + 목적격 보어 + that절'의 구조를 취한다. 그런데 목적어인 그가 예술계에서 경력을 쌓았다는 사실이 '놀란' 것이 아니라 '놀랍게 하는' 것이므로, 목적격 보어는 능동의 현재분사형 surprising으로 쓰여야 한다.
② 'What do you say to RVing?'는 '~하는 게 어때?'라는 의미를 나타내는 표현이다. 이때 to는 전치사이므로 동명사 getting의 쓰임은 적절하다.
③ 가이드북이 '설계된' 것이므로 수동태 is designed는 적절하게 쓰였으며, 준사역동사 help는 '(to) RV'를 목적격 보어로 취하므로 navigate의 쓰임도 적절하다.
④ 분사구문의 의미상 주어인 her body가 운동을 통해 '강화된' 것이므로 수동의 과거분사 Strengthened는 적절하게 쓰였으며, 2형식 동사로 쓰인 become이 형용사 resilient를 보어로 취하고 있는 것도 적절하다.
[어휘] pursue 해 나가다 navigate 길을 찾다 strengthen 강화하다 resilient 회복력 있는

[정답] ①

09 밑줄 친 부분에 들어갈 말로 가장 적절한 것은? 생활영어

A: Just look at this view. I'm so glad I took a trip here. I haven't seen anything so beautiful in my life.
B: I know! We should take an extra day off from work and look around some more. What do you think?
A: Hmm. Trust me, I'd love to do that as much as you do. But that seems like an impulsive decision.
B: Okay, you're right. I was too caught up in the moment. _____

① You need to stop being so impulsive.
② The view here isn't as great as I expected.
③ I'll tell my boss I'm taking an extra day off.
④ Let's make the most of our time here, then.

[해설] 여행을 하는 와중에 하루 더 휴가를 내자는 제안에 대해 대화를 나누고 있다. A가 그 제안이 너무 즉흥적인 결정 같다고 말하자, B는 이를 인정하고 있다. 따라서 빈칸에 들어갈 말로 가장 적절한 것은 ④ '그럼 여기에서 있는 시간을 최대한 누려보자.'이다.
① 너는 그렇게 충동적으로 행동하는 걸 멈춰야 해.
② 여기 경치는 내가 기대한 것만큼 좋지 않아.
③ 나 상사한테 하루 더 휴가 낸다고 말씀드릴게.

[해석] A: 이 경치를 좀 봐! 여기로 여행 와서 너무 좋다. 나 이렇게 아름다운 건 인생에서 처음 봤어.
B: 그러니까! 우리 하루 더 휴가 내서 좀 더 둘러보자. 어때?
A: 흠. 나도 너만큼이나 그렇게 하고 싶어, 정말이야. 근데 그건 충동적인 결정인 것 같아.
B: 알겠어, 네 말이 맞아. 내가 너무 이 순간에 빠져있었나 봐. 그럼 여기에서 있는 시간을 최대한 누려보자.

[어휘] take a day off 하루 휴가를 얻다 impulsive 충동적인 be caught up ~에 사로잡히다

[정답] ④

10 밑줄 친 부분에 들어갈 말로 가장 적절한 것은? 생활영어

A: Hey, do you make any investments with your money?
B: Yes, I invest in stocks. How about you?
A: I'm thinking of starting stock investments as well. _____
B: Only if you invest a small portion of your income. I don't advise putting too much money into it.
A: I see. That seems like a wise way to approach stock investments.

① Do you think it's a good idea?
② How much money are you investing?
③ What other investments do you make?
④ Since when have you started stock trading?

[해설] 주식 투자에 관한 대화를 나누는 상황이다. A는 자신도 주식 투자를 시작할까 생각 중이라고 말하며 빈칸 내용을 언급하였다. 이에 B는 수입에서 적은 비중만 투자하는 경우에만 그러하다며 너무 많은 돈을 투자하는 것을 추천하지 않는다고 조언하고 있다. 따라서 빈칸에 들어갈 말로 가장 적절한 것은 ① '이게 좋은 생각일까?'이다.
② 얼마나 많은 돈을 투자하고 있어?
③ 또 어떤 투자를 해?
④ 언제부터 주식 투자를 시작했어?

[해석] A: 저기, 너 네 돈으로 투자하는 거 있어?
B: 응, 나 주식에 투자해. 너는?
A: 나도 주식 투자를 시작할까 생각 중이야. 이게 좋은 생각일까?
B: 네 수입에서 적은 비중만 투자하는 경우에만. 너무 많은 돈을 거기에다 넣는 건 추천하지 않아.
A: 그렇구나. 그게 주식 투자에 대한 현명한 접근 방법인 것 같네.

[어휘] investment 투자; 투자하다 stock 주식 a portion of ~의 부분 trading 거래

[정답] ①

11. 두 사람의 대화 중 자연스럽지 않은 것은?

① A: You know, it was my birthday yesterday.
　B: Oh no, I'm sorry. It completely slipped my mind.
② A: The new employee makes so many mistakes.
　B: You should give him some slack. He's new, after all.
③ A: I heard Nicole didn't make it on the soccer team.
　B: No wonder she seemed so upset.
④ A: I am sick of having the same food for lunch every day.
　B: You should see a doctor and get some medicine.

해설 점심으로 매일 같은 음식을 먹는 게 지겹다는 A의 말에 의사에게 진찰을 받고 약을 받아보라는 B의 응답은 어색하다. 따라서 대화 중 자연스럽지 않은 것은 ④이다.

해석 ① A: 그거 알아? 어제가 내 생일이었어.
B: 아 이런, 미안해. 완전히 깜빡했어.
② A: 그 신입사원은 실수를 너무 많이 해.
B: 좀 봐줘야지. 어쨌든 신입이잖아.
③ A: Nicole이 축구팀에 들어가지 못했다고 들었어.
B: 그래서 그녀가 그렇게 속상해했구나.
④ A: 점심으로 매일 같은 음식을 먹는 게 지겨워.
B: 의사한테 진찰받고 약을 좀 받아봐.

어휘 slip one's mind 깜빡하다 give sb some slack ~을 봐주다 be sick of ~에 질린

정답 ④

12. 다음 글의 제목으로 가장 적절한 것은?

Anyone interested in the biology of trust has probably heard of the supposed magic of oxytocin, the hormone of trust, love, and basically anything that sounds warm and fuzzy. However, it is also known to have a darker side. To understand why, we need to take a look at one of its key roles — strengthening a mother's bond with her baby. If you think about it, there are two sides to this bond. She loves that baby dearly, and as a result believes the baby to be perfect and worth her undying nurturing efforts. But on the flip side, this means the mother sees her child as more perfect than any other baby and to be extremely protective. So, yes, oxytocin might increase attachment and willingness to trust those close to us, but it also might result in greater discriminatory behavior toward those we see as different. In the end, it may make us see the world in a slightly polarized way.

① The Meaning of Trust in a Polarized World
② Oxytocin: A Barrier to Maternal Bonding
③ How Oxytocin Increases Affection
④ The Two Faces of Oxytocin

해설 옥시토신은 가까운 사람들에 대한 신뢰나 애착을 강화하는 한편, 그 외 사람들을 차별하게 만드는 양면적 특성을 지니고 있다는 내용이다. 따라서 글의 제목으로 가장 적절한 것은 ④ '옥시토신의 두 얼굴'이다.
① 양극화된 세상에서 신뢰가 의미하는 것 → 옥시토신이 세상을 더 양극화된 방식으로 바라보게 만들 수 있다고 언급되었을 뿐, 양극화된 세상은 이 글의 전제가 아니다. 또한 그러한 세상에서 신뢰가 가지는 의미를 논하는 글도 아니다.
② 옥시토신: 모성 유대의 장애물 → 오히려 모성 유대를 강화하는 호르몬이므로 적절하지 않다.
③ 옥시토신이 애착을 높이는 방법 → 옥시토신이 애착을 높이는 작용 과정은 구체적으로 언급되지 않았다. 나아가 옥시토신이 차별을 강화하는 '양면'을 지녔다는 것을 포괄하지 못하는 선택지이므로 적절하지 않다.

해석 신뢰의 생물학에 관심이 있는 사람이라면 누구나 신뢰, 사랑, 그리고 기본적으로 따뜻하고 포근하게 들리는 모든 것의 호르몬인 옥시토신의 마법에 대해 들어본 적이 있을 것이다. 하지만 옥시토신에는 어두운 면이 있는 것으로도 알려져 있다. 그 이유를 이해하려면 옥시토신의 주요 역할 중 하나인 엄마와 아기의 유대감 강화에 대해 살펴볼 필요가 있다. 생각해 보면, 이 유대감에는 두 가지의 측면이 있다. 엄마는 아기를 지극히 사랑하며, 그 결과 아기가 완벽하고 끝없는 양육 노력을 기울일 가치가 있다고 믿는다. 그러나 반대로, 이것은 엄마가 자신의 아이를 다른 어떤 아기보다 더 완벽하다고 보며, 과잉보호하게 되는 것을 의미한다. 따라서 옥시토신이 가까운 사람에 대한 애착과 신뢰감을 높일 수 있는 것은 맞지만, 그것은 또한 우리와 다르다고 생각하는 사람에 대한 차별적인 행동을 더 많이 유발할 수도 있다. 결국, 옥시토신은 우리가 세상을 약간 양극화된 방식으로 바라보게 만들 수 있다.

어휘 biology 생물학 oxytocin 옥시토신 fuzzy 포근한, 보송보송한 role 역할 strengthen 강화하다 bond 유대감 dearly 지극히, 몹시 nurture 양육하다 attachment 애착 willingness 기꺼이 하는 마음 discriminatory 차별적인 slightly 약간 polarize 양극화하다

정답 ④

13 다음 글의 주제로 가장 적절한 것은?

We encounter many people in our day-to-day lives and, like many stimuli, this can sometimes lead to cognitive overload. We cope with this overload by making cognitive shortcuts that help us simplify and classify the stimuli we encounter. One such shortcut is the use of stereotypes; employing this technique probably gave us an advantage in our evolutionary past as it would have allowed us to establish very quickly who was friend (a member of our own in-group) and who was foe (a member of the out-group). Stereotypes can thus help us make sense of the world. They are a form of categorization that helps to simplify and systematize information. This makes information easier to identify, remember, predict, and respond to.

① positive aspects of using stereotypes
② ways biased information forms stereotypes
③ instances where stereotypes can be dangerous
④ inevitability of having cognitive overload in our lives

[해설] 고정관념은 일종의 지름길을 만듦으로써 정보를 단순화하고 분류하는 것을 돕는다고 말하는 등 고정관념의 긍정적인 측면에 관해 서술하는 글이다. 따라서 글의 주제로 가장 적절한 것은 ① '고정관념을 사용하는 것의 긍정적 측면'이다.
② 편향된 정보가 고정관념을 형성하는 방식 → 편향된 정보가 어떤 과정으로 고정관념을 형성하는지를 설명하는 글이 아니다.
③ 고정관념이 위험할 수 있는 경우들 → 고정관념의 긍정적인 측면을 서술하는 글로, 이것의 위험에 관해서는 언급하지 않았다.
④ 우리의 삶에서 인지 과부하가 있는 것의 필연성 → 많은 자극으로 인해 인지 과부하가 발생할 수 있다고 언급되긴 하나, 이는 고정관념의 이점을 서술하기 위한 서론일 뿐, 글의 요지는 아니다.

[해석] 우리는 일상적인 삶에서 많은 사람들을 우연히 마주치고, 많은 자극과 마찬가지로 그것은 때때로 인지 과부하를 유발할 수도 있다. 우리는 우리가 우연히 마주치는 자극을 단순화하고 분류하는 것을 돕는 인지적 지름길을 만듦으로써 이러한 과부하에 대처한다. 그러한 지름길 중 하나가 고정관념의 사용으로, 이러한 기법을 사용하는 것은 누가 친구(내집단의 구성원)이고 누가 적(외집단의 구성원)인지 매우 빠르게 구분할 수 있었기 때문에, 아마도 과거 진화 과정에서 우리에게 이점을 주었을 것이다. 따라서 고정관념은 우리가 세상을 이해하는 데 도움을 줄 수 있다. 그것은 정보를 단순화하고 체계화하는 것을 돕는 분류의 한 형태이다. 이는 정보를 식별하고, 기억하고, 예측하고, 반응하는 것을 더 쉽게 만든다.

[어휘] encounter 우연히 마주치다 stimuli 자극(pl. stimulus) cognitive overload 인지적 과부하 cope with ~에 대처하다 shortcut 지름길 simplify 단순화하다 classify 분류하다 stereotype 고정관념 employ 이용[사용]하다 evolutionary 진화의 in-group 내집단 foe 적 out-group 외집단 make sense of ~을 이해하다 categorization 분류 systematize 체계화하다 respond to ~에 반응[대응]하다

[정답] ①

14 다음 글의 요지로 가장 적절한 것은?

The ongoing global financial crisis has led some countries to consider reducing their commitment to international food aid. This has raised concerns that another food crisis could occur next year. The Director-General of the Food and Agriculture Organization of the United Nations has urged governments to continue their support for developing countries in need of external assistance due to crop failures, civil unrest, insecurity or escalating food costs. Currently, 36 countries are still in need of such assistance. Access to nutritious food is a fundamental human right; it's essential that everyone has access to adequate and healthy food, regardless of their circumstances or location. It's critical that we continue to provide food aid, as the global food crisis remains a pressing issue that cannot be overlooked.

① Conflicts within nations must end to solve the food crisis.
② Food aid should not stop despite the global financial crisis.
③ The global financial crisis is intensified by rising food costs.
④ Food aid is key in fostering positive relations among nations.

[해설] 전 세계적인 금융 위기로 인해 일부 국가들이 국제 식량 원조를 줄이는 것을 고려하고 있지만, 이러한 상황에서도 식량 원조가 지속되어야 할 필요성을 역설하는 글이다. 따라서 글의 요지로 가장 적절한 것은 ② '전 세계적인 금융 위기에도 불구하고 식량 지원이 중단되어서는 안 된다.'이다.
① 식량 위기 해결을 위해서는 국가 내 갈등이 종결되어야 한다. → 식량 위기를 해결하기 위해서 국제 식량 원조를 지속해야 할 필요성을 주장하는 글이다.
③ 금융위기는 증가하는 식비로 인해 심화된다. → 금융위기가 식비의 증가로 인해 심화되고 있다는 내용은 언급된 바 없으며, 글의 요지와도 거리가 멀다.
④ 식량 원조는 국가 간 긍정적인 관계를 조성하는 데 핵심이다. → 국가 간 긍정적인 관계를 조성하기 위해 식량 원조가 필요하다는 점을 서술하는 글이 아니다.

[해석] 계속되는 전 세계적 금융 위기는 일부 국가가 국제 식량 원조에 대한 약속의 축소를 고려하게 해왔다. 이로 인해 내년에 또 다른 식량 위기가 발생할 수 있다는 우려가 제기되었다. 유엔 식량농업기구 사무총장은 정부에 흉작, 내전, 치안 불안, 또는 식량 비용 상승 때문에 외부 지원이 필요한 개발도상국에 대한 지원을 계속할 것을 촉구했다. 현재, 36개국이 여전히 그러한 지원을 필요로 하고 있다. 영양가 있는 음식에 대한 접근은 기본적인 인권으로, 모든 사람이 자신의 상황이나 위치에 관계없이 적절하고 건강한 음식에 접근할 수 있는 것이 필수적이다. 우리가 식량 지원을 계속하는 것이 매우 중요한데, 세계 식량 위기는 간과할 수 없는 시급한 문제이기 때문이다.

[어휘] ongoing 계속 진행되는 financial crisis 금융 위기 commitment 약속, 헌신 food aid 식량 원조 concern 우려, 걱정 Director-General 사무총장 urge 촉구하다 external 외부의 assistance 도움 crop failure 흉작 civil unrest 내전 insecurity 불안(정) escalating 상승하는 currently 현재 access to ~에의 접근 adequate 적절한 regardless of ~에 상관없이 pressing 긴급한 overlook 간과하다

[정답] ②

15 다음 글의 내용과 일치하지 않는 것은?

Uruk is a well-studied Mesopotamian city. By 3,500 BCE, its population was around 10,000 people, which grew to a peak of 50,000. Surrounding Uruk was a massive brick wall seven meters high, its numerous gates and guard towers suggesting that Uruk was a city very conscious of defense. Monumental architecture included a prominent feature called a ziggurat, a pyramidal temple built to serve religious purposes. Commoners as well as slaves built and maintained the monumental buildings, showing the collective efforts that shaped the city's cultural and historical significance within the ancient world.

① Uruk는 인구가 최대 5만 명에 달하는 도시였다.
② Uruk 사람들은 도시를 방어하고자 하는 의식이 강했다.
③ Ziggurat는 주거 목적을 위해 세워진 기념비적인 건축물이다.
④ 노예뿐만 아니라 평민들도 기념비적인 건물을 건축하는 데 참여했다.

[해설] 4번째 문장에서 ziggurat는 종교적 목적에 쓰이기 위해 지어졌다고 언급되므로, 글의 내용과 일치하지 않는 것은 ③ 'Ziggurat는 주거 목적을 위해 세워진 기념비적인 건축물이다.'이다.
① Uruk는 인구가 최대 5만 명에 달하는 도시였다. → 2번째 문장에서 언급된 내용이다.
② Uruk 사람들은 도시를 방어하고자 하는 의식이 강했다. → 3번째 문장에서 언급된 내용이다.
④ 노예뿐만 아니라 평민들도 기념비적인 건물을 건축하는 데 참여했다. → 마지막 문장에서 언급된 내용이다.

[해석] Uruk는 잘 연구된 메소포타미아의 도시이다. 기원전 3,500년경에는 인구가 약 10,000명이었으며, 최고 50,000명까지 증가했다. Uruk를 둘러싸고 있는 7미터 높이의 거대한 벽돌 성벽과 수많은 성문과 감시탑은 Uruk가 방어를 매우 중요시하는 도시였음을 시사한다. 기념비적인 건축물로는 종교적 목적에 쓰이기 위해 지어진 피라미드형 신전인 ziggurat라고 불리는 유명한 구경거리가 있다. 노예뿐만 아니라 평민들도 기념비적인 건물을 짓고 유지 관리했으며, 이는 고대 세계에서 이 도시의 문화적, 역사적 중요성을 형성한 집단적 노력을 보여준다.

[어휘] well-studied 잘 연구된 a peak of 최고의 massive 거대한 brick 벽돌 monumental 기념비적인 architecture 건축물 prominent 눈에 띄는 feature 특징 religious 종교적인 commoner 평민 slave 노예 collective 집단적인

[정답] ③

16 다음 글의 흐름상 어색한 문장은?

Trend spotting is one popular use for data. ① Essentially, this comes down to spotting and monitoring patterns online, and using that information to predict where things might go in the future. ② In understanding and predicting trends, social media and the Internet play a large role. ③ Through social media like Instagram or blogs, we're used to sharing vast amounts of data about ourselves, our interests, habits, likes and dislikes, which companies use to spot the latest trends. ④ Before making use of any data, one must first be able to distinguish between good data and bad data. With individuals openly contributing data about their lives, companies are able to identify evolving trends and foresee future developments.

[해설] 소셜 미디어나 인터넷 등을 통해 공유되는 우리의 일상은 기업이 동향을 파악하기 위해 이용하는 하나의 데이터라는 내용의 글이다. 따라서 글의 흐름상 어색한 문장은 데이터를 활용하기 전에 좋은 데이터와 나쁜 데이터를 구분할 수 있어야 한다는 내용의 ④이다.

[해석] 동향 파악은 데이터의 인기 있는 한 가지 활용 사례이다. 기본적으로, 이것은 패턴을 파악하고 추적 관찰하며, 그 정보를 이용하여 향후 상황이 어디로 갈지 예측하는 것으로 요약된다. 동향을 이해하고 예측하는 데 있어 소셜 미디어와 인터넷이 큰 역할을 한다. 우리는 인스타그램이나 블로그와 같은 소셜 미디어를 통해 자기 자신, 우리의 관심사, 습관, 좋아하는 것과 싫어하는 것에 대한 방대한 양의 데이터를 공유하는 데 익숙하며, 기업들은 이를 이용하여 최신 동향을 파악한다. (데이터를 어떤 식으로든 활용하기 전에 먼저 좋은 데이터와 나쁜 데이터를 구분할 수 있어야 한다.) 개인들이 자신의 삶에 대한 데이터를 공개적으로 제공함으로써, 기업은 진화하는 동향을 파악하고 미래 전개를 예측할 수 있다.

[어휘] trend 경향, 추세 spot 파악[발견]하다 come down to ~으로 요약[설명]되다 monitor 추적 관찰하다 vast 방대한 make use of ~을 이용하다 distinguish 구별하다 contribute 제공하다, 주다 foresee 예측하다

[정답] ④

17 주어진 글 다음에 이어질 글의 순서로 가장 적절한 것은? [순서배열]

In 1994, a young woman asked for an order of restraint against her husband and filed for divorce.

(A) It was through writing fantasies that she was able to battle through the depression and eventually turn her life around. The woman's name was Joanne, but the world would come to know her as J.K. Rowling.

(B) But they were not enough to sustain her and her child, and she was constantly under financial pressure, suffering from depression and at times even having thoughts of suicide.

(C) With no job and little money to live on, she signed up for welfare benefits so that she could afford to care for her baby.

① (A) - (C) - (B)
② (B) - (A) - (C)
③ (C) - (A) - (B)
④ (C) - (B) - (A)

[해설] 주어진 글은 1994년에 한 젊은 여성이 남편을 상대로 접근금지 명령을 요청하고 이혼 소송을 제기했다는 내용으로, 뒤에는 이혼한 뒤 그녀의 힘든 상황을 서술하는 내용의 (C)가 오는 것이 자연스럽다. 그다음으로, (C)에서 언급된 welfare benefits를 they로 받아, 그것이 그녀와 그녀의 아이를 부양하기에는 불충분했다는 내용의 (B)가 와야 한다. 마지막으로, 그녀가 극심한 우울증을 겪었다고 서술한 (B) 다음에는, 그녀가 판타지를 쓰며 그 우울증을 극복하고 결국 삶을 뒤바꿀 수 있었다고 말한 뒤에 그녀가 누구였는지를 밝히는 내용의 (A)로 글이 마무리되어야 한다. 따라서 글의 순서로 가장 적절한 것은 ④ '(C) - (B) - (A)'이다.

[해석] 1994년, 한 젊은 여성이 남편을 상대로 접근금지 명령을 요청하고 이혼 소송을 제기했다. (C) 직업도 없고 생활비도 거의 없던 그녀는 아기를 돌볼 수 있도록 복지 혜택을 신청했다. (B) 그러나 그것은 그녀와 그녀의 아이를 부양하기에 충분하지 않았고, 그녀는 지속적으로 경제적 압박에 시달리며 우울증을 겪었고 때로는 자살 생각까지 하기도 했다. (A) 그녀가 우울증을 극복하고 결국 삶을 뒤바꿀 수 있었던 것은 판타지를 쓰는 것을 통해서였다. 이 여성의 이름은 Joanne이었지만 전 세계는 그녀를 유명한 Harry Potter 시리즈의 작가인 J.K. Rowling으로 알게 되었다.

[어휘] restraint 규제, 구속 divorce 이혼 depression 우울증 sustain 부양[유지]하다 suffer from ~을 겪다 suicide 자살 welfare 복지 benefit 혜택

[정답] ④

---

18 주어진 문장이 들어갈 위치로 가장 적절한 것은? [문장삽입]

But labor economists have been pessimistic about the possibility that middle-aged adults can be effectively retrained for a new career.

In our cities, many middle-aged adults are out of the labor force — and often for prolonged periods. (①) An optimist would presume that at any given moment, such displaced workers can be retrained so they can work in a booming sector. (②) We often hear, for example, about retraining coal miners to be computer programmers. (③) Their core argument is that, as we age, most of us have less ability to reinvent ourselves and learn new skills. (④) Also, the fact that unemployment periods tend to be longer in middle-aged adults than younger groups adds to the problem because a person's inclination and ability to find a job decrease the longer the person has been unemployed.

[해설] 주어진 문장은 But으로 시작하여, 노동 경제학자들은 중년층을 재교육하는 것이 효과적일지에 관해 비관적인 입장이라는 내용으로, 앞에는 그것에 관해 낙관적인 입장이 나와야 하며, 뒤에는 주어진 문장에 관한 부연이 나와야 자연스럽다. ③ 앞에서 중년층의 실직자들이 언제든 재교육을 받아 호황 분야에서 일할 수 있다고 생각하는 낙관주의자의 입장과 그에 관한 예시가 나왔다. 반면에 ③ 뒤에서는 나이가 들수록 자신을 재창조하고 새로운 기술을 배우는 능력이 떨어진다는 비관적인 입장이 나왔으므로 문맥상 단절이 있다는 것과 ③ 뒤에 나온 Their core argument가 주어진 문장에서 언급된 노동 경제학자의 주장이라는 것을 알 수 있다. 따라서 주어진 문장이 들어갈 위치로 가장 적절한 것은 ③이다.

[해석] 우리 도시에서는 많은 중년층이 노동력에서 이탈해 있으며, 그것이 장기간인 경우가 많다. 낙관주의자는 이러한 실직자들이 언제든 재교육을 받아 호황을 누리는 분야에서 일할 수 있다고 생각할 것이다. 예를 들어, 우리는 종종 탄광 노동자들을 컴퓨터 프로그래머로 재교육하는 것에 대해 듣곤 한다. 그러나 노동 경제학자들은 중년층이 새로운 직업을 위해 효과적으로 재교육을 받을 수 있는 가능성에 대해 비관적이다. 이들의 핵심 주장은 나이가 들수록 우리 대부분이 자신을 재창조하고 새로운 기술을 배우는 능력이 떨어진다는 것이다. 또한 실업 기간이 젊은 층보다 중년층에서 더 긴 경향이 있다는 사실은 문제를 더욱 악화시키는데, 이는 한 사람이 실직한 상태가 길어질수록 구직할 의향과 능력이 감소하기 때문이다.

[어휘] pessimistic 비관적인 middle-aged 중년의 retrain 재교육하다 labor force 노동력 prolonged 장기적인 optimist 낙관론자 booming 호황을 누리는 coal miner 탄광 노동자 core 핵심(의) reinvent 재발명하다 inclination 의향

[정답] ③

19 밑줄 친 부분에 들어갈 말로 가장 적절한 것은?

The estimates of others' attractiveness may change depending on the circumstances. In a study of singles bars, as closing time neared, both men and women showed increased ratings of attractiveness towards remaining individuals. Presumably, as the time deadline approached, people's freedom to decide on a possible partner was reduced and their liking for those remaining increased. This is an example of *reactance*, a response to reduced freedom of choice that leads to increased liking. This is common in marketing with advertisements such as "a one-day sale" or "supplies are limited." It is also applied in relationships where people intentionally act disinterested to avoid appearing too eager. In all of these cases, attraction toward a possible choice typically increases, as its _____ decreases.

① appeal
② reliability
③ availability
④ uniqueness

[해설] 선택할 수 있는 파트너 수가 줄어들 때 파트너에 대한 매력도 평가가 높아진다는 실험 내용과 기간이나 수량이 한정되어 있다는 점을 내세우는 마케팅 전략의 사례를 통해, 어떤 것을 얻기가 힘들어질수록 그것에 대한 선호가 증가한다는 결론을 내릴 수 있다. 따라서 빈칸에 들어갈 말로 가장 적절한 것은 ③ '이용 가능성'이다.
① 매력 → 매력이 줄어들 때 매력이 늘어난다는 말 자체가 성립되지 않는다.
② 신뢰도
④ 고유성 → 어떤 것의 고유성이 줄어든다는 것은 그것이 더 흔해진다는 것을 의미한다고 볼 수 있으므로, 오히려 반대된다.

[해석] 타인의 매력도에 대한 평가는 상황에 따라 달라질 수 있다. 싱글 바에 관한 한 연구에 따르면, 영업 종료 시간이 가까워짐에 따라, 남성과 여성 모두 남은 사람들에 대한 매력 평가가 높아지는 것으로 나타났다. 마감 시간이 다가올수록 사람들이 가능성 있는 파트너를 결정할 수 있는 자유가 줄어들고, 남은 사람들에 대한 호감도가 높아진 것으로 추정된다. 이것은 리액턴스, 즉 선호도 증가로 이어지는 선택의 자유의 감소에 대한 반응의 예시이다. 이것은 '단 하루 세일' 혹은 '수량이 한정되어 있습니다'와 같은 광고를 가지고 하는 마케팅에서 흔하다. 그것은 또한 사람들이 너무 열심인 것처럼 보이지 않으려고 일부러 무관심하게 행동하는 관계에도 적용된다. 이 모든 경우에, 가능한 선택지에 대한 매력은 일반적으로 그것의 이용 가능성이 줄어듦에 따라 증가한다.

[어휘] estimate 평가 attractiveness 매력 near 가까워지다 deadline 마감 시간 reactance 리액턴스(사람이 자유행동에 대한 위협을 경험할 때 나타나는 불쾌한 동기부여) intentionally 일부러 eager 열심인 attraction 매력, 끌림

[정답] ③

20 밑줄 친 부분에 들어갈 말로 가장 적절한 것은?

Our respiratory system _____.
The air we breathe goes down a single tube in our throat, and then divides into many smaller branches in our lungs. These branches end in small dead-end spaces filled with air sacs that allow gas exchange across a thin membrane. When we exhale, air follows the same pathway in reverse. This breathing process is not very efficient because stale air remains in our lungs even when fresh air is taken in. The old and new air mix together and reduce the oxygen content of the air that reaches our lungs. This means that the presence of stale air in our lungs limits the amount of oxygen that can be delivered to our body. To compensate for this, we need to go through the trouble of breathing deeper, especially during times of increased oxygen demand such as during exercise.

① decreases in efficiency as we age
② is not ideally designed for breathing
③ works to maximize our body's efficiency
④ closely interacts with organs outside its system

[해설] 신선한 공기를 들이마셔도 우리 폐 속에는 오래된 공기가 남아있어 우리 몸에 전달되는 산소의 양이 제한된다는 내용의 글이다. 이를 보완하기 위해 우리는 때로 숨을 더 깊이 들이마시는 수고를 감수해야 한다는 말에서도 유추할 수 있듯, 우리의 호흡계가 그다지 효율적이지 않다는 것을 알 수 있다. 따라서 빈칸에 들어갈 말로 가장 적절한 것은 ② '호흡을 위해 이상적으로 설계되어 있지 않다'이다.
① 우리가 나이가 듦에 따라 효율성이 감소한다. → 노화가 호흡계의 효율성에 미치는 영향에 관해서는 언급되지 않았다.
③ 우리 몸의 효율성을 극대화하기 위해 작동한다. → 오히려 우리의 호흡계가 그다지 효율적이지 않다는 내용의 글이므로 반대된다.
④ 그 계 외부에 있는 기관들과 밀접하게 상호작용한다. → 우리의 호흡계가 그 외부에 있는 기관들과 어떠한 상호작용을 하는지를 설명하는 글이 아니다.

[해석] 우리의 호흡계는 호흡을 위해 이상적으로 설계되어 있지 않다. 우리가 숨 쉬는 공기는 우리의 목구멍에 있는 하나의 관을 따라 내려간 다음 폐 속의 많은 더 작은 가지들로 나뉜다. 이 가지들은 얇은 막을 통해 가스를 교환하게 해주는 폐포로 가득한 작은 막다른 공간에서 끝난다. 우리가 숨을 내쉴 때, 공기는 똑같은 경로를 거꾸로 따라간다. 신선한 공기가 들어갈 때에도 오래된 공기가 폐에 남아 있기 때문에 이 호흡 과정은 그다지 효율적이지 않다. 오래된 공기와 새로운 공기가 함께 섞여버려서, 우리 폐에 도달하는 공기의 산소 함량을 감소시킨다. 이것은 폐 속의 오래된 공기의 존재가 우리 몸에 전달될 수 있는 산소의 양을 제한한다는 뜻이다. 이를 보완하려면, 우리는 특히 운동 중과 같이 산소 요구량이 증가하는 시간 동안 숨을 더 깊이 쉬어야 하는 수고를 감수해야 한다.

[어휘] respiratory 호흡계의 tube 관 throat 목구멍 branch 가지 lung 폐 dead-end 막다른 filled with ~으로 가득한 air sac 폐포 membrane 막 exhale 내쉬다 in reverse 거꾸로 stale 신선하지 않은, 오래된 presence 존재 compensate for ~을 보완[보충]하다

[정답] ②

회차 5
Answer

01	02	03	04	05
③	②	④	①	②
06	07	08	09	10
③	②	③	①	④
11	12	13	14	15
②	③	①	③	②
16	17	18	19	20
④	③	③	①	③

01 밑줄 친 부분의 의미와 가장 가까운 것은? [어휘]

The young inventor showcased his ingenious device at the science fair, leaving judges and attendees impressed.

① striking
② intricate
③ inventive
④ convenient

[해설] ingenious는 '독창적인'이라는 뜻으로, 이와 의미가 가장 가까운 것은 ③ 'inventive(독창적인)'이다.
① 인상적인 ② 복잡한 ④ 편리한
[해석] 그 젊은 발명가는 과학 박람회에서 독창적인 장치를 전시하여, 심사위원들과 참석자들에게 깊은 인상을 남겼다.
[어휘] showcase 전시하다 fair 박람회 attendee 참석자 impress 깊은 인상을 주다

[정답] ③

02 밑줄 친 부분의 의미와 가장 가까운 것은? [어휘]

Overreliance on single-use plastics continues to curtail the biodiversity of marine ecosystems.

① threaten
② diminish
③ sacrifice
④ devastate

[해설] curtail은 '줄이다'라는 뜻으로, 이와 의미가 가장 가까운 것은 ② 'diminish(줄이다)'이다.
① 위협하다 ③ 희생하다 ④ 완전히 파괴하다
[해석] 일회용 플라스틱에 대한 과한 의존은 해양 생태계의 생물 다양성을 계속해서 줄이고 있다.
[어휘] overreliance 과한 의존 biodiversity 생물 다양성

[정답] ②

03 밑줄 친 부분의 의미와 가장 가까운 것은? [이디엄]

After the celebrity appeared on a series of late-night talk shows, most of his mysteries seemed to come to light.

① become trivial
② remain unsolved
③ get a lot of attention
④ become widely known

[해설] come to light는 '밝혀지다'라는 뜻으로, 이와 의미가 가장 가까운 것은 ④ 'become widely known(널리 알려지다)'이다.
① 하찮아지다 ② 미궁으로 남아있다 ③ 많은 관심을 받다
[해석] 그 유명인이 심야 토크쇼에 연이어 출연한 이후, 그의 수수께끼가 대부분 밝혀지는 듯했다.
[어휘] celebrity 유명 인사 trivial 사소한, 하찮은

[정답] ④

04 밑줄 친 부분에 들어갈 말로 가장 적절한 것은? [어휘]

Social media platforms play a vital role in preventing the _____ of online interactions by implementing measures to combat cyberbullying and the spread of harmful content, essential for fostering a safe digital environment.

① abuse
② scarcity
③ isolation
④ complexity

[해설] 사이버 폭력과 유해 콘텐츠 확산은 모두 온라인상 교류의 잘못된 활용 예시들이므로, 빈칸에 들어갈 말로 가장 적절한 것은 ① 'abuse(오용)'이다.
② 부족 ③ 고립 ④ 복잡성
[해석] 소셜 미디어 플랫폼들은 안전한 디지털 환경 조성에 필수적인, 사이버 폭력과 유해 콘텐츠 확산을 방지하는 조치들을 시행함으로써 온라인 상호 작용의 오용을 막는 데 필수적인 역할을 한다.
[어휘] vital 필수적인 interaction 상호 작용 implement 시행하다 combat 싸우다, 방지하다 cyberbullying 사이버 폭력 foster 조성하다

[정답] ①

05 밑줄 친 부분에 들어갈 말로 가장 적절한 것은? [이어동사]

The hikers agreed to _____ each other, emphasizing the importance of safety.

① break off
② look after
③ fall behind
④ play up to

[해설] 빈칸에는 등산객들이 서로의 안전을 위해 취해야 하는 행동이 들어가야 함을 유추할 수 있다. 따라서 빈칸에 들어갈 말로 가장 적절한 것은 ② 'look after(보살피다)'이다.
① 분리시키다 ③ 뒤처지다 ④ 아첨하다

[해석] 그 등산객들은 안전의 중요성을 강조하며 서로를 보살피기로 합의했다.

[어휘] emphasize 강조하다

정답 ②

06 어법상 옳은 것은? [문법]

① How busy I am, don't hesitate to ask for assistance.
② The couple are having trouble to find a reliable babysitter.
③ The black cat chasing a bird was seen to climb the tall tree.
④ He told me the Battle of Gettysburg had brought a turning point in the Civil War.

[해설] 고양이가 새를 '쫓는' 것이므로 능동의 현재분사 chasing은 적절하게 쓰였으며, 지각동사로 쓰인 see가 수동태로 전환되면 to 부정사를 보어로 취하므로 to climb의 쓰임도 적절하다.
① (How → However) 명사절을 이끄는 how는 '얼마나 ~한지'라는 의미의 의문부사이고, 부사절을 이끄는 however는 '아무리 ~해도'라는 의미의 복합관계부사이다. 여기서는 쉼표 앞에 명사절이 단독으로 있을 수 없으며, 의미상으로도 '아무리 내가 바빠도'가 되어야 자연스러우므로 How를 However로 고쳐야 한다.
② (to find → (in) finding) '~하는 데 어려움을 겪다'라는 표현은 'have trouble (in) RVing' 구문을 사용해야 하므로, to find를 (in) finding으로 고쳐야 한다.
④ (had brought → brought) 게티즈버그 전투와 같은 역사적 사실은 항상 과거시제를 사용하므로, 대과거시제 had brought를 brought로 고쳐야 한다. 참고로 tell은 4형식 동사로 쓰여 직접목적어로 생략된 접속사 that이 이끄는 명사절을 취하고 있다.

[해석] ① 내가 아무리 바쁘더라도 주저하지 말고 도움을 요청해.
② 그 부부는 믿을 만한 보모를 찾는 데 어려움을 겪고 있다.
③ 새를 쫓는 검은 고양이가 높은 나무를 오르는 것이 보였다.
④ 그는 내게 게티즈버그 전투가 남북전쟁의 전환점을 가져왔다고 말했다.

[어휘] hesitate 주저하다 assistance 도움 reliable 믿을 만한 turning point 전환점

정답 ③

07 다음 글의 내용과 일치하지 않는 것은? [불일치]

Bats don't just live in caves — they could find their way into your place of lodging. If you find a bat in your room after you wake up, you should see a medical professional as rabies can be transmitted through a bat bite. Though most bats don't have rabies, bats are the leading cause of rabies deaths in the United States. Because bat bites are small and don't cause much pain, some people neglect them. Don't make this mistake! Always seek medical advice if you've been bitten by a bat or think you may have been bitten by one. It's imperative to act right away because once a person shows any signs of the illness, rabies is almost always fatal. Bats are normally unaggressive and avoid contact with humans, but bats with rabies can bite without being provoked. So if a cave is inhabited by bats, it's best to avoid it.

① It is not common for a bat to have rabies.
② Though bat bites are small, they are very painful.
③ Being highly dangerous, rabies must be treated instantly.
④ Bats that don't have rabies generally don't attack humans.

[해설] 4번째 문장에서 박쥐에게 물린 곳이 작고, 큰 고통을 유발하지는 않는다고 했으므로, 글의 내용과 일치하지 않는 것은 ② '박쥐에게 물린 곳은 작지만, 매우 고통스럽다.'이다.
① 박쥐가 광견병에 걸리는 것은 흔하지 않다. → 3번째 문장에서 언급된 내용이다.
③ 광견병은 매우 위험하기 때문에 즉시 치료해야 한다. → 7번째 문장에서 언급된 내용이다.
④ 광견병에 걸리지 않은 박쥐들은 일반적으로 사람을 공격하지 않는다. → 마지막 2번째 문장에서 언급된 내용이다.

[해석] 박쥐는 동굴에서만 사는 것이 아니라, 당신의 숙소로 들어갈 수도 있다. 당신이 잠에서 깬 후 방에서 박쥐를 발견하면, 박쥐에게 물린 곳을 통해 광견병에 전염될 수도 있기 때문에 전문 의료진에게 가봐야 한다. 대부분의 박쥐들은 광견병에 걸리지 않지만, 미국에서 박쥐들은 광견병 사망의 주요 원인이다. 박쥐에게 물린 곳이 작고 큰 고통을 유발하지 않기 때문에, 몇몇 사람들은 그것들을 방치한다. 이런 실수를 하지 마라! 박쥐에게 물렸거나 물렸을 수도 있다고 생각한다면 항상 의사의 진찰을 받아라. 일단 사람이 병의 증세를 보이면 광견병은 거의 언제나 치명적이기 때문에 즉시 행동하는 것이 필수다. 박쥐들은 보통 공격적이지 않고 인간과의 접촉을 피하지만, 광견병에 걸린 박쥐들은 자극을 받지 않아도 물 수 있다. 따라서 만약 동굴에 박쥐가 서식한다면, 피하는 게 가장 좋다.

[어휘] find their way into ~으로 들어가다 lodging 숙소 rabies 광견병 transmit 전염시키다 neglect 대수롭지 않게 여기다 imperative 필수의, 긴급한 fatal 치명적인 unaggressive 공격적이지 않은 provoke 자극하다 inhabit 서식하다

정답 ②

08 밑줄 친 부분 중 어법상 옳지 않은 것은? [문법]

The first dinosaur fossils with structures that could be considered ① as feathers were found in the 1990s. Other discoveries ② followed. By 2011 some studies were even suggesting that all dinosaurs had some type of feathery covering on at least some parts of their bodies — in much the same way ③ which all mammals have hair but not all mammals are hairy. ④ Despite the first dinosaurs being thought to have emerged some 245 million years ago, dinosaurs with feathers have been dated to only 180 million years ago.

[해설] (which → in which) 관계대명사 which 뒤에는 불완전한 문장이 와야 하는데 여기서는 완전한 문장이 오고 있다. 따라서 which를 완전한 문장을 이끌 수 있는 '전치사 + 관계대명사'로 만들고, 선행사인 the same way와 어울리게끔 전치사 in을 사용하여 in which로 고쳐야 한다.
① consider는 5형식 동사로 쓰여 'consider + O + (as) + 형/명'의 구조를 취할 수 있는데, 수동태로 전환하면 'be considered + (as) + 형/명' 형태가 된다.
② follow가 '뒤따르다'라는 의미의 자동사로 적절하게 쓰였다.
④ 전치사 Despite 뒤에 의미상 주어 the first dinosaurs를 동반한 동명사 being thought가 온 것은 적절하다.

[해석] 깃털로 간주될 수 있는 구조를 가진 최초의 공룡 화석이 1990년대에 발견되었다. 다른 발견들이 뒤따랐다. 2011년까지 몇몇 연구들은 심지어 모든 포유동물들이 털이 있지만 모든 포유동물들이 털이 많은 것은 아닌 것과 거의 같은 방식으로, 모든 공룡들이 적어도 몸의 일부에 깃털 모양의 외피를 가졌음을 시사하고 있었다. 최초의 공룡들이 약 2억 4천 5백만 년 전에 출현했다고 여겨짐에도 불구하고, 깃털을 가진 공룡들은 불과 1억 8천만 년 전으로 연대가 추정된다.

[어휘] fossil 화석 feather 깃털 mammal 포유동물 hairy 털이 많은 emerge 출현하다 date ~의 연대를 추정하다

[정답] ③

09 다음 글의 제목으로 가장 적절한 것은? [제목]

The devil's advocate technique is a critical thinking approach where someone deliberately takes on an opposing viewpoint to challenge and question prevailing opinions within a group. Its origin lies in the practice of the Roman Catholic Church when considering a candidate for sainthood. Understandably, the Church doesn't want to make a mistake. They don't want to learn later that the candidate behaved in ways that were not saintly. Thus, in 1587, they introduced a practice of exploring everything negative about the candidate, which was what the devil's advocate was assigned to do. His job was to find any evidence that would cast doubt on the candidate's holiness by questioning witnesses, scrutinizing documents, and uncovering potential flaws. By employing the devil's advocate, the Church aimed to ensure that only truly deserving individuals were declared saints.

① The Origin of the Devil's Advocate Technique
② Does the Devil's Advocate Technique Really Work?
③ How the Church Eliminated the Devil's Advocate Practice
④ The Controversy over Who Should Play the Devil's Advocate

[해설] 로마 가톨릭교회가 성인 후보자를 검증하기 위해 시작된 악마의 변호인 기법의 유래를 설명하는 글이다. 따라서 글의 제목으로 가장 적절한 것은 ① '악마의 변호인 기법의 기원'이다.
② 악마의 변호인 기법이 정말 효과가 있을까? → 악마의 변호인 기법의 효과가 아닌 기원에 대한 글이므로 적절하지 않다.
③ 교회는 어떻게 악마의 변호인 관행을 없앴는가 → 이 글은 악마의 변호인 기법의 기원을 소개할 뿐, 그 관행이 어떻게 사라졌는지에 대해 설명하고 있지는 않다.
④ 누가 악마의 변호인 역할을 해야 하는지에 대한 논란 → 누가 악마의 변호인을 해야 하는지에 관한 논란을 서술하는 글이 아니다.

[해석] 악마의 변호인 기법은 누군가가 의도적으로 집단 내의 지배적인 의견에 이의를 제기하고 그것을 의심하기 위해 의도적으로 반대 입장을 취하는 비판적 사고방식이다. 그 기원은 성인이 될 후보자를 고려할 때의 로마 가톨릭교회 관습에 있다. 당연히, 교회는 실수하고 싶지 않다. 그들은 그 후보자가 성인답지 않은 방식으로 행동했다는 것을 나중에 알게 되기를 원하지 않는다. 따라서, 1587년에 그들은 후보자에 대한 부정적인 모든 것을 살펴보는 관행을 도입했는데, 이것이 바로 악마의 변호인이 해야 할 일이었다. 그의 역할은 증인을 심문하고, 문서를 세밀히 조사하고, 잠재적인 결함을 밝혀냄으로써 후보자의 신성함에 의심을 품을만한 그 어떤 증거든 찾아내는 것이었다. 악마의 변호인을 이용함으로써, 교회는 진정으로 자격이 있는 사람들만이 성인으로 선언되도록 보장하고자 했다.

[어휘] devil's advocate technique 악마의 변호인 기법 deliberately 의도적으로 challenge 이의를 제기하다 prevailing 지배적인, 우세한 candidate 후보자 saintly 성인다운 cast doubt on ~을 의심하다 scrutinize 세밀히 조사하다

[정답] ①

10. 다음 글의 흐름상 가장 어색한 문장은?

Bonding is so good for us that the most reliable way to extend one's life expectancy is to marry and stay married. The flip side is the risk we run after losing a partner. ① The death of a spouse often leads to despair and a reduced will to live, which can trigger social isolation and depressive symptoms. ② It can also leave a physical vulnerability, including a statistically higher risk of developing diseases like heart complications or cancer. ③ It is actually known that mortality remains elevated for about half a year following a spouse's death. ④ In coping with the death of a spouse, it is important to lean on others for support, whether they are family, friends, or counselors. It is worse for younger than older people, and worse for men than women.

[해설] 배우자를 잃은 후에 겪는 아픔으로 인한 여러 심리적, 신체적 악영향에 관해 서술하는 글이다. 따라서 글의 흐름상 가장 어색한 문장은 배우자의 죽음에 대처하는 방법을 설명하는 내용의 ④이다. 참고로, 마지막 문장의 It은 문맥상 ③ 뒤에서 언급된 mortality를 가리키는 것을 알 수 있으므로 ④의 내용이 들어간다면 문맥이 단절되는 것을 알 수 있다.

[해석] 기대 수명을 연장하는 가장 확실한 방법이 결혼을 하고 결혼 생활을 유지하는 것일 만큼, 유대감은 우리에게 매우 좋은 것이다. 그것의 이면은 배우자를 잃은 후에 우리가 무릅쓰는 위험이다. 배우자의 죽음은 종종 절망과 삶의 의욕 저하로 이어져 사회적 고립과 우울 증상을 유발할 수 있다. 그것은 심장 합병증이나 암과 같은 질병에 걸릴 위험이 통계적으로 더 높아지는 등 신체적 취약성을 남길 수도 있다. 실제로 배우자의 사망 후 약 반년 동안 사망률이 높아지는 것으로 알려져 있다. (배우자의 죽음에 대처할 때, 지지를 위해 가족이든 친구든 상담사든 다른 사람에게 의지하는 것이 중요하다.) 나이가 많은 사람보다 젊은 사람이, 여성보다 남성이 더 심하다.

[어휘] extend 연장하다 life expectancy 기대 수명 despair 절망적인 isolation 고립 symptoms 증상 vulnerability 취약성 heart complications 심장 합병증 mortality 사망률 elevate 높이다 spouse 배우자 cope with ~에 대처하다

[정답] ④

11. 밑줄 친 부분에 들어갈 말로 가장 적절한 것은?

A: Rick, did you burn something in the microwave?
B: How did you know?
A: _____
B: Really? I cleaned up everything and left it open for quite a while, though.
A: You must have burnt something pretty badly. What did you burn anyway?
B: A sweet potato. I'll be more careful next time.

① Not that I know of.
② It's stinking in there.
③ The microwave works fine.
④ I microwaved it for too long.

[해설] 전자레인지로 음식을 태운 것에 관해 대화를 나누는 상황이다. 전자레인지에 무언가를 태운 사실을 어떻게 아냐는 B의 질문에 A는 빈칸 내용을 언급하였다. 따라서 빈칸에 들어갈 말로 가장 적절한 것은 ② '거기 안에서 악취가 나.'이다.

① 내가 알기로는 아니야.
③ 그 전자레인지는 잘 작동해.
④ 내가 그걸 전자레인지에 너무 오래 돌렸어.

[해석] A: Rick, 전자레인지에 뭐 태웠어?
B: 어떻게 알았어?
A: 거기 안에서 악취가 나.
B: 진짜? 근데 난 다 치우고 그걸 꽤 오랫동안 열어뒀는데.
A: 뭔가를 꽤 심하게 태웠나 보네. 그나저나 뭘 태운 거야?
B: 고구마. 다음부터는 더 조심할게.

[어휘] microwave 전자레인지 stink 악취가 나다

[정답] ②

12 밑줄 친 부분에 들어갈 말로 가장 적절한 것은? 생활영어

A: Um, Mr. Royko, I was wondering if I could transfer to a different department.
B: Oh, is there any problem?
A: I feel that I'm showing a poor performance at the sales department, and that I could contribute more elsewhere.
B: Well, it's only been 3 months since you started. No one is good at their job at first, and your performance isn't actually that bad. _____
A: Wow, I didn't expect to hear that. Okay, I will. Thank you.

① I'm glad I've been doing well in sales.
② Your performance here has been declining.
③ How about you take some time to reconsider?
④ Which department would you like to be transferred to?

해설 A가 자신이 부족하다고 판단하여 부서 이동을 할 수 있는지 B에게 물어보는 상황이다. 이러한 상황에서 B는 A를 격려한 뒤에 빈칸 내용을 언급했는데, 이에 A는 그렇게 하겠다고 말하며 감사를 전하고 있다. 따라서 빈칸에 들어갈 말로 가장 적절한 것은 ③ '다시 생각해 보는 시간을 좀 갖는 게 어때요?'이다.
① 제가 영업에서 잘 해오고 있어서 다행이네요.
② 이곳에서 실적이 계속 떨어지고 있어요.
④ 어느 부서로 이동하고 싶으신가요?

해석 A: Royko 님, 제가 다른 부서로 옮길 수 있는지 궁금해요.
B: 아, 무슨 문제라도 있나요?
A: 제가 영업 부서에서 형편없는 실적을 내는 것 같고, 다른 곳에서 더 많이 기여할 수 있을 것 같아요.
B: 음, 시작한 지 3개월밖에 안 됐잖아요. 처음부터 일을 잘하는 사람은 아무도 없고, 성과도 사실 그렇게 나쁘지 않아요. 다시 생각해 보는 시간을 좀 갖는 게 어때요?
A: 와, 그런 말씀을 들을 줄은 몰랐어요. 네, 그렇게 하겠습니다. 감사합니다.

어휘 transfer 옮기다 department 부서 reconsider 다시 생각하다

정답 ③

13 우리말을 영어로 잘못 옮긴 것은? 문법

① 이제 우리가 다가오는 행사 계획을 세우기 시작할 때이다.
→ It is about time we start planning for the upcoming event.
② 현재 상황을 고려하면, 그 계획은 재고되는 것이 당연하다.
→ Given the current circumstances, the plan may well be reconsidered.
③ John은 시험 결과에 만족하지 못했고, 그의 부모님도 마찬가지였다.
→ John wasn't satisfied with the exam results, and neither were his parents.
④ 새는 날개를 엄청 빠르게 움직여 공중에 떠 있을 수 있다.
→ The bird moves its wings incredibly fast, allowing itself to float in the air.

해설 (start → started 또는 should start) '~할 시간이다'를 의미하는 It is (about) time 가정법은 'It is (about) time + S + 과거동사' 또는 'It is time + S + should + RV'의 형태로 쓰이며, 후자의 경우엔 should를 생략할 수 없다. 따라서 start를 started 또는 should start로 고쳐야 한다.
② '~을 고려하면'이라는 뜻의 분사형 전치사 given과 '~하는 것도 당연하다'라는 뜻의 'may well RV'가 주어진 우리말에 맞게 적절히 쓰였다. '~하는 것이 더 낫다'라는 뜻을 지닌 'may as well RV'와의 구별에 유의해야 한다. 또한 계획이 '재고하는' 것이 아니라 '재고되는' 것이므로 수동태 be reconsidered의 쓰임도 적절하다.
③ 부정 동의를 나타낼 때는 'and neither + V + S'의 형태로 도치가 일어나고, 대동사는 앞에 나온 동사 was를 대신하면서 복수 명사 his parents에 수일치해야 하므로 and neither were his parents의 쓰임은 적절하다. 참고로 여기서 neither는 접속사가 아닌 부사이므로 등위접속사 and와 같이 쓰는 것이다.
④ 부사구 incredibly fast가 동사 moves를 적절하게 수식하고 있다. 또한 분사구문의 의미상 주어인 The bird가 자신을 '뜰 수 있게 하는' 것이므로, 능동의 현재분사 allowing과 재귀대명사 itself는 적절하게 쓰였다. allow가 5형식 동사로 사용되면 to 부정사를 목적격 보어로 취하므로, to float가 쓰인 것도 적절하다.

어휘 upcoming 다가오는 circumstance 상황 incredibly 엄청나게 float 뜨다

정답 ①

14 우리말을 영어로 잘못 옮긴 것은? [문법]

① 학생의 3분의 1은 도서관에서 공부하는 것을 선호한다.
→ One third of the students prefer studying in the library.
② 예산안이 부결된 이유를 제게 설명해 주실 수 있나요?
→ Can you explain to me why the budget proposal was rejected?
③ 베개에 머리를 대고 누우면 수면의 질이 향상될 수도 있다.
→ Lying with your head placing on a pillow may improve sleep quality.
④ 직무 능력 평가는 4개월마다 시행된다.
→ Employee performance evaluations are conducted every four months.

[해설] (placing → placed) 부대 상황을 나타내는 'with + O + OC'의 분사구문이 사용되었는데, your head가 베개에 '놓이는' 것이므로 수동의 과거분사 placed가 쓰여야 한다.
① '부분명사 + of + 전체명사'가 주어로 쓰이면 of 뒤의 전체명사에 동사를 수일치하는데, 여기서는 복수 명사 the students가 오고 있으므로 그에 수일치한 복수 동사 prefer의 쓰임은 적절하다. 또한 prefer가 동명사 studying을 목적어로 취하고 있는 것도 적절하다.
② explain은 4형식으로 쓸 수 없는 3형식 동사이므로 간접목적어 앞에 전치사 to를 써야 한다. 또한 의문사 why가 이끄는 간접의문문은 '의문사 + S + V'의 평서문 어순을 취하며, 예산안이 '거절당한' 것이므로 수동태 was rejected도 적절하게 쓰였다.
④ 주어인 Employee performance evaluations가 '수행하는' 것이 아니라 '수행되는' 것이므로 수동태 are conducted는 적절하게 쓰였다. 또한 every는 '~마다'라는 뜻으로 쓰일 때, 'every + 기수 + 복수 명사' 또는 'every + 서수 + 단수 명사'의 형태를 취하므로, every four months의 쓰임도 적절하다.

[어휘] budget proposal 예산안 pillow 베개 evaluation 평가 conduct 수행하다

[정답] ③

15 밑줄 친 (A), (B)에 들어갈 말로 가장 적절한 것은? [연결사]

Social surveys are powerful tools that offer a quick and efficient means of collecting valuable information from a sub-sample of the population. However, to do this effectively is expensive, because of the time and cost involved in drawing up sampling frames, selecting a sample and then carrying out the fieldwork. Much survey work, __(A)__, doesn't need to meet these demanding standards as it is typically done on a one-time basis by organizations that want quick snapshots of particular groups of people, such as employees or local residents. In these instances, the conclusions drawn from the survey data are often difficult to generalize. __(B)__, the results do provide basic descriptions of the people involved in the survey, which gives some indication of the prevalence of behaviours and attitudes in the particular group.

	(A)	(B)
①	however	For instance
②	however	Nevertheless
③	therefore	By contrast
④	therefore	In addition

[해설] 사회 조사를 수행하는 방법 및 그 의의에 관해 설명하는 글이다. (A)가 속한 문장 앞은 사회 조사를 효과적으로 수행하는 데 비용이 많이 든다고 하며 그 이유를 설명하는 내용인데, 그 뒤에서 대부분의 조사 작업은 이러한 까다로운 기준을 충족할 필요가 없다고 하였으므로, (A)에 들어갈 연결사로 가장 적절한 것은 however이다. 또한, (B) 앞에서는 간단히 수행하는 조사에서 도출된 결론을 일반화하기는 어렵다고 했는데, (B) 뒤에서 그 결론이 기본적인 설명은 제공한다는 상반되는 의견을 제시했으므로, (B)에 들어갈 연결사로 적절한 것은 Nevertheless이다.

[해석] 사회 조사는 인구의 일부 표본으로부터 가치 있는 정보를 빠르고 효율적으로 수집할 수 있는 강력한 도구이다. 그러나 이를 효과적으로 수행하는 데는 비용이 많이 드는데, 그 이유는 표본 추출 프레임을 작성하고 표본을 선택한 다음 현장 조사를 수행하는 데 드는 시간과 비용 때문이다. 그러나, 대부분의 설문 조사 작업은 일반적으로 직원이나 지역 주민과 같은 특정 집단 사람들에 대한 빠른 짤막한 정보를 원하는 조직에서 일회성으로 수행하기 때문에 이러한 까다로운 기준을 충족할 필요가 없다. 이러한 경우에는 설문 조사 데이터에서 도출된 결론을 일반화하기 어려운 경우가 많다. 그럼에도 불구하고, 그 결론은 설문 조사에 참여한 사람들에 대한 기본적인 설명을 제공하는 것은 맞으며, 그 설명은 특정 그룹의 행동과 태도의 유행을 어느 정도 파악할 수 있게 한다.

[어휘] fieldwork 현장 조사 demanding 까다로운 typically 일반적으로 snapshot 짤막한 정보 resident 주민 generalize 일반화하다 prevalence 유행

[정답] ②

16. 밑줄 친 부분에 들어갈 말로 가장 적절한 것은?

A poor farmer had a lot of moldy hay. Instead of wasting it, he tried to feed it to his cows, but the cows would rather go hungry than eat the bad-tasting grass. So the farmer mixed the moldy hay with some fresh hay and gave it to his cows. The cows simply separated the good hay from the bad and ate the good stuff. Still, the moldy hay remained. Then the farmer noticed something strange. Even though there was plenty of grass in the paddock, the cows would often be seen pushing their heads between the wires of the fence to eat the grass just outside the paddock. So the farmer left the moldy hay just outside of the fence, close enough for a cow to reach with a stretch. The moldy hay was all eaten in a couple of days. _____ hay, even when moldy, tastes sweet.

*paddock: 울타리를 쳐 놓은 들판

① Mixed
② Wasted
③ Borrowed
④ Forbidden

17. 다음 글의 제목으로 가장 적절한 것은?

Drug addiction is an old problem for society, leading to crime, diminished productivity, mental illness and, more recently, to an expanding prison population. Most countries deal with the problem of drug addiction by criminalizing it. A few decades ago, 38,000 Americans were in prison for drug-related offenses. Today, it's half a million. On the face of it, that might sound like success in the War on Drugs but this mass imprisonment hasn't slowed the drug trade. This is because, for the most part, the people in jail aren't the cartel bosses, the mafia dons, or the big-time dealers. Instead, the prisoners have been locked up for possession of a small amount of drugs, usually less than two grams. They're just the users, the addicts. Simply locking them up in prison doesn't solve the problem.

① The Legal Basis for Criminalizing Drug Abuse
② How Jail Became a Major Route for Drug Trades
③ Is Imprisonment the Answer to the War on Drugs?
④ The Vicious Cycle of Drug Use and Crime: How It Works

18 주어진 문장이 들어갈 위치로 가장 적절한 곳은? 문장삽입

In contrast, other athletes may view success purely in terms of comparisons with others; their standard for a high perception of ability and achievement is beating the opposition.

Task-involved athletes are concerned with the development of their competence and use levels of effort and task completion to assess their competence in a self-reflective manner. (①) They view ability as something that is improvable. (②) Therefore, they are satisfied if they perform at a level that extracts the best of their current ability by mastering a particular technique, increasing tactical awareness, or making personal improvements in a given skill. (③) In other words, to feel successful and competent, these athletes have to demonstrate ability superior to somebody else, regardless of personal improvements or developments that may have occurred in the process. (④) In this case, the athletes are ego-involved.

[해설] 주어진 문장은 In contrast로 시작하여, 다른 운동선수들은 남을 이겨야 유능감과 성취감을 느끼는 등 다른 사람들과의 비교를 통해 성공을 바라본다는 내용으로, 앞에는 이 운동선수들의 특성과 대조되는, 즉 남들과 비교를 통해서가 아닌 자신의 발전을 기준으로 삼는 운동선수들에 관한 설명이 나와야 하며, 뒤에서는 주어진 문장에서 언급된 운동선수들에 관한 부연이 이어져야 자연스럽다. ③ 앞에는 자신의 능력을 개선하는 것을 목표로 삼는 과제 지향적인 운동선수들이 나왔으며, ③ 뒤에서 이 선수들은 다른 사람보다 더 뛰어난 능력을 보여줘야만 성공했다고 느낀다고 했으므로, 문맥이 단절되는 것을 알 수 있다. 또한 ③ 뒤의 these athletes가 주어진 문장에서 나온 other athletes를 가리키는 것을 알 수 있으므로, 주어진 문장이 들어갈 위치로 가장 적절한 곳은 ③이다.

[해석] 과제 지향적인 운동선수들은 자기 역량 개발에 관심이 있으며, 자기 성찰적인 방식으로 자신의 능력을 평가하기 위해 노력 및 과제 완수 수준을 이용한다. 그들은 능력을 개선 가능한 것으로 여긴다. 그렇기에 그들은 특정 기술을 익히거나, 전술에 대한 이해를 높이거나, 특정 기술에 있어 개인적인 향상을 이뤄냄으로써 현재 자기 능력의 최고를 뽑아내는 수준으로 경기하는 경우에 만족한다. 이와는 대조적으로, 다른 선수들은 성공을 순전히 다른 사람들과 비교하는 측면에서 바라볼 수 있으며, 능력과 성취가 높다는 인식에 대한 그 사람의 기준은 상대편을 이기는 데 있다. 다시 말해, 성공적이고 유능하다고 느끼려면, 이 선수들은 과정에서 일어났을 수도 있는 개인적 향상이나 발전과는 관계없이, 다른 어떤 사람보다 더 뛰어난 능력을 보여줘야만 한다. 이 경우에, 그 운동선수들은 자아 지향적인 것이다.

[어휘] in terms of ~의 관점에서 comparison 비교 beat 이기다 competence 능력, 역량 completion 완수 self-reflective 자아 성찰적인 improvable 개선 가능한 extract 뽑다, 추출하다 tactical 전략적인 demonstrate 입증하다, 보여주다 superior to ~보다 뛰어난 regardless of ~에 관계없이

[정답] ③

19 다음 글의 요지로 가장 적절한 것은? 요지

In today's world, we are constantly bombarded with information. With the Internet and social media at our fingertips, we have access to an infinite amount of information about anything and everything. While this may seem like a good thing, it can actually be overwhelming and lead to indecision. When we have too much information, we may feel that we need to gather more and more information before we can make a decision. This can get us stuck in a cycle of constantly researching and analyzing without actually taking action. In addition, in a state of information overload, we struggle to process and retain all the information we receive, making it difficult to prioritize information and determine what is truly relevant to our decision-making process. As a result, we may become overwhelmed with details and fail to make a clear decision.

① Information overload can lead to decision paralysis.
② It's important to check the validity of every information.
③ Access to vast amount of information facilitates learning.
④ Details should not be overlooked when making a decision.

[해설] 과다한 정보는 결정을 내리는 것을 어렵게 만들어 오히려 우리의 의사 결정 과정에 방해가 된다는 내용의 글이다. 따라서 글의 요지로 가장 적절한 것은 ① '정보 과부하는 결정 마비로 이어질 수 있다.'이다.
② 모든 정보의 유효성을 확인하는 것이 중요하다. → 이 글은 너무 많은 정보는 해가 된다고 말할 뿐, 그 논지가 모든 정보의 유효성을 확인해야 한다는 주장으로까지 이어지지는 않았다.
③ 방대한 양의 정보에 대한 접근 기회는 학습을 용이하게 한다. → 정보가 너무 방대한 경우에 생기는 부정적인 측면을 서술하는 글이므로 적절하지 않다.
④ 결정을 내릴 때 세부사항이 간과되어서는 안 된다. → 오히려 과다한 세부적인 정보들로 인해 의사 결정을 내리는 것이 어려워진다고 하였으므로 적절하지 않다.

[해석] 오늘날의 세상에서, 우리는 끊임없이 퍼부어지는 정보와 함께 살고 있다. 인터넷과 소셜 미디어를 손쉽게 이용할 수 있기 때문에, 우리는 무엇이든지 다 그것에 관한 무한한 양의 정보에 접근할 수 있다. 이것은 좋은 일처럼 보일 수 있지만, 실제로는 압도적일 수 있으며 우유부단함으로 이어질 수 있다. 우리가 너무 많은 정보를 가지고 있는 경우에는, 결정을 내릴 수 있기 전에 더욱 더 많은 정보를 수집해야 한다고 느낄 수 있다. 이것은 실제로 행동을 취하지 않은 채 계속해서 연구하고 분석하는 순환에 갇히게 만들 수 있다. 게다가, 정보 과부하 상태에서 우리는 우리가 받는 모든 정보를 처리하고 기억하는 데 애를 써서, 정보의 우선순위를 정하고 의사결정 과정에 진정으로 관련 있는 것을 결정하기가 어렵게 된다. 결과적으로, 우리는 세부사항에 압도되어 명확한 의사결정을 내리지 못할 수도 있다.

[어휘] bombard (질문 등을) 퍼붓다 at one's fingertips ~을 손쉽게 이용할 수 있는 infinite 무한한 anything and everything 무엇이든지 다 overwhelming 압도적인 indecision 우유부단함 get stuck in ~에 갇히다 overload 과부하 prioritize 우선순위를 정하다 paralysis 마비 facilitate 용이하게 하다

[정답] ①

20 주어진 글 다음에 이어질 글의 순서로 가장 적절한 것은? `순서배열`

When people can witness the work done for them, they believe more effort is involved and see the service provider as more skilled. Furthermore, showing the process can make people prefer even "delayed" results.

(A) By doing this, they show how hard they're working for those using the site, making them wait until the search is finished. As a result, people trust *Kayak.com* to deliver a better outcome for travelers.

(B) Researchers call this observed pattern *operational transparency*. Ryan Buell and Michael Norton report in their article that the travel website *Kayak.com* is beloved in part because of this psychological principle.

(C) When searching for a holiday, the site laboriously illustrates which airline is being examined, providing visual updates of results throughout the search rather than offering an instantaneous reveal.

① (A) - (C) - (B) ② (B) - (A) - (C)
③ (B) - (C) - (A) ④ (C) - (A) - (B)

[해설] 주어진 글은 사람들이 자신을 위해 행해지는 일을 직접 목격하는 경우에 서비스 제공자가 더 노력하고 있으며 더 숙련되었다고 느끼며, 심지어 지연된 결과물조차 선호하게 된다는 내용으로, 뒤에는 이 현상을 this observed pattern으로 받아, 이를 연구자들이 '운영 투명성'이라고 부른다는 내용의 (B)가 이어져야 한다. 그다음으로, (B)에서 언급된 Kayak.com이라는 웹 사이트가 어떻게 운영 투명성을 이용하는지 구체적으로 설명하는 (C)가 와야 한다. 마지막으로, 그 과정을 this로 받아, 이를 통해 사람들은 그 웹 사이트를 더 신뢰하게 된다는 내용의 (A)로 글이 마무리되어야 한다. 따라서 글의 순서로 가장 적절한 것은 ③ '(B) - (C) - (A)'이다.

[해석] 사람들이 자기를 위해 행해지는 일을 보면, 그들은 더 많은 노력이 수반된다고 믿고, 서비스 제공자가 더 숙련되었다고 생각한다. 더구나, 과정을 보여주는 것은 사람들이 '지연된' 결과물조차 선호하게 만들 수 있다. (B) 연구원들은 이 관찰된 패턴을 '운영 투명성'이라고 부른다. Ryan Buell과 Michael Norton은 그들의 논문에서, 여행 웹 사이트 'Kayak.com'이 부분적으로 이러한 심리적 원리 때문에 사랑받는다고 밝힌다. (C) 휴일을 위해 검색할 때, 이 사이트는 즉각적인 (정보) 노출을 제공하는 대신, 검색 내내 결과물의 시각적 업데이트를 제공하면서 어떤 항공사를 검토하고 있는지 공들여서 보여준다. (A) 이렇게 함으로써 그들은 그들이 사이트 이용자들을 위해 얼마나 열심히 일하는지 보여주고, 검색이 끝날 때까지 그들을 기다리게 한다. 결과적으로, 사람들은 'Kayak.com'이 여행자를 위한 더 좋은 결과를 도출해 줄 것이라고 믿는다.

[어휘] witness 목격하다, 보다 skilled 숙련된 deliver 도출하다 operational 운영의 transparency 투명성 article 논문 psychological 심리[정신]적인 laboriously 공들여 instantaneous 즉각적인

[정답] ③

회차 6
Answer

01	02	03	04	05
①	②	④	②	④
06	07	08	09	10
②	①	②	④	③
11	12	13	14	15
③	②	④	④	②
16	17	18	19	20
③	②	②	①	②

01 밑줄 친 부분의 의미와 가장 가까운 것은? [어휘]

Most subordinate tasks were assigned efficiently to team members, maximizing productivity in the workplace.

① secondary ② appropriate
③ independent ④ sophisticated

[해설] subordinate는 '부차적인'이라는 뜻으로, 이와 의미가 가장 가까운 것은 ① 'secondary(부차적인)'이다.
② 적절한 ③ 독자적인 ④ 정교한
[해석] 대부분의 부차적인 업무가 팀원들에게 효율적으로 배정되어 업무 현장의 생산성을 극대화했다.
[어휘] assign 배정하다 maximize 극대화하다 productivity 생산성

[정답] ①

02 밑줄 친 부분의 의미와 가장 가까운 것은? [어휘]

The indigenous communities are actively engaging in preserving and promoting their precious heritage.

① ritual ② legacy
③ integrity ④ commodity

[해설] heritage는 '유산'이라는 뜻으로, 이와 의미가 가장 가까운 것은 ② 'legacy(유산)'이다.
① 의식 ③ 정직, 온전함 ④ 상품
[해석] 원주민 공동체들은 자신들의 소중한 유산을 보존하고 홍보하는 데 적극적으로 나서고 있다.
[어휘] indigenous 원산의, 토착의 promote 홍보하다 precious 소중한

[정답] ②

03 밑줄 친 부분의 의미와 가장 가까운 것은? [이디엄]

Successful project management requires teams to take into account potential risks in multiple ways.

① become aware of ② previously remove
③ be ready to suffer ④ think carefully about

[해설] take into account는 '고려하다'라는 뜻으로, 이와 의미가 가장 가까운 것은 ④ 'think carefully about(신중히 생각하다)'이다.
① 알아채다 ② 미리 없애다 ③ 겪을 준비가 되어 있다
[해석] 성공적인 프로젝트 관리를 위해서는 팀이 잠재적인 위험을 다방면으로 고려해야 한다.
[어휘] management 관리 potential 잠재적인 multiple 다양한

[정답] ④

04 밑줄 친 부분에 들어갈 말로 가장 적절한 것은? [어휘]

The COVID-19 pandemic led to _____ job losses, which means that a lot of businesses were forced to close or reduce operations. Even employees of companies that were originally large and stable could not avoid layoffs.

① precise ② inevitable
③ distinctive ④ confidential

[해설] which means that 이하의 많은 기업이 강제로 사업을 중단하거나 줄여야 했다는 내용과, 안정적인 기업에 다니던 직원들도 실업을 피할 수 없었다는 내용으로 보아, 실직이 맞닥뜨릴 수밖에 없는 것이었음을 알 수 있다. 따라서 빈칸에 들어갈 말로 가장 적절한 것은 ② 'inevitable(불가피한)'이다.
① 정확한 ③ 독특한 ④ 비밀의
[해석] 코로나19 대유행은 불가피한 실직을 초래했는데, 이는 많은 기업이 문을 닫거나 사업을 축소할 수밖에 없었음을 의미한다. 원래 규모가 크고 안정적이었던 기업의 직원들마저 해고를 피할 수는 없었다.
[어휘] pandemic 전 세계적인 유행병 operation 사업 stable 안정적인 layoff 해고

[정답] ②

05 밑줄 친 부분에 들어갈 말로 가장 적절한 것은? [이어동사]

To promote a balanced lifestyle, you should _____ unhealthy habits.

① hold on
② hold by
③ keep up with
④ keep away from

[해설] 균형 잡힌 생활 방식을 고취하려면 건강에 안 좋은 습관을 피해야 할 것을 추측할 수 있으므로, 빈칸에 들어갈 말로 가장 적절한 것은 ④ 'keep away from(멀리하다)'이다.
① 붙잡다; 기다리다 ② 고수하다 ③ 따라가다
[해석] 균형 잡힌 생활 방식을 촉진하기 위해서는 건강하지 못한 습관을 멀리해야 한다.
[어휘] promote 촉진하다

[정답] ④

06 어법상 옳은 것은? [문법]

① His speech is often thought as a powerful message of inspiration.
② The more goals you set, the more motivated you'll be to achieve them.
③ The theory requiring vast statistical analyses are likely to be proven credible.
④ The director encouraged the actors to rise their voices during the performance.

[해설] '~하면 할수록 더 ~하다'라는 의미의 'the 비교급, the 비교급' 구문이 쓰였다. The more goals는 set의 목적어로, the more motivated는 be의 형용사 보어로 적절하게 쓰였다. 문맥상 you가 '의욕을 갖게 하는' 것이 아니라 '의욕을 갖는' 것이므로 수동의 과거분사형 motivated의 쓰임은 적절하며, them은 복수 명사 goals를 받는 대명사로 적절하게 쓰였다.
① (thought → thought of) think가 5형식 동사로 쓰일 때 'think of A as B'의 구조를 취할 수 있는데, 이를 수동태로 바꾸면 'A be thought of as B'의 구조가 된다. 이때 전치사 of가 생략되지 않도록 유의해야 한다.
③ (are → is) 주어인 The theory는 단수 명사이므로, 동사도 그에 수일치하여 단수 동사 is가 되어야 한다. 한편 이론이 방대한 통계 분석을 '요구하는' 것이므로 능동의 현재 분사 requiring은 적절하게 쓰였으며, 믿을 만한 것으로 '입증되는' 것이므로 5형식 동사로 쓰인 prove의 수동형 be proven과 형용사 보어 credible의 쓰임도 적절하다.
④ (rise → raise) rise는 '오르다, 일어나다'라는 뜻의 완전 자동사이므로, '올리다'라는 뜻의 타동사 raise로 고쳐야 한다. 참고로 5형식 동사로 쓰인 encourage는 to 부정사를 목적격 보어로 취하며, 전치사 during 뒤에 명사구가 온 것은 적절하다.
[해석] ① 그의 연설은 종종 강력한 영감의 메시지로 여겨진다.
② 목표를 더 많이 세울수록 그것들을 달성하려는 의욕이 강해질 것이다.
③ 방대한 통계 분석을 요구하는 이론은 믿을 만한 것으로 입증될 가능성이 크다.
④ 그 연출가는 배우들이 공연 중에 목소리를 높이도록 부추겼다.
[어휘] inspiration 영감 motivate 의욕을 갖게 하다 vast 방대한 statistical 통계의 credible 믿을 만한

[정답] ②

07 Arnold Schwarzenegger에 관한 다음 글의 내용과 일치하지 않는 것은? [불일치]

Arnold Schwarzenegger's political career began in 2003 when he ran for the Governor of California and won a seat in a special election, marking a remarkable transition from Hollywood to public service. Despite lacking prior political experience, Schwarzenegger brought his charisma to the forefront and demonstrated his competence in managing the responsibilities of public office. He successfully implemented measures to improve California's economic situation by working to bridge political parties and emphasize cooperation. He's also notable for his efforts to address environmental issues, including the passage of the Global Warming Solutions Act. As a result, he was able to secure an easy win in the 2006 reelection.

① His experience in politics contributed to his win in the 2003 election.
② He tackled California's economic issues by promoting cooperation.
③ He dedicated efforts to confronting environmental issues.
④ He faced little difficulty in winning the 2006 reelection.

[해설] 2번째 문장에서 그는 이전 정치 경험이 없었다고 언급되므로, 글의 내용과 일치하지 않는 것은 ① '그의 정치 경험이 2003년 선거에서 그의 승리에 기여했다.'이다.
② 그는 협력을 촉진하여 캘리포니아의 경제 문제를 해결했다. → 3번째 문장에서 언급된 내용이다.
③ 그는 환경 문제에 맞서는 데 노력을 바쳤다. → 마지막 2번째 문장에서 언급된 내용이다.
④ 그는 2006년 재선거에서 승리하는 데 어려움이 거의 없었다. → 마지막 문장에서 언급된 내용이다.
[해석] Arnold Schwarzenegger의 정치 경력은 2003년에 그가 캘리포니아 주지사 선거에 출마하여 특별 선거에서 당선되면서 시작되었으며, 이는 할리우드에서 공직으로의 놀라운 전환을 표했다. Schwarzenegger는 이전 정치 경험이 없었음에도 불구하고 카리스마를 앞세워 공직의 책임을 다하는 데 탁월한 역량을 발휘했다. 그는 정당 간 다리 역할을 하고 협력을 강조함으로써 캘리포니아의 경제 상황을 개선하기 위한 조치를 성공적으로 시행했다. 또한 그는 지구 온난화 해결 법안 통과 등 환경 문제 해결을 위한 노력으로도 유명하다. 그 결과 그는 2006년 재선거에서 손쉬운 승리를 얻어낼 수 있었다.
[어휘] run for ~에 출마하다 Governor 주지사 remarkable 놀라운 transition 변화 lack 부족하다 forefront 맨 앞 competence 능력 measure 조치 notable 유명한, 눈에 띄는 reelection 재선 tackle 해결하다 confront 맞서다

[정답] ①

08 밑줄 친 부분 중 어법상 옳지 않은 것은?

On November 29, 1947, the UN voted to partition the British mandate of Palestine into a Jewish state and an Arab state, ① which immediately caused clashes between Jews and Arabs in Palestine. As British troops prepared to withdraw from Palestine, conflict continued to escalate. Among the most infamous events ② were the attack on the Arab village on April 9, 1948. The news of a massacre there spread ③ widely and inspired both panic and revenge. Days later, Arab forces attacked a Jewish convoy ④ approaching a hospital, killing 78.

[해설] (were → was) 장소의 부사구 Among the most infamous events가 문두에 위치하여 주어와 동사가 도치된 문장이다. 따라서 문장의 주어는 단수 명사인 the attack이므로, 동사 were를 수일치에 맞게 was로 고쳐야 한다.
① 관계대명사 which는 ,(콤마) 다음에 계속적 용법으로 쓸 수 있으며, 불완전한 절을 이끌고 있는 것도 적절하다.
③ '널리'라는 뜻의 부사 widely가 동사 spread를 적절하게 수식하고 있다.
④ 유대인 호송대가 병원에 '접근한' 것이므로 능동의 현재분사 approaching은 적절하게 쓰였으며, approach는 완전타동사이므로 전치사 없이 바로 목적어를 취하고 있는 것도 적절하다.

[해석] 1947년 11월 29일, UN은 팔레스타인에 대한 영국의 권한을 유대 국가와 아랍 국가로 분할하기로 가결했는데, 이는 즉시 팔레스타인에서 유대인과 아랍인 사이에 충돌을 일으켰다. 영국군이 팔레스타인으로부터 철수를 준비하면서 갈등은 계속 고조되었다. 가장 악명 높은 사건들 중 하나는 1948년 4월 9일에 있었던 아랍 마을에 대한 공격이었다. 그곳에서의 대학살 소식은 널리 퍼졌고 공황과 보복 모두를 고취했다. 며칠 후, 아랍 군대는 병원으로 접근하는 유대인 호송대를 공격하여 78명을 죽였다.

[어휘] partition 분할 mandate 권한 immediately 즉시 clash 충돌 troops 군대 withdraw 철수하다 escalate 고조되다 infamous 악명 높은 massacre 대학살 inspire 고취하다 revenge 보복 convoy 호송대

[정답] ②

09 다음 글의 제목으로 가장 적절한 것은?

The reason the human race has been so successful is not because we're the strongest animals — far from it. Size and might alone do not guarantee success. We've succeeded as a species because of our ability to form groups that share a common set of values and beliefs. And when we share values and beliefs with others, we form trust. In these trust circles, we rely on others to help protect our children and ensure our personal survival. The ability, for example, to leave the den to hunt or explore with confidence that the community would protect your family until you returned was one of the most important factors in the survival of our species. Through mutual trust, we pool our resources, keep each other safe, and take on challenges that we could not deal with on our own. It is through trust that we create a network of support for the betterment of all.

① Diverse Aspects of World Cultures
② How to Earn Trust from Other People
③ Wisdom Beats Strength in Survival Games
④ Power of Human Prosperity: Trust in Others

[해설] 타인을 신뢰하는 무리 안에서 생활했기에 인류가 번영할 수 있었다는 내용의 글이다. 따라서 글의 제목으로 가장 적절한 것은 ④ '인류 번영의 힘: 타인에 대한 신뢰'이다.
① 세계 문화의 다양한 측면
② 타인의 신뢰를 얻는 방법 → 타인의 신뢰를 얻는 방법을 소개하는 글이 아니다.
③ 생존 게임에서는 지혜가 힘을 이긴다 → '지혜'가 아닌 '신뢰'가 생존에 중요했다는 내용의 글이다.

[해석] 인류가 그토록 성공한 이유는 우리가 가장 강한 동물이기 때문이 아니며, 그것과는 거리가 멀다. 크기와 힘만으로는 성공이 보장되지 않는다. 우리가 종으로서 성공할 수 있었던 것은 공통된 가치와 신념을 공유하는 집단을 형성하는 능력 덕분이다. 그리고 다른 사람들과 가치와 신념을 공유할 때 우리는 신뢰를 형성한다. 이러한 신뢰 무리 속에서, 우리는 남들이 우리의 자녀를 보호하고 개인의 생존을 보장하는 데 도움을 줄 것이라고 믿는다. 예를 들어, 당신이 돌아올 때까지 공동체가 당신의 가족을 보호해 줄 것이라는 확신을 가지고 사냥을 하거나 탐험을 하기 위해 굴을 떠날 수 있었던 힘은 우리 종의 생존에 있어서 가장 중요한 요소 중 하나였다. 우리는 상호 신뢰를 통해 자원을 모으고, 서로를 안전하게 지키며, 혼자서는 감당할 수 없는 어려움에 도전한다. 우리가 모두의 향상을 위한 지원 네트워크를 구축할 수 있는 것은 신뢰를 통해서이다.

[어휘] guarantee 보증하다, 보장하다 species 종(pl. species) den 굴, 소굴 confidence 신용, 신뢰 factor 요인, 요소 betterment 향상, 개선 prosperity 번영

[정답] ④

10

Many runners, believing that arm movements help propel them forward, use rather expansive arm swings while running. Scientific research convincingly shows that this is not a good strategy. ① Swinging the arms in big movements like across the front of the body is energy-consuming and inefficient. ② Faster, more economical runners actually tend to have less arm movement than slower runners. ③ It is common for runners to find it challenging to alter their established running form during a run. ④ Quick, *little* arm movements carried out in synchrony with the swings of the legs appear to be the ones that produce the most economical running. The key to efficient running lies in minimal, not maximal, arm movements.

11

A: Good evening, this is Shim's Steakhouse.
B: Hi, I'd like to book a table for four people for Saturday evening.
A: I'm sorry, but all tables are fully booked during that time as of now.
B: Oh, that's a shame. _____
A: Sure, absolutely. We tend to have a few cancellations on Saturday evenings, so I'll give you a call as soon as a table becomes available.

① How would you like your steak?
② Which times are available that evening?
③ Could you put me on the waiting list then?
④ Would it be okay if I cancel my reservation?

12 밑줄 친 부분에 들어갈 말로 가장 적절한 것은? [생활영어]

A: Are you coming to the class reunion this Friday?
B: _____
A: What's making you hesitate?
B: Well, it could be fun but I haven't been in touch with a lot of people after graduating. It'll probably be really awkward for me.
A: Hey, you have me, right? And I have no doubt you'll be able to mingle easily. You won't regret coming.
B: Hmm. Okay, but promise you'll stick with me.

① Count me in.
② I'm on the fence.
③ I'd like to make a toast.
④ I'm planning to show up.

[해설] 동창회 참석 여부에 관해 대화를 나누는 상황이다. B가 빈칸 내용을 언급한 것에 대해 A는 무엇 때문에 망설이는 건지 물어보고 있으므로, 빈칸에 들어갈 말로 가장 적절한 것은 ② '난 고민 중이야.'이다.
① 나도 끼워줘.
③ 나 건배하고 싶어.
④ 난 참석할 예정이야.

[해석] A: 너 이번 금요일에 동창회에 와?
B: 난 고민 중이야.
A: 무엇 때문에 망설이는 거야?
B: 음, 재미있을 수도 있는데 내가 졸업한 후엔 많은 사람들과 연락을 주고받진 않아서. 아마 나한테는 정말 어색할 것 같아.
A: 야, 내가 있잖아, 그렇지? 그리고 난 네가 쉽게 어울릴 수 있다는 데 한 치도 의심하지 않아. 오는 걸 후회하지 않을 거야.
B: 흠. 알았어, 근데 나랑 꼭 붙어있겠다고 약속해 줘.

[어휘] reunion 동창회 hesitate 망설이다 awkward 어색한 mingle (사람들과) 어울리다 count sb in ~을 끼워주다 be on the fence 고민 중인, 결정하지 못한 make a toast 건배하다

[정답] ②

13 우리말을 영어로 잘못 옮긴 것은? [문법]

① 당신의 부주의가 하마터면 재앙을 불러올 뻔했다.
→ Your carelessness came near to causing a disaster.
② 그 팀은 소프트웨어 개발 프로젝트를 완수하려고 노력했다.
→ The team tried to get the software development project completed.
③ 이 걸작들을 그린 예술가가 전시회를 열고 있다.
→ The artist who painted these masterpieces is holding an exhibition.
④ 그 회사는 확장되었을 뿐만 아니라, 공로로 상을 타기도 했다.
→ Not only has the firm expanded, but it has also awarded for its contribution.

[해설] (awarded → been awarded) 'A뿐만 아니라 B도'라는 뜻의 'not only A but also B' 구문이 사용되고 있으며, 문두에 부정어인 not only가 나와 주어와 동사가 의문문의 어순으로 도치되었다. 그런데 but 이하에서 it이 가리키는 것은 the firm이고, 회사가 '상을 준' 것이 아니라 '상을 받은' 것이므로 수동태로 쓰여야 한다.
① 'come near to RVing'는 '거의 ~할 뻔하다'라는 뜻을 지닌 관용표현으로 주어진 우리말에 맞게 쓰였다. 이때 to는 전치사이므로 뒤에 동명사가 오는 것에 유의해야 한다.
② 주어진 우리말에 따라 '~하기 위해 노력하다'라는 의미의 'try to RV'가 쓰인 것은 적절하다. '시험 삼아 ~해보다'라는 뜻인 'try RVing'와의 구분에 유의해야 한다. 또한 준사역동사 get은 목적어와 목적격 보어의 관계가 능동이면 to RV를, 수동이면 p.p.를 목적격 보어로 취하는데, 여기서는 프로젝트가 '완수되는' 것이므로 수동을 나타내는 completed가 적절하게 쓰였다.
③ The artist를 선행사로 받는 주격 관계대명사 who가 불완전한 절을 이끄는 것은 적절하다. 또한 주어가 단수 명사인 The artist이고, 예술가가 전시회를 '여는' 것이므로 능동태 단수 동사 is holding은 적절하게 쓰였다.

[어휘] carelessness 부주의 complete 완수하다 masterpiece 걸작 exhibition 전시회 expand 확장되다 contribution 기여, 공로

[정답] ④

14 우리말을 영어로 잘못 옮긴 것은? [문법]

① 한 소년이 던진 공이 호수에 떨어졌다.
→ The ball thrown by a boy landed in the lake.
② 내가 정보를 찾은 웹 사이트는 평판이 좋다.
→ The website on which I found the information is reputable.
③ 만약 내가 결과를 알았다면 그런 위험을 감수하지 않았을 것이다.
→ If I had known the results, I wouldn't have taken such a risk.
④ 그들이 인터넷에서 보는 모든 것을 믿는 것은 어리석은 짓이다.
→ It's stupid for them to believe everything they look at on the internet.

[해설] (for → of) stupid와 같은 사람의 성격을 나타내는 형용사의 의미상 주어는 'of + 목적격'으로 표현해야 한다. 참고로 everything과 they 사이에는 목적격 관계대명사가 생략되어 있어, look at의 목적어 자리가 비어 있다.
① 주어인 The ball이 소년에 의해 '던져진' 것이므로 수동의 과거분사 thrown은 적절하게 쓰였다. 참고로 land는 '떨어지다'라는 뜻의 자동사로 쓰였다.
② which는 The website를 선행사로 받고 있으며, '전치사 + 관계대명사' 형태인 on which 뒤에 완전한 절이 온 것은 적절하다. 또한 주어가 단수 명사인 The website이므로 그에 수일치한 단수 동사 is의 쓰임도 적절하다.
③ 주어진 우리말에 따라 if절에 'had p.p.', 주절에 '조동사 과거형 + have p.p.'가 오는 가정법 과거완료가 적절하게 쓰였다. 또한 such는 'such + a(n) + 명사'의 어순을 취하므로 such a risk의 쓰임도 적절하다.

[어휘] reputable 평판이 좋은

[정답] ④

---

15 밑줄 친 (A), (B)에 들어갈 말로 가장 적절한 것은? [연결사]

Cancer is a major cause of human deaths worldwide. Most cancers generally follow an exponential increase with age, being prevalent mostly during the post-reproductive period of the lifespan. Thus, aging is the most straightforward risk factor for cancer. __(A)__, some specific types of cancer disobey this pattern. The incidence of testicular cancer is mostly concentrated within the reproductive portion of life, when spermatogenic cells are most active. Bone cancers also have a substantial peak of incidence during early ages when the skeleton is growing. __(B)__, the natural incidence of cancers can be significantly influenced by risk factors related to lifestyle choices. Smoking, alcohol abuse, and obesity are among the many factors linked with elevated cancer risk.

	(A)	(B)
①	However	That is
②	However	Additionally
③	For instance	Instead
④	For instance	As a result

[해설] 암은 대체로 연령이 증가함에 따라 발생률이 증가하는데, 일부 암의 경우에는 이러한 경향을 따르지 않으며, 암의 발생률이 생활 방식의 영향을 크게 받을 수 있다는 내용의 글이다. (A) 앞은 노화가 암의 가장 직접적인 위험 요인이라는 내용이고, (A) 뒤는 일부 특정 유형의 암은 이를 따르지 않는다는 상반되는 내용이므로, (A)에 들어갈 연결사로 가장 적절한 것은 However이다. 또한 (B) 앞에서 노화와 관계없이 발생하는 암들에 관해 설명한 후에 (B) 뒤에서 생활 방식이 암의 발생률에 큰 영향을 줄 수 있다고 하였는데, 이 또한 노화가 암의 직접적인 위험 요인이라는 전제에 해당하지 않는 사례임을 알 수 있다. 따라서 (B)에 들어갈 연결사로 가장 적절한 것은 Additionally이다.

[해석] 암은 전 세계적으로 사망의 주요 원인이다. 대부분의 암은 일반적으로 연령이 증가함에 따라 기하급수적으로 증가하며, 주로 생식기 이후 생애에 걸쳐 만연한다. 따라서 노화는 암의 가장 직접적인 위험 요인이다. 그러나, 일부 특정 유형의 암은 이러한 패턴을 따르지 않는다. 고환암의 발생률은 대부분 정자 생성 세포가 가장 활발한 생식기에 집중되어 있다. 뼈암도 골격이 성장하는 어린 시절에 동안 발생률이 상당한 정점에 이른다. 또한, 암의 자연 발생률은 생활 방식 선택과 관련된 위험 요소에 의해 크게 영향을 받을 수 있다. 흡연, 알코올 남용, 비만은 증가된 암 위험과 관련된 여러 요인 중 하나이다.

[어휘] exponential 기하급수적인 lifespan 수명 aging 노화 straightforward 직접의, 정직한 disobey 따르지 않다 spermatogenic 정자 생성의 cell 세포 substantial 상당한 incidence 발생 abuse 남용 obesity 비만

[정답] ②

16 밑줄 친 부분에 들어갈 말로 가장 적절한 것은? [빈칸완성]

Social psychologist Stanley Milgram's groundbreaking study on obedience aimed to investigate the extent to which individuals would comply with authority figures. In his experiment, he asked participants to give electric shocks to another person, believed to be a fellow participant, whenever they answered questions incorrectly. The person receiving the shocks was actually an actor, and no real harm was inflicted. The shocks were progressively increased in intensity and the actor would react with increasing signs of distress, pleading for the experiment to stop. Many participants continued to give the shocks as instructed even when they believed the shocks could be lethal, although they reported feeling guilty and disturbed. Milgram found that approximately 65% of participants obeyed the authority figure and continued to deliver shocks until the maximum voltage. This demonstrated the power of authority to _____ personal moral beliefs and individual conscience.

① boost
② restore
③ surpass
④ combine

[해설] 소개된 실험에 따르면, 많은 참가자들은 죄책감을 느낌에도 불구하고 권위자의 지시에 따라 계속해서 충격을 가했으므로, 권위의 힘이 도덕적 신념과 양심을 능가한 것으로 볼 수 있다. 따라서 빈칸에 들어갈 말로 가장 적절한 것은 ③ '능가하는'이다.
① 증진하는 → 권위의 힘에 복종하여 도덕적 신념과 양심을 저버린 것이므로 반대된다.
② 복구하는 → 사라진 도덕적 신념과 양심이 권위의 힘으로 인해 다시 생겨난 것이 아니므로 적절하지 않다.
④ 결합하는

[해석] 사회 심리학자 Stanley Milgram의 복종에 관한 획기적인 연구는 개인이 권위자의 말에 어느 정도까지 순응할지를 조사하는 것을 목표로 했다. 그는 그의 실험에서 참가자들에게, (그들이) 동료라고 믿는 또 다른 사람이 질문에 틀리게 대답할 때마다 전기 충격을 가하도록 요청했다. 전기 충격을 받는 사람은 실제로는 배우였으며, 실제 해를 입지는 않았다. 충격의 강도는 점점 더 높아졌고 배우들은 점점 더 고통스러운 반응을 보이며 실험을 중단해 달라고 빌었다. 많은 참가자가 죄책감과 불안을 느꼈지만, 그 충격이 치명적일 수 있다고 생각하면서도 지시에 따라 계속 충격을 가했다. Milgram은 참가자의 약 65%가 권위자의 말에 순종하여 최대 전압이 될 때까지 계속 충격을 가했다는 사실을 발견했다. 이는 개인의 도덕적 신념과 개인의 양심을 능가하는 권위의 힘을 보여주었다.

[어휘] social psychologist 사회심리학자 groundbreaking 획기적인 obedience 순응 investigate 조사하다 authority figures 권위자, 실세 intensity 강도 distress 고통 plead for ~을 호소하다 guilty 죄책감 disturb 불안하게 하다 voltage 전압 conscience 양심

[정답] ③

17 다음 글의 제목으로 가장 적절한 것은? [제목]

In 1993, a major flood in Missouri caused roughly $15 billion worth of damage and fifty deaths. 10,000 homes were totally destroyed, and hundreds of towns were hit hard, with at least seventy-five towns completely under flood waters. And yet today, more than $2.2 billion worth of new development stands on that land. Why so much development in an area that was severely flooded only less than two decades ago? The federal government, both through disaster relief and by providing flood insurance, has led developers to feel comfortable building in a zone that is really unsafe. The building boom did bring jobs, services, and tax revenue to the region, which was what the government had intended. But many are concerned this could lead to more damage in future floods. Encouraging development in a flood plain is risky, but that's exactly what the federal government's actions did.

① The Outcome of Federal Efforts on Flood Prevention
② Flood Plain Development: Federal Promotion of Danger
③ Disaster Recovery as a Prescription for Economic Growth
④ How Can We Reduce Flood Risk in Development Projects?

[해설] 대홍수가 발생한지 채 20년도 안 된 지역에 수백억 달러의 개발 사업이 진행된 상황을 비판하며, 그 원인이 연방 정부에 있음을 지적하는 글이다. 따라서 글의 제목으로 가장 적절한 것은 ② '홍수 범람 지역의 개발: 위험에 대한 연방 정부의 부추김'이다.
① 홍수 예방을 위한 연방 정부의 노력의 결과 → 연방 정부가 홍수 예방을 위해 노력했다는 내용은 언급되지 않았다.
③ 경제 성장을 위한 처방으로서의 재난 복구 → 연방 정부가 재난 복구를 하려 했다는 내용이 언급되나, 이를 통해 개발자들이 안심하고 수많은 건물을 지은 것을 비판하는 글이므로 적절하지 않다.
④ 개발 프로젝트에서 홍수 위험을 어떻게 줄일 수 있을까? → 개발 프로젝트에서 홍수의 위험을 줄이는 방법을 소개하는 글이 아니다.

[해석] 1993년 Missouri에서 발생한 대홍수로 약 150억 달러의 피해와 50명의 사망자가 발생했다. 10,000채의 주택이 완전히 파괴되었고, 수백 개의 마을이 큰 피해를 입었으며, 최소 75개의 마을이 홍수 속에 완전히 잠겼다. 그런데도 오늘날 그 땅에는 22억 달러의 가치가 넘는 새 개발 사업이 세워져 있다. 불과 20년도 채 되지 않았는데도 심각한 홍수가 있었던 지역에 이렇게 많은 개발이 이루어진 이유는 무엇일까? 연방 정부는 재난 구호와 홍수 보험 제공을 통해 개발자들이 실제로는 안전하지 않은 지역에 건물을 짓는 것에 안심할 수 있도록 유도했다. 건설 붐은 그 지역에 일자리와 서비스 사업 및 세수를 가져다주었고, 이는 정부가 의도했던 바였다. 그러나 많은 사람들은 이것이 향후 홍수 발생 시 더 많은 피해를 초래할 수 있다고 우려하고 있다. 홍수 범람 지역에 개발을 장려하는 것은 위험하지만, 그것이 정확히 연방 정부의 조치가 한 것이었다.

[어휘] flood 홍수 roughly 약, 거의 billion 10억 federal government 연방 정부 insurance 보험 tax revenue 세수

[정답] ②

18 주어진 문장이 들어갈 위치로 가장 적절한 곳은?

Once they got the animal's attention, a researcher modeled an action — either touching the object with their nose or hand.

Dr. Fugazza and her team tested whether puppies and other young animals might imitate people's actions. They gathered 42 puppies, 39 kittens and 8 young wolves, all of which lived with human families. (①) In each test, the researchers showed an animal an object. (②) Then, the scientists watched whether the animal copied it. (③) It often took a while to get the attention of kittens and young wolves, Fugazza says. (④) But "the dog puppies were immediately looking at the human even before we started to call their attention." After showing the actions, cats rarely mimicked what humans did. Wolves sometimes copied, but the dogs were much more reliable.

[해설] 이 글은 동물들이 사람의 행동을 모방하는지 시험한 한 실험을 설명하고 있다. 주어진 문장은 연구원이 동물의 주의를 끌고 나서 코나 손으로 그 물건을 건드리는 행동을 시범으로 보였다는 내용으로, 앞에는 the object가 가리키는 대상이 나와야 하며, 뒤에는 이러한 내용에 관한 부연이 이어져야 한다. ② 앞에서 연구원들이 동물에게 어떤 물건을 보여주었다고 했는데, 이것이 주어진 문장의 the object 임을 알 수 있다. 또한 ② 뒤에서 언급된 it은 문맥상 주어진 문장의 an action을 가리키므로, 주어진 문장이 들어갈 위치로 가장 적절한 곳은 ②이다.

[해석] Fugazza와 그녀의 팀은 강아지와 다른 어린 동물들이 사람들을 모방할 수도 있는지 실험했다. 그들은 강아지 42마리, 고양이 39마리와 어린 늑대 8마리를 모았다. 이 모든 동물은 인간 가족과 살았다. 각 실험에서, 연구원들은 한 동물에게 어떤 물건을 보여줬다. 그들이 동물의 주의를 끌면, 한 연구원이 코나 손으로 그 물건을 건드리는 행동을 시범으로 보였다. 그다음, 과학자들은 동물이 그것을 모방하는지 지켜보았다. Fugazza가 말하길, 고양이와 어린 늑대의 주의를 끄는 것은 시간이 조금 걸렸다고 한다. 하지만 "강아지들은 우리가 그들의 주의를 끌기도 전에 즉시 인간을 보고 있었다." 행동들을 보여준 뒤, 고양이들은 드물게 인간들이 한 것을 모방했다. 늑대들은 가끔 모방했지만, 강아지들이 훨씬 믿을 만했다.

[어휘] attention 관심, 집중 researcher 연구원, 조사원 model 시범을 보이다 imitate 모방하다, 흉내 내다 copy 모방하다, 복사하다 immediately 즉시 rarely 드물게 mimic 모방하다 reliable 믿을 만한

[정답] ②

19 다음 글의 요지로 가장 적절한 것은?

Receiving criticism, even constructive criticism, can be a difficult experience. It's natural to feel defensive or hurt when someone points out areas where we can improve. However, feeling this way can be counterproductive and prevent us from learning and growing. It's important to try to approach criticism with an open mind and a willingness to learn. Instead of reacting immediately, take some time to process the feedback and consider its validity. It may be helpful to ask clarifying questions to better understand the feedback and find solutions to the problem. Remember that healthy criticism can help you grow and learn new skills. By being open to feedback, you can be more successful in your personal and professional life.

① Accept healthy criticism as an opportunity to improve.
② Stand up for yourself when you receive unfair criticism.
③ Never hesitate to question authority if you want to grow.
④ Don't criticize anyone without offering practical solutions.

[해설] 비판을 받을 때 상처를 받는 것은 당연하지만, 열린 마음으로 비판을 받아들이면 성장할 수 있다는 내용의 글이다. 따라서 글의 요지로 가장 적절한 것은 ① '건전한 비판을 발전의 기회로 받아들여라.'이다.
② 부당한 비판을 받을 때 자기 자신을 옹호하라. → 부당한 비판을 받을 때 이에 맞서야 한다는 내용의 글이 아니다.
③ 성장하고 싶다면 주저하지 말고 권위자에게 의문을 제기하라. → 성장하고 싶다면 건전한 비판을 수용하라는 내용이지, 권위자에게 의문을 제기하라는 내용이 아니다.
④ 실질적인 해결책을 제시하지 않고서 그 누구도 비판하지 마라. → 남을 비판할 때에는 실질적인 해결책을 같이 제시해야 한다는 취지의 글이 아니다.

[해석] 건설적인 비판이라 할지라도, 비판을 받는다는 것은 힘든 경험일 수 있다. 누군가가 우리가 개선될 수 있는 부분을 지적할 때 방어적으로 되거나 상처를 받는 것은 당연한 일이다. 하지만 이렇게 느끼는 것은 역효과를 내며 우리가 학습하고 성장하는 것을 방해할 수 있다. 열린 마음과 기꺼이 배우고자 하는 마음으로 비판에 접근하려고 하는 것이 중요하다. 즉각적으로 반응하는 대신에, 시간을 갖고 피드백을 처리하고 그것의 타당성을 고려하라. 피드백을 더 잘 이해하고 문제에 대한 해결책을 찾기 위해 (피드백의 요점을) 명확하게 하는 질문을 하는 것이 도움이 될 수도 있다. 건전한 비판은 당신이 성장하고 새로운 기술을 배우는 데 도움이 될 수 있다는 점을 기억하라. 피드백에 열린 자세로 임함으로써, 당신은 개인적인 삶과 직장 생활에서 더 성공할 수 있다.

[어휘] constructive 건설적인 defensive 방어적인 counterproductive 역효과를 내는 willingness to 기꺼이 ~하려는 마음 immediately 즉시 process 처리하다 validity 타당성 clarifying 명확하게 하는 practical 실질[현실]적인

[정답] ①

20 주어진 글 다음에 이어질 글의 순서로 가장 적절한 것은? [순서배열]

Imagine that seven out of ten working Americans got fired tomorrow. What would they all do? It's hard to believe you'd have an economy at all if you laid off more than half the labor force.

(A) Since then, wave upon wave of new occupations have arrived — appliance repair person, food chemist, photographer, web designer — each building on previous automation. Today, the majority of us are doing jobs that no farmer from the 1800s could have imagined.

(B) But that, in slow motion, is what the industrial revolution did in the early 19th century. Two hundred years ago, 70 percent of American workers were farmers. Today automation has eliminated all but 1 percent of their jobs, replacing them with machines.

(C) But the displaced workers did not sit idle. They found new jobs in factories that manufactured farm equipment, cars, and other industrial products as automation created hundreds of millions of jobs in entirely new fields.

① (B) - (A) - (C)
② (B) - (C) - (A)
③ (C) - (A) - (B)
④ (C) - (B) - (A)

[해설] 주어진 글은 노동자들을 대량 해고할 경우에 경제라는 것이 존재하리라 믿기는 어렵다는 내용으로, 그다음에는 이러한 상황을 that으로 받아, 그것이 느리게 진행된 경우가 바로 산업혁명이었다는 내용의 (B)가 오는 것이 자연스럽다. 자동화가 농부들의 일자리를 1%만 남겨두고 없애버렸다는 (B)의 마지막 문장 뒤에는 이를 But으로 반전시켜, 그 해고된 사람들은 한가롭게 앉아 있지 않았으며 자동화가 새 일자리를 창출함에 따라 그와 관련된 직업을 새로 찾았다는 내용의 (C)가 와야 한다. 마지막으로는 이 시기를 then으로 받아, 그 이후로 새로운 직업의 물결이 계속해서 도래했다는 내용의 (A)가 와야 한다. 따라서 글의 순서로 가장 적절한 것은 ② '(B) - (C) - (A)'이다.

[해석] 일하는 미국인 10명 중 7명이 내일 해고된다고 상상해 보라. 이들은 모두 어떻게 할까? 노동력의 절반 이상을 해고할 때 경제 (체계)가 존재할 것이라 믿기는 어렵다. (B) 그러나 그것을 느린 속도로 진행한 것은 산업 혁명이 19세기 초에 했던 일이다. 200년 전, 미국 노동자의 70%는 농부였다. 오늘날 자동화는 (그들의 일자리를) 기계로 대체하며 그들 일자리의 1%를 제외하고 다 없애버렸다. (C) 그러나 쫓겨난 노동자들은 앉아서 놀지 않았다. 자동화가 완전히 새로운 분야에서 수억 개의 일자리를 창출하면서 그들은 농기구, 자동차 및 기타 공산품을 제조하는 공장에서 새로운 일자리를 찾았다. (A) 그 이후로, 가전제품 수리 담당자, 식품 화학자, 사진사, 웹 디자이너 등 새로운 직업의 물결이 계속해서 도래했는데, 각각의 물결은 그 이전의 자동화에 기반을 두고 있었다. 오늘날, 우리 대부분은 1800년대의 농부 그 누구도 상상하지 못했을 일을 하고 있다.

[어휘] get fired 해고되다 lay off 내보내다, 해고하다 labor force 노동력 occupation 직업 appliance 가전 chemist 화학자 automation 자동화 eliminate 제거하다, 없애다 replace 대체하다 displace 대체하다, 쫓아내다 idle 놀고 있는, 한가한

[정답] ②

회차 7
Answer

01	02	03	04	05
③	③	②	①	①
06	07	08	09	10
①	③	④	②	④
11	12	13	14	15
④	④	④	③	②
16	17	18	19	20
③	②	①	②	③

01 밑줄 친 부분의 의미와 가장 가까운 것은? [어휘]

The architects considered how to confine the modern elements within the historical structure.

① reflect
② remove
③ restrict
④ embrace

[해설] confine은 '제한하다'라는 뜻으로, 이와 의미가 가장 가까운 것은 ③ 'restrict(제한하다)'이다.
① 반영하다 ② 제거하다 ④ 수용하다
[해석] 건축가들은 역사적 구조물 안에 현대적인 요소들을 어떻게 제한할지 고려했다.
[어휘] architect 건축가

[정답] ③

02 밑줄 친 부분의 의미와 가장 가까운 것은? [어휘]

The new policy is highly adverse to the interests of the workers.

① inferior
② advantageous
③ opposed
④ corresponding

[해설] adverse는 '반대의'라는 뜻으로, 이와 의미가 가장 가까운 것은 ③ 'opposed(반대의)'이다.
① 열등한 ② 이로운 ④ 상응하는
[해석] 그 새로운 정책은 근로자들의 이익에 매우 불리하다.
[어휘] interest 이익

[정답] ③

03 밑줄 친 부분의 의미와 가장 가까운 것은? [이디엄]

The ecosystem is on the verge of collapse, requiring conservation efforts.

① owing to
② at the point of
③ relating to
④ in the event of

[해설] on the verge of는 '~의 직전에'라는 뜻으로, 이와 의미가 가장 가까운 것은 ② 'at the point of(~의 직전에)'이다.
① ~때문에 ③ ~에 관해 ④ ~의 경우에
[해석] 생태계는 붕괴 직전에 있어 보존 노력이 필요하다.
[어휘] collapse 붕괴 conservation 보존

[정답] ②

04 밑줄 친 부분에 들어갈 말로 가장 적절한 것은? [이어동사]

The chef was careful not to _____ all ingredients before the reserved guests arrived.

① use up
② stand by
③ stick to
④ make out

[해설] 주방장이 예약 손님 도착 전에 모든 재료를 대상으로 주의해야 하는 행위는 소진하지 않는 것이리라고 추측할 수 있다. 따라서 빈칸에 들어갈 말로 가장 적절한 것은 ① 'use up(다 쓰다)'이다.
② 지지하다; 대기하다 ③ 고수하다 ④ 이해하다
[해석] 그 주방장은 예약 손님들이 오기 전에 모든 재료를 다 쓰지 않도록 조심했다.
[어휘] ingredient 재료

[정답] ①

05 어법상 옳지 않은 것은?

① The city has widely known for its iconic landmarks.
② Scarcely had he entered the hall when everyone got silent.
③ Each of the volunteers is expected to follow the guidelines.
④ The streets crowded with visitors during the annual festival are lively.

[해설] (has → has been) 맥락상 주어인 The city가 '아는' 것이 아니라 '알려진' 것이므로 수동태인 has been widely known으로 쓰여야 한다. 참고로 전치사 for는 알려진 이유를 나타내고 있다.
② '~하자마자 ~했다'라는 뜻의 'Scarcely + had + S + p.p. ~ when + S + 과거동사' 구문이 적절하게 쓰였다. 또한 enter는 전치사 없이 목적어를 바로 취하는 완전타동사이고, get은 2형식 동사로 쓰여 형용사 silent를 보어로 취하고 있다.
③ each가 대명사로 쓰이는 경우 'each + of + 복수 명사 + 단수 동사'의 구조를 취하므로 the volunteers와 is는 적절하게 쓰였으며, 자원봉사자가 지침을 따를 것으로 '예상되는' 것이므로 수동태 is expected의 쓰임도 적절하다.
④ The streets가 방문객들로 '가득 메워진' 것이므로 수동의 과거분사 crowded는 적절하게 쓰였고, 전치사 during 뒤에 명사구 the annual festival이 오는 것도 적절하다. 또한 문장의 주어는 복수 명사인 The streets이므로 그에 수일치한 복수 동사 are는 적절하게 쓰였으며, 그 보어로 형용사 lively가 온 것도 적절하다. 참고로 lively는 ly로 끝나지만 품사가 형용사인 것에 유의해야 한다.

[해석] ① 그 도시는 상징적인 랜드마크로 널리 알려져 있다.
② 그가 홀에 들어서자마자 모두 조용해졌다.
③ 각 자원봉사자는 그 지침을 따라야 한다.
④ 매년 축제 기간에 방문객들로 붐비는 거리는 활기가 넘친다.

[어휘] iconic 상징적인 crowd 가득 메우다 annual 매년의 lively 활기 넘치는

[정답] ①

06 어법상 옳지 않은 것은?

① She found joy in that others perceived as a boring job.
② The program aims to provide the elderly with social activities.
③ So shocked were they by the news that they couldn't believe it.
④ Predicting when a pandemic will end requires constant analysis.

[해설] (that → what) 관계대명사 that은 전치사의 목적어 자리에 위치할 수 없고, 뒤에 perceived의 목적어가 없는 불완전한 절이 오고 있으므로 선행사를 포함하는 관계대명사 what으로 고쳐야 한다. 참고로 일이 '지루하게 하는' 것이므로 능동의 현재분사형 boring은 적절하게 쓰였다.
② 'A에게 B를 제공하다'라는 뜻의 'provide A with B' 구문이 사용되고 있다. '~한 사람들'이라는 의미의 'the + 형용사'가 쓰여, the elderly로 '노인들'을 표현한 것도 적절하다.
③ '너무 ~해서 ~하다'라는 뜻의 'so ~ that' 구문이 사용되고 있는데, be동사 were의 보어로 쓰인 형용사가 문두에 나와 주어와 동사가 의문문의 어순으로 적절하게 도치되었다. they가 '충격을 받은' 것이므로 수동의 과거분사형 shocked의 쓰임도 적절하며, it은 불가산명사 news를 받는 대명사로 적절하게 쓰였다.
④ 의문부사 when이 '의문사 + S + V' 어순의 간접의문문을 이끌어 predict의 목적어로 적절하게 쓰였다. 이때 when절은 부사절이 아닌 명사절이므로, 현재시제가 미래시제를 대신하지 않고 미래시제 그대로 쓴 것은 적절하다. 또한 주어가 동명사인 Predicting이므로 단수 동사 requires의 쓰임도 적절하다.

[해석] ① 그녀는 다른 사람들이 지루한 일로 인식하는 것에서 즐거움을 발견했다.
② 그 프로그램은 노인들에게 사회 활동을 제공하는 것을 목표로 한다.
③ 그들은 그 소식에 너무 충격받아서 그것을 믿을 수가 없었다.
④ 전 세계적 유행병이 언제 끝날지 예측하려면 지속적인 분석이 필요하다.

[어휘] elderly 나이 든 pandemic 전 세계적 유행병 constant 지속적인 analysis 분석

[정답] ①

07 우리말을 영어로 잘못 옮긴 것은?

① 그들이 결혼한 지 10년이 되었다.
→ It is ten years since they got married.
② 그는 오류가 생기지 않도록 계산을 두 번 확인했다.
→ He checked the calculations twice lest there be an error.
③ 나는 그 웹 사이트에서 보여주는 업데이트된 메뉴를 자주 확인한다.
→ I frequently check the updated menu displaying on the website.
④ 우리는 행사를 준비한 후, 손님들이 도착하기를 기다렸다.
→ Having organized the event, we awaited the arrival of the guests.

[해설] (displaying → displayed) 메뉴가 '보여주는' 것이 아니라 웹 사이트에 '보이는' 것이므로 수동의 과거분사 displayed가 쓰여야 한다. 참고로 메뉴가 '갱신되는' 것이므로 과거분사형 updated는 적절하게 쓰였다.
① '~한 지 ~가 되었다'를 의미하는 표현은 'It is[has been] + 시간 + since + S + 과거동사' 구문으로 쓰일 수 있다.
② '~하지 않도록'이라는 뜻의 접속사 lest가 이끄는 절 내의 동사는 '(should) + RV'의 형태를 취하므로 be는 적절하게 쓰였다.
④ 행사를 준비한 시점이 손님들을 기다리는 시점보다 더 이전이므로 완료분사구문 Having organized ~가 쓰인 것은 적절하다. 또한 await는 전치사 없이 바로 목적어를 취하는 완전타동사로 적절하게 쓰였다.

[어휘] calculation 계산 frequently 자주 display 보여주다 organize 준비하다

[정답] ③

08 우리말을 영어로 잘못 옮긴 것은? [문법]

① 적절한 안전 조치를 시행하는 것이 필수적이다.
   → It is essential that proper safety measures be implemented.
② 그 선수는 팬들의 관심을 유지하기 위해 때때로 그들과 대화를 나눈다.
   → The player talks to the fans now and then to keep them engaged.
③ 갑작스러운 사태 전환으로 인해 나는 신중하게 세운 계획을 변경해야 했다.
   → The sudden turn of events made me change my carefully laid plans.
④ 그곳은 다양한 액티비티를 제공했는데, 그중 대부분이 패키지에 포함되어 있었다.
   → It offered various activities, most of them were included in the package.

[해설] (them → which) 두 개의 절을 연결하는 접속사가 없으므로 접속사 역할을 하는 관계대명사가 필요하다. 따라서 전치사 of의 목적어 자리에 있는 인칭 대명사 them을 목적격 관계대명사 which로 고쳐야 한다. 참고로 관계사절의 주어인 복수 명사 activities가 패키지에 '포함된' 것이므로 수동태 were included의 쓰임은 적절하다.
① essential과 같은 이성적 판단의 형용사가 포함된 가주어(It)-진주어(that절) 구문에서, that절 내의 동사는 '(should) + RV'를 사용하며, 안전 조치가 '시행되는' 것이므로 수동태 be implemented는 적절하게 쓰였다.
② talk는 자동사로 쓰여 목적어 the fans 앞에 전치사 to가 있는 것은 적절하다. 또한 5형식 동사로 쓰인 keep이 분사형 형용사를 보어로 취하고 있는데, them이 가리키는 the fans가 '관심을 끄는' 것이 아니라 '관심을 사로잡히는' 것이므로 수동의 과거분사형 engaged도 적절하게 쓰였다.
③ 사역동사 make는 목적어와 목적격 보어의 관계가 능동이면 RV를, 수동이면 p.p.를 목적격 보어로 취한다. 여기서는 '나'가 계획을 '바꾸는' 것이므로 change가 적절하게 쓰였다. 참고로 my carefully laid는 plans를 수식하는 형용사구인데, 계획은 '놓이는' 것이므로 '놓다'라는 뜻의 타동사 lay의 과거분사 laid가 쓰이고 있다.

[어휘] measure 조치 implement 시행하다 now and then 가끔 engage 관심을 끌다

[정답] ④

09 두 사람의 대화 중 가장 어색한 것은? [생활영어]

① A: It's so hard to get through to you these days.
   B: I know, I'm just so busy. Let's catch up soon.
② A: The tip you gave me is coming in handy for me.
   B: Oh, I'm sorry to hear it's not working out for you.
③ A: Would you like your food for here or to go?
   B: To go, please. Could you also pack in extra napkins?
④ A: Who's in charge of our next project?
   B: It's up to our boss to decide but he hasn't yet.

[해설] 상대방이 자신에게 준 팁이 도움 되고 있다는 A에 말에 그게 효과가 없다니 아쉽다고 말한 B의 응답은 모순된다. 따라서 대화 중 가장 어색한 것은 ②이다.

[해석] ① A: 요즘 너랑 연락 닿기가 너무 어렵네.
B: 맞아, 내가 너무 바빠서 말이야. 곧 얘기 나누자.
② A: 네가 준 팁이 나한테 도움이 되고 있어.
B: 아, 그게 너한테 효과가 없다니 아쉽네.
③ A: 음식을 여기서 드실 건가요 아니면 가져가실 건가요?
B: 가져가겠습니다. 여분의 냅킨도 같이 넣어 주실 수 있나요?
④ A: 다음 프로젝트는 누가 담당하나요?
B: 저희 상사가 결정할 일인데 아직 결정하지 않으셨어요.

[어휘] get through 연락이 닿다 come in handy 효과[쓸모]가 있다 extra 여분의 in charge of ~을 담당하는

[정답] ②

10 밑줄 친 부분에 들어갈 말로 가장 적절한 것은? [생활영어]

A: Ugh, my computer just crashed!
B: What? What happened?
A: I downloaded something silly from the internet which must have been a virus.
B: Oh, no. _____?
A: It's my work computer so all my work-related files were on there. This is so frustrating!
B: I feel you. But don't worry, I had a similar issue last year, and this technician worked wonders. He even recovered all of my files. Here, I'll give you his number.

① What was it that you downloaded
② Did you try restarting your computer
③ Have you tried calling someone to fix it
④ Was there anything important on your computer

[해설] 바이러스로 인해 컴퓨터가 다운되어 곤란을 겪는 상황이다. B가 빈칸 내용을 물어보자 A가 업무용 컴퓨터라며 업무 관련 파일이 다 거기에 있었다고 답하였다. 따라서 빈칸에 들어갈 말로 가장 적절한 것은 ④ '컴퓨터에 중요한 게 있었어'이다.
① 네가 다운로드한 게 뭐였어
② 컴퓨터를 다시 시작해 봤어
③ 그걸 고치려고 누군가에게 전화해 봤어

해석 A: 이런, 내 컴퓨터가 지금 고장 났어!
B: 뭐라고? 무슨 일이야?
A: 인터넷에서 우스꽝스러운 걸 다운로드했는데, 바이러스였던 게 틀림없어.
B: 아, 이런. 컴퓨터에 중요한 게 있었어?
A: 내 업무용 컴퓨터라서 업무 관련 파일이 다 거기에 있었어. 너무 짜증 나!
B: 공감해. 근데 걱정하지 마, 나한테 작년에 비슷한 문제가 있었는데, 이 기술자가 기적을 해냈어. 그는 심지어 내 파일을 모두 복구해 줬어. 여기, 그의 전화번호를 줄게.

어휘 crash 고장 나다 work-related 업무 관련 frustrate 좌절시키다, 불만스럽게 만들다 recover 복구하다, 되찾다

정답 ④

11 주어진 글 다음에 이어질 글의 순서로 가장 적절한 것은? 순서배열

In 425 BCE, Athens was in a long and destructive war with Sparta.

(A) Some of them were morally wrong, like killing all the citizens of a conquered city, while others were strategically bad, such as launching a doomed expedition to Sicily. Athens eventually lost the war.

(B) Athens rejected this proposal and the war continued. However, as the war went on, Sparta increasingly gained the advantage, turning the game around. This was just one of many poor decisions made by Athens.

(C) During the Battle of Pylos, Athens succeeded in capturing many of Sparta's top soldiers. When Spartan leaders realized this, they asked for peace with favorable terms.

① (B) - (A) - (C) ② (B) - (C) - (A)
③ (C) - (A) - (B) ④ (C) - (B) - (A)

해설 주어진 글은 기원전 425년에 아테네가 스파르타와 전쟁을 치렀다는 내용이고, 그다음엔 그에 대한 구체적인 부연으로, Pylos 전투에서 아테네가 스파르타의 최정예 병사들을 다수 생포하여 스파르타의 지도자들이 유리한 조건으로 평화를 요청했다는 내용의 (C)가 오는 것이 자연스럽다. 그다음으로, 이 요청을 this proposal로 받아, 아테네가 그 제안을 거절했다는 내용의 (B)가 와야 한다. 마지막으로, 그것이 아테네가 내린 수많은 형편없는 결정들 중 하나일 뿐이었다고 한 (B)의 마지막 문장 뒤에는 그 형편없는 결정들을 them으로 받아, 그중 일부는 도덕적으로 잘못되었으며, 일부는 전략적으로 잘못되었다고 하면서 결국 아테네가 전쟁에서 패했다는 내용의 (A)로 글이 마무리되어야 한다. 따라서 글의 순서로 가장 적절한 것은 ④ '(C) - (B) - (A)'이다.

해석 기원전 425년, 아테네는 스파르타와 길고도 파괴적인 전쟁을 치르고 있었다. (C) Pylos 전투에서 아테네는 스파르타의 최정예 병사들을 다수 생포하는 데 성공했다. 스파르타의 지도자들이 이를 깨닫자, (아테네에) 유리한 조건을 들고 평화를 요청했다. (B) 아테네는 이 제안을 거절했고 전쟁은 계속되었다. 그러나 전쟁이 계속되면서 스파르타는 점점 더 우위를 점했고 전세를 역전시켰다. 이것은 아테네가 내린 수많은 형편없는 결정들 중 하나일 뿐이었다. (A) 그중 일부는 정복한 도시의 시민들을 모두 죽이는 것과 같이 도덕적으로 잘못된 것도 있었고, 시칠리아로 파멸의 원정을 떠나는 것과 같이 전략적으로 잘못된 것도 있었다. 아테네는 결국 전쟁에서 패했다.

어휘 destructive 파괴적인 morally 도덕적으로 conquer 정복하다 strategically 전략적으로 doomed 불운한 expedition 원정, 탐험 proposal 제안 advantage 우위 succeed in ~에 성공하다 favorable 유리한 term 조건

정답 ④

12 주어진 문장이 들어갈 위치로 가장 적절한 곳은? 문장삽입

If you are clearly of a higher status than they are, they will conceal their envy by appearing to admire your success.

As social animals we humans are very sensitive to our rank and position within any group. (①) We constantly measure our status by monitoring differences and comparing ourselves with others. (②) And for some people, status is more than a way of measuring social position — it is the most important determinant of their self-worth. (③) These people will try to measure their status against yours by asking about how much money you make, whether you own your home, and all of the other little things that can be used as points of comparison. (④) In contrast, if they sense a potential rivalry, they will attack you in secret and dishonest ways, trying to undermine your position within the group.

해설 주어진 문장은 만약 당신이 그들보다 명백히 더 높은 지위에 있는 경우에 그들은 당신을 존경하는 것처럼 보임으로써 질투를 감출 것이라는 내용으로, 앞에는 they가 지칭하는 대상이 와야 하며, 뒤에는 부연 설명이 이어져야 한다. ④ 앞에 언급된 These people은 여러 질문을 하며 당신과 자신의 지위를 비교하려는 사람들로, 주어진 문장의 they가 가리키는 대상임을 알 수 있다. 또한, ④ 뒤에서는 그들이 잠재적인 경쟁 관계를 감지하는 경우에 어떠한 행동을 하는지에 관한 내용이 나왔으므로, 주어진 문장의 경우와 대조되는 상황임을 알 수 있다. 이때 주어진 문장과 ④ 뒤의 내용이 In contrast로 적절히 연결되므로, 주어진 문장이 들어갈 위치로 가장 적절한 곳은 ④이다.

해석 사회적 동물인 인간은 어떤 집단 내에서의 우리의 지위와 위치에 매우 민감하다. 우리는 끊임없이 차이를 관찰하고 우리 자신을 다른 사람들과 비교하면서 자신의 지위를 측정한다. 그리고 어떤 사람들에게 지위는 사회적 위치를 측정하는 방법 그 이상으로, 그것은 자존감을 결정하는 가장 중요한 요소이다. 이러한 사람들은 당신이 돈을 얼마나 버는지, 당신이 자신의 집을 소유하고 있는지, 그리고 비교의 잣대로 사용될 수 있는 다른 모든 사소한 것들에 대해 질문하며 자신의 지위를 당신의 지위와 비교하며 평가하려 할 것이다. 만약 당신이 그들보다 명백히 더 높은 지위에 있다면, 그들은 당신의 성공을 존경하는 것처럼 보임으로써 질투를 감출 것이다. 반대로, 그들이 잠재적인 경쟁 관계를 감지한다면 그들은 집단 내에서의 당신의 지위를 약화시키려 당신을 은밀하고 정직하지 못한 방식으로 공격할 것이다.

어휘 status 지위, 위치 conceal 감추다 envy 질투 sensitive 민감한 monitor 추적 관찰하다 determinant 결정 요인 comparison 비교 potential 잠재적인 rivalry 경쟁 관계 dishonest 부정직한 undermine 약화시키다

정답 ④

13 다음 글의 제목으로 가장 적절한 것은?

In the historical past, children were ill-treated and often regarded as the property of their parents. In Roman times, the father had the absolute power of life and death over his children. As possessions of their father, children were left unprotected by the law, subject to the practice of maltreatment. In medieval and early modern Europe, although conditions for children were not so severe, the property concept continued to apply. Parents still had almost unlimited power over their children, and children remained subject to abandonment and abuse. Even in the 17th and 18th centuries, children still had the status of property. They could be cared for in a relatively humane way by their parents, but they were typically seen as parental possessions and the private domain of their parents.

① The Definition and Elements of Possession in Law
② The Advancement of Parental Rights over Children
③ Kids in Ancient Times: A Source of Family Support
④ Children as Property: A Prevalent Notion in the Past

14 글의 흐름상 가장 어색한 문장은?

The universe contains immense amounts of water. In our solar system alone, the interiors of many planets and moons have enormous quantities of water. ① Mars has ice caps on its poles, just like Earth, as well as belts of glaciers in its southern and northern latitudes. ② The moons of Saturn and Jupiter also have oceans beneath their icy surfaces. ③ The radar reflections observed on the icy moons of Jupiter and Saturn exhibit unique characteristics that could potentially suggest the existence of extraterrestrial life. ④ But what makes Earth's water unique is that it exists in a glorious liquid state between ice and vapor, and it's not too salty or too acidic or too alkaline. And we have a lot of it. The Earth's oceans cover about 70 percent of the surface of our planet. Without this vast reserve of water, life as we know it would not exist.

*alkaline: 알칼리성의

15 다음 글의 내용과 일치하지 않는 것은?

For decades, India suffered from what was called the "Hindu rate of economic growth" which was a little more than 1 percent per capita. But this slow rate of economic growth turned out to owe less to Hindu culture than to imported British socialist economic planning. After independence in 1947, India followed an inward-looking policy focused on heavy industry. Then, after market-oriented reforms in the 1990s, the pattern changed and growth rates rose to 7 percent, with projections of double-digit rates in the future. British columnist Martin Wolf calls India a "premature superpower," saying that the Indian economy will be bigger than Britain's in a decade and bigger than Japan's in two. That India has an emerging middle class of several hundred million, and that English is an official language spoken by some 50-100 million people position India to play a major role in global markets.

① 힌두 경제 성장률은 주로 영국의 사회주의 경제 계획에서 비롯되었다.
② 인도는 독립 이후에 중공업 중심의 산업 구조로부터 탈피하였다.
③ 1990년대 시장 중심의 개혁 이후 인도의 경제 성장률이 높아졌다.
④ 많은 신흥 중산층 인구는 세계 시장에서 인도에 이점이 된다.

[해설] 3번째 문장에서 인도가 1947년에 독립한 이후에 중공업에 중점을 둔 내향적 정책을 따랐다고 언급되므로, 글의 내용과 일치하지 않는 것은 ② '인도는 독립 이후에 중공업 중심의 산업 구조로부터 탈피하였다.'이다.
① 힌두 경제 성장률은 주로 영국의 사회주의 경제 계획에서 비롯되었다. → 첫 두 문장에서 언급된 내용이다.
③ 1990년대 시장 중심의 개혁 이후 인도의 경제 성장률이 높아졌다. → 4번째 문장에서 언급된 내용이다.
④ 많은 신흥 중산층 인구는 세계 시장에서 인도에 이점이 된다. → 마지막 문장에서 언급된 내용이다.

[해석] 수십 년 동안, 인도는 1인당 1%를 조금 넘는, 이른바 '힌두 경제 성장률'로 인해 어려움을 겪었다. 그러나 이러한 느린 경제 성장률은 힌두 문화보다는 영국의 사회주의 경제 계획의 도입에서 비롯된 것으로 밝혀졌다. 1947년 독립 이후, 인도는 중공업에 중점을 둔 내향적 정책을 따랐다. 그러다가 1990년대 시장 중심의 개혁 이후 그 패턴은 바뀌었고, 성장률은 7%로 상승했으며, 앞으로도 두 자릿수 성장률이 예상된다. 영국의 칼럼니스트 Martin Wolf는 인도 경제가 10년 후에는 영국보다, 20년 후에는 일본보다 더 커질 것이라 말하며 인도를 '미숙한 초강대국'이라고 불렀다. 인도에는 수억 명의 신흥 중산층이 있다는 점과 영어가 약 5천만 명에서 1억 명의 인구가 사용하는 공식 언어라는 점은 세계 시장에서 인도가 중요한 역할을 하도록 자리매김 해준다.

[어휘] decade 10년 suffer from ~을 겪다 per capita 1인당 owe A to B A는 B 덕분이다 import 도입하다, 들여오다 independence 독립 inward-looking 내향적인, 내정중시의 market-oriented 시장 중심의 projection 예상 premature 미숙한 superpower 초강대국

[정답] ②

16 다음 글의 내용과 일치하지 않는 것은?

Learning plays a large part in making honeybees such efficient foragers. When honeybees find a profitable flower patch, they learn the location so they can find it again. Other honeybees can also learn the location from the dances of recently returned foragers. As some flower species are better sources of nectar, they pay special attention to learning the shape, colour, and scent of those flowers. They even learn the optimal time of day to visit particular flower patches. Learning is rapid and accurate: in the first five seconds of a nectar sip, the bee learns to accurately associate the nectar reward with the features of the flower. This association is remembered for days, and, if the learning is repeated, the association will influence the bee's choices for the rest of its three-week-long life of foraging.

① Honeybee dances provide information to other bees.
② Honeybees learn the best time to visit specific flowers.
③ The nectar-flower link is inexact when made in a few seconds.
④ Associations honeybees learn can last for days and even weeks.

[해설] 마지막 2번째 문장에서 꿀을 마시는 처음 5초 동안 벌이 꿀의 보상과 꽃의 특징을 정확하게 연관시킨다고 언급되므로, 글의 내용과 일치하지 않는 것은 ③ '꿀-꽃 연관성은 몇 초 안에 이루어질 땐 부정확하다.'이다.
① 꿀벌의 춤은 다른 꿀벌들에게 정보를 제공한다. → 3번째 문장에서 언급된 내용이다.
② 꿀벌은 특정 꽃을 방문하기 가장 좋은 시간을 학습한다. → 5번째 문장에서 언급된 내용이다.
④ 꿀벌이 학습한 연관성은 며칠 또는 심지어 몇 주 동안 지속될 수 있다. → 마지막 문장에서 언급된 내용이다.

[해석] 학습은 꿀벌들이 효율적인 사냥꾼이 되는 데 큰 역할을 한다. 꿀벌들이 얻을 것이 많은(꿀이 많이 나오는) 꽃밭을 찾으면, 그들은 그곳을 다시 찾을 수 있도록 그 위치를 학습한다. 다른 꿀벌들도 최근에 돌아온 사냥꾼들의 춤으로부터 그 위치를 학습할 수 있다. 어떤 종의 꽃은 더 좋은 꿀 공급원이기 때문에, 그것들은 그 꽃의 모양, 색깔, 향기를 학습하는 데 각별한 주의를 기울인다. 그것들은 심지어 특정 꽃밭을 찾아가기 최적인 시간대까지 학습한다. 배움은 빠르고 정확한데, 꿀을 마시는 처음 5초 동안 벌은 꿀의 보상을 꽃의 특징들과 정확하게 연관시키는 법을 학습한다. 이 연상은 며칠 동안 기억되며, 만일 학습이 반복된다면, 남은 3주간의 사냥 생활 동안 그 벌의 선택에 영향을 미치게 된다.

[어휘] play a part in ~에 역할을 하다 efficient 효율적인 forager 먹이를 구하는 사람, 사냥꾼 profitable 얻을 것이 많은, 수익성이 좋은 patch (식물 등을 키우는) 작은 땅 nectar (꽃의) 꿀 sip 홀짝 마심, 한 모금 associate A with B A와 B를 연관 짓다 inexact 부정확한

[정답] ③

17. 다음 글의 요지로 가장 적절한 것은?

Intelligence is often seen as a critical factor in determining one's success in life. It is generally assumed that those with high IQs are destined for greatness and are more likely to achieve great things in their careers. However, intelligence alone is no guarantee of success. While a high IQ may give individuals an advantage in certain areas, it does not necessarily translate into exceptional skills or accomplishments. In fact, many individuals with high IQs may not necessarily be considered gifted, as there are other factors that contribute to success, such as creativity, determination, and hard work. Therefore, it is important to recognize that intelligence is only one piece of the puzzle, and that other qualities are equally important in achieving success in life. In the end, it is the combination of intelligence, hard work, and personal qualities that determines an individual's success in life, not just their IQ.

① IQ can be increased by persistent repetition and training.
② Intelligence is not the only factor that determines success.
③ Success in life is meaningless if it is gained without effort.
④ Intelligence is mostly determined in childhood and fixed thereafter.

18. (A)와 (B)에 들어갈 말로 가장 적절한 것은?

Stress is often very helpful. The classic stress response mobilizes energy to your muscles by increasing your heart rate, blood pressure, and breathing. High stress also helps your sensory system. __(A)__, policemen report that during shoot-outs their visual acuity and focus improves, leading the mind to focus intently on the task at hand for a short burst. This reaction is valuable in extraordinary circumstances. Stress has an adverse effect, __(B)__, if it is constant. Unfortunately, most human stress comes from the chronic, emotional strains of job deadlines, financial worries, and relationship issues. These kinds of ongoing stress pose health risks overtime. While mobilizing your body to respond to a short-term threat is an amazing feat, the same response is detrimental to your health if it is always on.

(A)	(B)
① For example	however
② For example	therefore
③ Instead	furthermore
④ Instead	conversely

19 밑줄 친 부분에 들어갈 말로 가장 적절한 것은? [빈칸완성]

Most mothers would say that being a good mother is extremely important to them; most mothers believe they act in the best interests of their children, at least most of the time. Yet, sometimes as hard as they try to do right by their kids, bad things happen; sometimes they say or do things that hurt the very kids they so desperately love; sometimes they get uncontrollably angry with their kids and they behave badly. So often, thus, they feel burdened by the weight of guilt over their mothering. Even the best moms — those gracious, calm magicians, perfectly dressed, bringing home-baked brownies and clean-faced toddlers to their older child's school events in between their jobs — have feelings of regret about some aspects of their mothering. Indeed, it seems that _____.

① moms benefit from emotional space when angry
② guilt is an inseparable companion of motherhood
③ every child feels some guilt towards their mother
④ juggling between career and parenting is inevitable

[해설] 엄마들이 양육 과정에서 자연스럽게 느끼는 죄책감을 설명하는 글로, 아무리 양육을 완벽하게 해내려고 해도 죄책감이 생기는 것은 불가피하다는 점을 서술하고 있다. 따라서 빈칸에 들어갈 말로 가장 적절한 것은 ② '죄책감은 모성애와 떼려야 뗄 수 없는 동반자인'이다.
① 엄마들은 화가 났을 때 감정적 공간의 도움을 받는 → 엄마들이 화가 났을 때 무엇이 도움 되는지를 설명하는 글이 아니다.
③ 모든 아이는 엄마에 대해 조금이라도 죄책감을 느낀다는 → 역으로 모든 엄마가 자신의 아이에 대해 죄책감을 느낀다는 내용의 글이다.
④ 일과 양육을 동시에 하는 것은 불가피한

[해석] 대부분의 엄마들은 좋은 엄마가 되는 것이 그들에게 매우 중요하다고 말할 것이다. 엄마들 대부분은 자신이 적어도 대부분의 경우 자녀의 최선의 이익을 위해 행동한다고 믿는다. 하지만 그들이 아이들에게 잘하려고 열심히 노력하는데도 불구하고, 가끔 나쁜 일들이 생긴다. 즉, 때때로 그들은 자신이 매우 절실히 사랑하는 바로 그 아이들에게 상처를 주는 말이나 행동을 하며, 때때로 그들은 아이들에게 걷잡을 수 없이 화를 내고, 나쁜 행동을 한다. 그래서 너무도 흔히, 그들은 엄마 노릇에 대한 죄책감의 무게에 짓눌리는 기분을 느낀다. 심지어 최고의 엄마들, 즉 완벽하게 옷을 입고, 집에서 구운 브라우니를 들고 얼굴이 깨끗한 어린 아기를 데리고 일이 비는 시간에 더 큰 아이의 학교 행사에 오는, 우아하고 침착한 그 마술사들조차 자신의 엄마 노릇의 일부 측면에 대해 후회의 감정을 지니고 있다. 실로, 죄책감은 모성애와 떼려야 뗄 수 없는 동반자인 것 같다.

[어휘] extremely 매우, 몹시 in the interest of ~(의 이익)을 위하여 desperately 절실하게, 간절히 uncontrollably 걷잡을 수 없이 burden 부담을 지우다 guilt 죄책감 mothering 엄마 노릇, 보살피기 gracious 우아한 inseparable 떼려야 뗄 수 없는 companion 동반자 motherhood 모성애 juggle (두 가지 이상의 일을 곡예 하듯) 하다 inevitable 불가피한

[정답] ②

20 밑줄 친 부분에 들어갈 말로 가장 적절한 것은? [빈칸완성]

Great evolution can be achieved in the face of tremendous constraints, and one of the best examples of this is the vertebrate wing. Wings have been invented in many separate lineages. The wings of bats, birds, and pterosaurs all evolved separately and therefore have big structural differences. However, in all of those cases, the wing evolved from a forelimb. Those animals lost many uses of their forelimbs in order to get wings. Neither birds nor bats can grasp things very well; they have to use their feet and mouths to manipulate objects, which is obviously uncomfortable. It would have been far better for those animals to grow wholly new wings while retaining their forelimbs, but evolution rarely works that way. For an animal with a complex body plan, the option was to slowly reshape existing limbs. In light of this, a conclusion can be drawn that evolution is a constant game of _____.

*vertebrate: 척추동물

① defense
② probability
③ compromise
④ accumulation

[해설] 날개를 얻기 위해 앞다리의 쓰임을 포기해야 했던 동물들의 예를 통해, 진화란 '하나를 얻기 위해 다른 하나를 포기하는' 과정임을 이해할 수 있다. 따라서 빈칸에 들어갈 말로 가장 적절한 것은 ③ '타협'이다.
① 방어 → 오히려 앞다리의 쓰임을 지키지 못하고 포기해야 했기 때문에 반대된다고 볼 수 있다.
② 확률 → 앞다리가 날개로 진화한 것이 확률에 의한 것이었음을 주장하는 글이 아니다.
④ 축적 → 날개가 생기면서 앞다리의 쓰임을 잃은 것을 축적으로 볼 수는 없다.

[해석] 위대한 진화는 엄청난 제약 속에서도 이뤄질 수 있는데, 이것의 가장 좋은 예시 중 한 가지가 척추동물의 날개이다. 날개는 다양한 계보에서 만들어졌다. 박쥐, 새, 익룡의 날개는 모두 따로 진화했고, 그래서 큰 구조적 차이가 있다. 하지만 이 모든 경우에서, 날개는 앞다리로부터 진화했다. 이 동물들은 날개를 얻고자 앞다리의 용도를 많이 잃었다. 새도 박쥐도 물건을 잘 잡지 못한다. 이들은 물건을 조작하기 위해 발과 입을 사용해야 하는데, 이는 당연히 불편하다. 이런 동물들이 앞다리를 유지하면서 완전히 새로운 날개를 성장시켰다면 훨씬 더 좋았겠지만, 진화란 그런 식으로 거의 작용하지 않는다. 복잡한 신체 체계를 가진 동물에게 선택지는 기존의 팔다리를 천천히 변형하는 것이었다. 이에 비춰 보면, 진화는 지속적인 타협의 게임이라는 결론이 도출될 수 있다.

[어휘] in the face of ~에도 불구하고 tremendous 엄청난 constraint 제약 lineage 계보 pterosaur 익룡 separately 따로, 각자 forelimb 앞다리 grasp 잡다, 쥐다 manipulate 조작하다 wholly 완전히 retain 보유하다 existing 현존하는, 기존의 constant 지속적인 compromise 타협

[정답] ③

회차 8
Answer

01	02	03	04	05
③	①	③	③	④
06	07	08	09	10
③	④	①	①	③
11	12	13	14	15
③	④	②	④	②
16	17	18	19	20
④	②	①	③	③

01 밑줄 친 부분의 의미와 가장 가까운 것은? [어휘]

In the creative writing workshop, participants focused on developing <u>coherent</u> narratives.

① novel
② central
③ consistent
④ compelling

[해설] coherent는 '일관성 있는'이라는 뜻으로, 이와 의미가 가장 가까운 것은 ③ 'consistent(일관된)'이다.
① 새로운 ② 중심의 ④ 설득력 있는
[해석] 창의적 글쓰기 워크숍에서, 참여자들은 <u>일관성 있는</u> 서사를 개발하는 데 집중했다.
[어휘] narrative 이야기, 서사

정답 ③

02 밑줄 친 부분의 의미와 가장 가까운 것은? [어휘]

In the park, the gardener uses organic methods to <u>nurture</u> the plants.

① rear
② exhibit
③ classify
④ protect

[해설] nurture는 '기르다'라는 뜻으로, 이와 의미가 가장 가까운 것은 ① 'rear(기르다)'이다.
② 전시하다 ③ 분류하다 ④ 보호하다
[해석] 그 공원에서 정원사는 식물을 <u>기르기</u> 위해 유기농 방법을 사용한다.
[어휘] organic 유기농의

정답 ①

03 밑줄 친 부분의 의미와 가장 가까운 것은? [이디엄]

The application was rejected <u>on the grounds of</u> lack of experience.

① in spite of
② in place of
③ in virtue of
④ in search of

[해설] on the grounds of는 '~의 이유로'라는 뜻으로, 이와 의미가 가장 가까운 것은 ③ 'in virtue of(~때문에)'이다.
① ~에도 불구하고 ② ~대신에 ④ ~을 찾아서
[해석] 그 지원서는 경험 부족을 <u>이유로</u> 거절되었다.
[어휘] application 지원서

정답 ③

04 밑줄 친 부분에 들어갈 말로 가장 적절한 것은? [이어동사]

We should value diversity rather than _____ those with different lifestyles.

① carry out
② depend on
③ look down on
④ come down to

[해설] rather than에 유의해서 보면, 빈칸에는 다양성을 중시하는 것에 반대되는 표현이 와야 한다. 즉, 다른 생활방식을 가진 사람들을 무시한다는 내용이 되어야 하므로, 빈칸에 들어갈 말로 가장 적절한 것은 ③ 'look down on(얕보다)'이다.
① 수행하다 ② 의존하다 ④ 결국 ~이 되다
[해석] 우리는 다른 생활방식을 가진 사람들을 <u>얕보기</u>보다 다양성을 중시해야 한다.
[어휘] diversity 다양성

정답 ③

05 어법상 옳지 않은 것은? [문법]

① My parents have gone to Europe, so I'm alone now.
② Should she study abroad, she could gain valuable experiences.
③ The cake he baked is as delicious as the one from the bakery.
④ Trust your instincts to avoid taking advantage of in any situation.

[해설] (taking → being taken) avoid는 동명사를 목적어로 취하는 동사이다. 그런데 여기서는 of 뒤에 목적어가 없으며 맥락상 '이용당하는' 것을 피한다는 뜻이 되어야 자연스러우므로, 수동형인 being taken advantage of로 쓰여야 한다.
① 문맥상 '~에 가고 없다'라는 뜻의 결과를 나타내는 have gone to가 적절하게 쓰이고 있다. '~에 간 적 있다'라는 뜻의 경험을 나타내는 have been to와의 구별에 유의해야 한다. 또한 '혼자'라는 뜻의 alone은 서술적 용법으로만 쓰이는 형용사이므로 be동사 am의 보어로 오고 있는 것도 적절하다.
② 'Should + S + RV'는 가정법 미래에서 if가 생략된 도치 표현으로, 주절엔 '조동사 현재형/과거형 + RV'나 현재형 동사를 사용할 수 있다.
③ The cake와 he 사이에는 목적격 관계대명사가 생략되어 있어 baked의 목적어 자리가 비어 있는 것은 적절하다. 또한 'as ~ as' 원급 비교 구문이 쓰여, 그 사이에 is의 보어로 형용사 delicious가 들어간 것도 적절하다. 불특정한 것을 지칭하는 부정대명사 one도 적절하게 쓰였다.
[해석] ① 부모님이 유럽으로 가셔서 나는 지금 혼자 있다.
② 그녀는 유학한다면 소중한 경험을 얻을 수 있을 것이다.
③ 그가 구운 케이크는 빵집의 케이크만큼 맛있다.
④ 어떤 상황에서도 이용당하지 않도록 자신의 본능을 믿어라.
[어휘] valuable 소중한 instinct 본능 take advantage of ~을 이용하다

[정답] ④

06 어법상 옳지 않은 것은? [문법]

① He finally noticed the small note left on his desk.
② It takes me three hours to get to work every day.
③ The film received acclaim for its intense, humor, and sensitivity.
④ Participating in a coding class, we practiced developing applications.

[해설] (intense → intensity) 세 개의 단어가 등위접속사 and로 병렬되고 있다. 이때 전치사인 for 뒤에는 명사(구)가 와야 하고, 병렬 대상의 급은 동일해야 한다. 따라서 명사 humor, sensitivity와 급이 동일하도록 형용사 intense를 명사 intensity로 고쳐야 한다.
① 지각동사 notice는 목적어와 목적격 보어의 관계가 능동이면 RV나 RVing를, 수동이면 p.p.를 목적격 보어로 취한다. 여기서는 the small note가 책상 위에 '남겨진' 것이므로 left는 적절하게 쓰였다.
② '~하는 데 시간이 걸리다'라는 표현은 'It takes + (사람) + 시간 + to RV' 구문으로 쓰일 수 있다.
④ 분사구문의 의미상 주어인 we가 수업에 '참여한' 것이므로 능동의 현재분사 Participating은 적절하게 쓰였으며, 완전자동사 participate는 목적어를 취할 때 전치사를 함께 사용해야 하므로 뒤에 in이 온 것도 적절하다. 또한 practice는 동명사를 목적어로 취하는 동사이므로 developing 역시 옳게 쓰였다.

[해석] ① 그는 마침내 작은 쪽지가 책상 위에 남겨진 것을 알아차렸다.
② 나는 매일 출근하는 데 3시간이 걸린다.
③ 그 영화는 강렬함, 유머, 감수성으로 호평을 받았다.
④ 우리는 코딩 수업에 참여하면서 애플리케이션을 개발하는 연습을 했다.
[어휘] acclaim 찬사, 호평 intense 강렬한 sensitivity 감수성

[정답] ③

07 우리말을 영어로 잘못 옮긴 것은? [문법]

① 협업에 있어서 성공은 정직함에 달려있다.
→ Success relies on honesty when it comes to collaborating.
② 그녀는 수영 초보자임에도 불구하고 물에 빠진 아이를 구했다.
→ Beginner swimmer as she was, she saved a drowning child.
③ 나는 지난주에 들었던 강의에서 얻은 통찰을 공유할 것이다.
→ I'm going to share insights from the lecture I listened to last week.
④ 토론을 유발하는 소설을 쓴 그 작가의 영향력이 커졌다.
→ The writer whose novels spark discussions have become influential.

[해설] (have → has) The writer를 선행사로 받는 소유격 관계대명사 whose 뒤에 명사 novels와 함께 완전한 절이 오고 있다. 그런데 문장의 주어는 단수 명사인 The writer이므로 동사도 그에 수일치하여 단수 동사 has become이 되어야 한다. 참고로 become이 2형식 동사로 쓰여 형용사 influential을 보어로 취하고 있는 것은 적절하다.
① '~에 의존하다'라는 뜻의 rely on이 '자동사 + 전치사'로 수에 맞게 적절히 쓰였다. 또한 'when it comes to RVing'는 '~에 관해서라면'이라는 의미의 관용표현으로 주어진 우리말에 맞게 쓰였다. 이때 to는 전치사이므로 뒤에 (동)명사가 오는 것에 유의해야 한다.
② '형용사/부사/무관사명사 + as + S + V'는 '비록 ~이지만'을 의미하는 양보 도치 부사절이다. be동사 was의 보어로 명사 Beginner swimmer가 오면서 관사가 없는 것은 적절하다.
③ the lecture와 I 사이에 목적격 관계대명사가 생략되어 to의 목적어 자리가 비어 있는 것은 적절하다. 또한 last week이라는 확실한 과거 시점 부사구가 있는데, 주절의 동사 am going to가 아닌 관계사절의 동사 listened to를 수식하고 있으므로 시제 일치도 적절하다.
[어휘] collaborate 협력하다 drown 물에 빠지다 insight 통찰, 이해 spark 유발하다 discussion 토론 influential 영향력이 큰

[정답] ④

08 우리말을 영어로 잘못 옮긴 것은? [문법]

① 그들은 높은 수준에서 경쟁할 수 있을 정도로 열심히 훈련했다.
→ They trained enough hard to compete at a high level.

② 그는 계속 정보를 얻도록 업계 뉴스를 읽는 것을 원칙으로 삼는다.
→ He makes a point of reading industry news to stay informed.

③ 두 후보 모두 경험이 부족하다는 비판을 받았다.
→ Both of the candidates were criticized for their lack of experience.

④ 그녀의 공연에 감동한 관객들은 앙코르를 외쳤다.
→ Touched by her performance, the audience cried out for an encore.

[해설] (enough hard → hard enough) enough는 형용사나 부사를 수식할 경우 후치 수식하므로 부사 hard 뒤에 위치해야 한다.
② 'make a point of RVing'는 '~하는 것을 원칙으로 삼다'라는 뜻의 동명사 관용표현이므로 reading은 적절하게 쓰였다. 또한 2형식 동사로 쓰인 stay의 보어로 분사형 형용사가 오고 있는데, 의미상 주어인 He가 '알리는' 것이 아니라 '알게 되는' 것이므로 수동의 과거분사 informed도 적절하게 쓰였다.
③ '두 후보 모두'라는 주어진 우리말에 따라 Both가 쓰이고 있는데, both는 대명사로 쓰이는 경우 'both + of + 복수 명사 + 복수 동사'의 구조를 취하므로 the candidates와 were의 쓰임은 적절하다. 또한 'criticize A for B'는 'A를 B에 대해 비난하다'라는 뜻을 가진 구문으로, 이를 수동태로 바꾸면 'A be criticized for B'가 된다. 대명사 their의 수일치 역시 옳다.
④ 분사구문의 의미상 주어인 the audience가 '감동받은' 것이므로 수동의 과거분사 Touched는 적절하게 쓰였다.

[어휘] compete 경쟁하다 candidate 후보자 touch 감동시키다 cry out ~을 외치다

[정답] ①

09 두 사람의 대화 중 가장 어색한 것은? [생활영어]

① A: Could you help me organize these files?
B: Yes I can, since my hands are tied at the moment.

② A: BTS raised the bar for Korean pop music.
B: Yeah, they definitely set a new standard.

③ A: Why does your brother pick on you all the time?
B: I think he finds it enjoyable to watch me get angry.

④ A: Would you like to see a baseball game this weekend?
B: I'd love to, but I can't. Can I take a raincheck on that?

[해설] 파일을 정리하는 데 도움을 요청하는 A에게 자신의 손발이 묶여 있어서 도움을 줄 수 있다는 B의 응답은 모순된다. 따라서 대화 중 가장 어색한 것은 ①이다.
[해석] ① A: 이 파일들을 정리하는 것을 도와주실 수 있나요?
B: 네, 지금 제 손발이 묶여 있어서 가능해요.
② A: BTS는 한국 음악의 기준을 높였어.
B: 응, 확실히 새로운 기준을 세웠지.
③ A: 네 오빠는 왜 항상 널 괴롭혀?
B: 내가 화내는 걸 보고 즐거워하는 것 같아.
④ A: 이번 주말에 야구 경기 보러 갈래?
B: 그러고 싶지만 그럴 수 없어. 다음 기회로 미뤄도 될까?

[어휘] organize 정리하다 raise 높이다, 올리다 pick on ~을 괴롭히다 take a rain check 다음을 기약하다

[정답] ①

10 밑줄 친 부분에 들어갈 말로 가장 적절한 것은? [생활영어]

A: I'm in trouble. My biology exam is tomorrow and I haven't even started studying yet.
B: What? Didn't you have plenty of time?
A: Yeah, but you know, I have a habit of cramming for tests.
B: You should really plan out your studies next time.
A: _____

① No, I didn't get a good grade on the exam.
② You're right. There's no need to break my habit.
③ Yeah, I'm seeing the importance of that right now.
④ I beg to differ. I'll make sure to follow your advice.

[해설] 내일 있을 생물학 시험을 앞두고 공부를 시작하지도 않아 걱정하고 있는 A에게 B가 조언을 하는 상황이다. 빈칸에는 다음부터는 공부 계획을 잘 세우라는 B의 조언에 적합한 대답이 와야 한다. 따라서 빈칸에 들어갈 말로 가장 적절한 것은 ③ '응, 지금 그 중요성을 느끼고 있어.'이다.
① 아니, 그 시험에서 좋은 성적을 받지 못했어.
② 네 말이 옳아. 내 습관을 고칠 필요는 없어.
④ 내 생각은 달라. 네 조언을 따르도록 할게.
[해석] A: 나 문제가 있어. 내일 생물학 시험이 있는데 아직 공부를 시작하지도 않았어.
B: 뭐라고? 시간이 충분하지 않았어?
A: 응, 근데 너도 알다시피 난 시험을 벼락치기로 보는 버릇이 있잖아.
B: 다음부터는 정말 공부 계획을 잘 세우도록 해.
A: 응, 지금 그 중요성을 느끼고 있어.
[어휘] plenty of 많은 cram 벼락치기 공부하다 break (a) habit 습관을 고치다 advice 조언

[정답] ③

11 주어진 글 다음에 이어질 글의 순서로 알맞은 것은? [순서배열]

Dan Ariely, an MIT professor of psychology, used self-imposed restriction and rewards in his own life to rid himself of hepatitis C.

(A) To ensure he'd withstand these side effects and go through with the treatment, Ariely, a movie lover, allowed himself to watch an unlimited number of movies on the days of his injections, only after he had taken the dose.

(B) That way, he made a full recovery, and, in fact, was the only patient to stick to the treatment plan. Introducing a positive association with the injection allowed him to tolerate short-term agony to achieve long-term health.

(C) To treat himself, Ariely had to inject himself three days a week with Interferon, a drug known for its extreme side effects, including fever, vomiting, nausea, and headaches.

*hepatitis: 간염

① (A) - (C) - (B) ② (B) - (A) - (C)
③ (C) - (A) - (B) ④ (C) - (B) - (A)

[해설] 주어진 글은 심리학 교수인 Dan Ariely가 스스로 부여한 제한과 보상을 활용해 C형 간염을 치료했다는 내용으로, 뒤에는 그 치료법을 소개하며 그것이 얼마나 고통스러운지를 설명하는 내용의 (C)가 오는 것이 자연스럽다. 그다음으로, (C)에서 언급된 부작용들을 these side effects로 받아, 그가 그러한 부작용들을 견디기 위해 스스로 부여한 보상 체계를 설명하는 (A)가 와야 한다. 마지막으로, 그 보상 방법을 That way로 받아, 이로 인해 그가 완전히 회복할 수 있었다는 결론을 제시하는 (B)가 오는 것이 적합하다. 따라서 글의 순서로 가장 적절한 것은 ③ '(C) - (A) - (B)'이다.

[해석] MIT의 심리학 교수인 Dan Ariely는 C형 간염을 자신에게서 없애기 위해 자기 삶에서 스스로 부여한 제한과 보상을 이용했다. (C) 자신을 치료하기 위해서, Ariely는 일주일에 3일을 발열, 구토, 메스꺼움, 두통을 포함한 극심한 부작용으로 알려진 약인 인터페론을 스스로 주사해야 했다. (A) 이러한 부작용을 견디고 치료를 완수할 것을 확실히 하기 위해서, 영화광인 Ariely는 주사를 맞는 날에는 스스로 영화를 무제한으로 볼 수 있도록 했는데, 오로지 그 용량을 맞고 난 후에만 그렇게 했다. (B) 그렇게 해서 그는 완치되었고, 사실상 그는 그 치료 계획을 지킨 유일한 환자였다. 주사에 긍정적인 연상을 도입한 것이 그가 단기간의 고통을 참아내고 장기간의 건강을 얻게 해주었다.

[어휘] self-imposed 스스로 부과한 restriction 제한 reward 보상 rid A of B A에서 B를 없애다 withstand 견디어 내다 side effect 부작용 treatment 치료 unlimited 무한정의 injection 주사 dose 투여량, 복용량 stick to ~을 고수하다 association 연상 tolerate 참아내다 agony (극도의) 고통, 괴로움 vomiting 구토 nausea 메스꺼움

[정답] ③

12 주어진 문장이 들어갈 위치로 가장 적절한 곳은? [문장삽입]

But the Pluto/planet link cannot be rapidly erased and will likely remain deep-rooted in my brain circuits for the rest of my life.

One day in 2006 I was informed that some powerful people had decided that Pluto was no longer a planet. (①) After a lifetime of being told that Pluto was a planet, my brain had created strong links between the neural representation of "planets" and the celestial object "Pluto." (②) But now I was being told that this link was incorrect. Unfortunately, the brain is well-designed to form new links between concepts, but the converse is not true: there is no specific mechanism for "unlinking." (③) Of course, my brain may adjust to the new turn of events by creating new links between "Pluto" and "not a planet." (④) And there may come a day late in my life in which I will return to my first belief and insist to my grandchildren that Pluto is a planet.

[해설] 주어진 문장은 But으로 시작하여, 명왕성/행성 연결고리는 금방 지워지지 않고 뇌에 남아 있을 가능성이 크다는 내용으로, 앞에는 이와 대조적인 내용이 와야 하며, 뒤에는 부연 설명이 이어져야 한다. ④ 앞에서 뇌가 '명왕성'과 '행성이 아님' 사이에 새로운 연결고리를 만들어 낼 수도 있다고 했는데, 이 새로운 연결고리는 '명왕성'과 '행성' 사이의 연결고리와 대조적인 것을 알 수 있다. 따라서 주어진 문장이 ④에 들어간다면, 새로운 연결고리가 생겨난다고 할지라도 명왕성/행성 연결고리는 없어지지 않을 것이라는 문맥이 자연스럽게 이어진다. 또한 ④ 뒤는 자신이 말년에는 명왕성이 행성이라고 주장할지도 모른다는 내용으로, 주어진 문장을 부연하는 것을 알 수 있다. 따라서 주어진 문장이 들어갈 위치로 가장 적절한 곳은 ④이다.

[해석] 2006년 어느 날, 나는 몇몇 힘 있는 사람들이 명왕성이 더 이상 행성이 아니라고 결정했다는 소식을 들었다. 평생을 명왕성이 행성이라는 말을 들은 후에, 내 뇌는 '행성'이라는 신경상의 표상과 천체 '명왕성' 사이의 강한 연관성을 만들어 냈다. 그러나 지금 나는 이 연결고리가 잘못되었다는 말을 듣고 있었다. 안타깝게도, 뇌는 개념들 사이에 새로운 연결고리를 형성하도록 잘 설계되었지만, 그 정반대는 사실이 아니다. 즉 '연결 해제'를 위한 구체적인 메커니즘은 없다. 물론 내 뇌는 '명왕성'과 '행성이 아님' 사이에 새로운 연결고리를 만들어 냄으로써 새로운 사건의 전환에 적응할 수 있다. 하지만 명왕성/행성 연결고리는 금방 지워지지 않고 남은 삶 동안 내 뇌 회로에 깊이 뿌리 박힌 채 남아 있을 가능성이 크다. 그리고 말년에는 내 첫 믿음으로 돌아가 내 손자들에게 명왕성이 행성이라고 주장할 날이 올지도 모른다.

[어휘] Pluto 명왕성 erase 지우다 deep-rooted 뿌리 깊이 박힌 circuit 회로 representation 표상, 재현 celestial 천체의 form 형성하다 converse 정반대 adjust to ~에 적응하다 insist 주장하다

[정답] ④

13 다음 글의 제목으로 가장 적절한 것은?

Juries are a big deal in the legal world. They force lawyers and judges to break down the law so that ordinary people can understand it. If we didn't have juries, the legal people in the courtroom might talk in confusing ways. That would make it hard for people on trial to understand what they're being accused of and how the trial works. Although jurors aren't legal experts, they bring a down-to-earth viewpoint that expert panels may lack. This prevents the legal proceeding from being overly technical and ensures a more balanced setting. So juries are there to provide different points of view. They help keep the law clear and fair. With juries, we get a mix of perspectives that keeps things in check and makes sure everyone gets a fair shot.

*juror: (한 사람의) 배심원

① Benefits and Drawbacks of Incorporating Juries
② Why Juries Exist: Their Role in the Legal System
③ How to Resolve Conflicts between Different Jurors
④ Common Problems Found during the Trial Process

[해설] 배심원단이 법정에서 하는 역할과 그 이점에 관해 서술하는 글이다. 따라서 글의 제목으로 가장 적절한 것은 ② '배심원단이 존재하는 이유: 법률 체제에서 그들의 역할'이다.
① 배심원단을 도입하는 것의 이점과 결점 → 배심원단의 이점만을 설명할 뿐, 결점은 언급되지 않았다.
③ 서로 다른 배심원들 간 갈등을 해결하는 방법
④ 재판 과정에서 발견되는 흔한 문제점들 → 재판 과정에서 생기는 문제점들을 배심원단을 통해 해소할 수 있다고 볼 수는 있으나, 이 글은 그 문제점 자체에 초점을 맞추지는 않았으므로 적절하지 않다.

[해석] 배심원단은 법조계에서 중요한 존재이다. 배심원단은 변호사와 판사가 일반인이 이해할 수 있도록 법을 세분화하도록 만든다. 배심원단이 없다면 법정에서 법조인들이 헷갈리는 방식으로 말할지도 모른다. 그것은 재판받는 사람들이 자신이 어떤 혐의를 받고 있는지, 재판이 어떻게 진행되는지 이해하기 어렵게 만들 것이다. 배심원이 법률 전문가는 아니지만, 전문가 패널에게 부족할지도 모르는 현실적인 관점을 제시한다. 이는 법적 절차가 지나치게 전문적으로 치우치는 것을 방지하고 보다 균형 잡힌 환경을 보장한다. 따라서 배심원은 다양한 관점을 제공하기 위해 존재한다. 그들은 법을 명확하고 공정하게 유지하는 것을 돕는다. 배심원단이 있으면, 상황을 견제하고 모든 사람이 공정한 기회를 가질 수 있도록 하는 다양한 관점을 얻는다.

[어휘] jury 배심원단 big deal 중요한 존재 legal 법률의 lawyer 변호사 judge 판사 break down 세분화하다, 분해하다 courtroom 법정 confusing 헷갈리게 하는 trial 재판 be accused of ~의 혐의를 받다 down-to-earth 현실적인 proceeding 절차 perspective 관점 shot 기회

[정답] ②

14 글의 흐름상 가장 어색한 문장은?

A strategic alliance, the newest form of international business structure, is a partnership formed between two or more organizations to create competitive advantage on a worldwide basis. ① The number of strategic alliances is growing at an estimated rate of about 20 percent per year. ② In fact, in the automobile and computer industries, strategic alliances are becoming the predominant means of competing. Why is this happening? ③ International competition is so fierce and the costs of competing on a global basis are so high that few firms have all the resources needed to do it alone. ④ Increasing international competition makes creativity more important than ever in the battle for technological leadership. Thus, individual firms that lack the internal resources essential for international success may seek to collaborate with other companies to gain a competitive edge.

[해설] 국제적으로 경쟁이 계속해서 과열되는 상황에서 기업들이 경쟁력을 확보하기 위해 서로 맺는 파트너십의 한 형태인 전략적 제휴에 관한 글이다. 따라서 글의 흐름상 가장 어색한 문장은 기술 리더십을 확보하기 위한 전투 속에서 창의성이 그 어느 때보다 더 중요해지고 있다는 내용의 ④이다.

[해석] 최신 국제 비즈니스 구조의 형태인 전략적 제휴는 전 세계적으로 경쟁 우위를 창출하기 위해 두 개 이상의 조직이 맺는 파트너십이다. 전략적 제휴의 수는 매년 약 20%의 비율로 증가하고 있다. 실제로, 자동차와 컴퓨터 산업에서는 전략적 제휴가 지배적인 경쟁 수단이 되고 있다. 왜 이런 일이 일어나고 있을까? 국제 경쟁이 너무 치열하고 전 세계적으로 경쟁에 드는 비용이 너무 많이 들어서 그것을 하기 위해 필요한 모든 자원을 가지고 있는 기업은 거의 없다. (증가하는 국제 경쟁은 기술 리더십을 확보하기 위한 전투 속에서 창의성을 그 어느 때보다 더 중요하게 만든다.) 따라서 국제적 성공에 필수적인 내부 자원이 부족한 개별 기업은 경쟁 우위를 확보하기 위해 다른 기업과의 협업을 추구할 수 있다.

[어휘] strategic 전략적 alliance 제휴 structure 구조 competitive advantage 경쟁 우위 estimated 약, 대략 predominant 지배적인 means 수단 fierce 치열한 resource 자원 essential 필수적인 collaborate with ~과 협업하다

[정답] ④

15 다음 글의 내용과 일치하지 않는 것은?   [불일치]

Soviet astronaut Valentina Tereshkova was born on March 6, 1937, in Russia. She started school at eight and left school at sixteen, but continued her education through correspondence courses while working. Since a young age, she developed skills in parachute jumping, which eventually led to her selection as an astronaut. In 1962, she was recruited into a space program and selected for spaceflight training with four other candidates. Tereshkova was the sole individual to complete that training. On June 16, 1963, Tereshkova made history as the first woman to fly in space when she was launched aboard Vostok 6. In this historic 70.8-hour flight, she orbited Earth 48 times. Her achievement earned her the title "Hero of the Soviet Union." Although she never went to space again, Tereshkova became a Soviet spokesperson, and received the United Nations Gold Medal of Peace while in office.

① 젊은 시절에 Tereshkova는 일하면서도 학업을 계속하였다.
② 1962년에 Tereshkova는 우주 비행 훈련에 혼자 선발되었다.
③ Tereshkova는 1963년에 우주 비행을 한 최초의 여성이 되었다.
④ Tereshkova는 첫 우주 비행 이후로 다시는 우주에 가지 않았다.

[해설] 4번째 문장에서 1962년에 그녀는 다른 네 명의 후보들과 함께 우주 비행 훈련에 선발되었다고 언급되므로, 글의 내용과 일치하지 않는 것은 ② '1962년에 Tereshkova는 우주 비행 훈련에 혼자 선발되었다.'이다.
① 젊은 시절에 Tereshkova는 일하면서도 학업을 계속하였다. → 2번째 문장에서 언급된 내용이다.
③ Tereshkova는 1963년에 우주 비행을 한 최초의 여성이 되었다. → 6번째 문장에서 언급된 내용이다.
④ Tereshkova는 첫 우주 비행 이후로 다시는 우주에 가지 않았다. → 마지막 문장에서 언급된 내용이다.

[해석] 소련의 우주 비행사 Valentina Tereshkova는 1937년 3월 6일에 러시아에서 태어났다. 그녀는 8살에 학교를 시작하여 16살에 학교를 그만두었지만, 일하면서도 원격 강좌를 통해 학업을 계속했다. 어렸을 때부터, 그녀는 낙하산 점프 기술을 익혔고, 이것은 결국 그녀가 우주 비행사로 선발되게 했다. 1962년에 그녀는 한 우주 프로그램에 모집되었고, 다른 네 명의 후보들과 함께 우주 비행 훈련에 선발되었다. Tereshkova는 그 훈련을 끝낸 유일한 사람이었다. 1963년 6월 16일에, Tereshkova는 Vostok 6호에 탑승해 우주로 가게 되어, 우주 비행을 한 첫 번째 여성으로서 역사에 남았다. 70.8시간에 걸친 그 역사적인 비행을 하며, 그녀는 지구 궤도를 48번 돌았다. 그녀의 업적은 그녀에게 '소련의 영웅'이라는 칭호를 안겨주었다. 비록 다시 우주에 가지 않았지만, Tereshkova는 소련의 대변인이 되었고, 재임 중에 유엔 평화 금메달을 받았다.

[어휘] Soviet 소련의 astronaut 우주 비행사 correspondence course 통신 강좌 parachute 낙하산 eventually 결국 selection 선발 recruit 모집하다 spaceflight 우주비행 historic 역사적으로 중요한 orbit 궤도를 돌다 achievement 업적, 성취 spokesperson 대변인 while in office 재직 도중

[정답] ②

16 다음 글의 내용과 일치하지 않는 것은?   [불일치]

Austria has a relatively low youth criminal rate compared to other European countries, and the rate is declining according to Austrian crime statistics. However, what's concerning is the increasing brutality displayed by these young perpetrators: "today, they don't stop when the other one starts bleeding," researchers reported. One contributing factor to the rising brutality is the involvement of a significant proportion of young offenders in substance abuse, which often acts as a pathway to further criminal behavior. However, despite the urgency of the problem, the authorities including the police, prosecutor's office, youth welfare offices, and family courts, seem to pass the responsibility of dealing with these young offenders back and forth. This is creating a fragmented framework for handling youth offenders, hindering any viable solutions.

① The criminal rate of Austrian youths is decreasing.
② The level of violence young Austrian offenders show is intensifying.
③ Increasing brutality of youth criminals is linked to substance abuse.
④ Austrian authorities are effectively dealing with youth criminal issues.

[해설] 마지막 두 문장에서 당국 기관들이 서로에게 책임을 떠넘기면서 유효한 해결책이 나오는 것을 어렵게 하고 있다고 언급되므로, 글의 내용과 일치하지 않는 것은 ④ '오스트리아 당국은 청소년 범죄 문제에 효과적으로 대처하고 있다.'이다.
① 오스트리아 청소년의 범죄율은 감소하고 있다. → 첫 문장에서 언급된 내용이다.
② 오스트리아 청소년 범죄자들이 보이는 폭력성이 심화되고 있다. → 2번째 문장에서 언급된 내용이다.
③ 청소년 범죄자의 잔인성 증가는 약물 남용과 관련이 있다. → 3번째 문장에서 언급된 내용이다.

[해석] 오스트리아는 다른 유럽 국가에 비해 상대적으로 낮은 청소년 범죄율을 가지고 있으며, 오스트리아 범죄 통계에 따르면 그 비율은 감소하고 있다. 그러나 우려스러운 점은 이 젊은 가해자들이 보여주는 증가하는 잔인성이다. 연구자들은 "오늘날 그들은 상대방이 피를 흘리기 시작해도 멈추지 않는다"라고 보고했다. 증가하는 잔인성에 기여하는 요인 중 하나는 상당수의 청소년 범죄자가, 종종 추가 범죄 행위로 이어지는 경로로 작용하는 약물 남용에 연루되어 있다는 것이다. 그러나 이 문제의 시급성에도 불구하고 경찰, 검찰, 청소년 복지관, 가정법원 등 관계 당국은 이러한 청소년 범죄자들에 대처하는 책임을 서로에게 떠넘기고 있는 것으로 보인다. 이것은 청소년 범죄자를 다루는 데 있어 파편화된 체계를 만들고 있으며, 실행 가능한 해결책이 나오는 것을 방해하고 있다.

[어휘] youth 청소년 criminal 범죄자 statistics 통계 brutality 잔인성 perpetrator 가해자 contributing 기여하는 offender 범죄자 authorities 당국 responsibility 책임 deal with ~을 다루다 back and forth 여기저기 hinder 방해하다 viable 실행 가능한 violence 폭력성

[정답] ④

17 다음 글의 요지로 가장 적절한 것은?

It is widely believed that by 2030, up to two-thirds of the world's countries will face severe water shortages, leading to water stress. Water is a scarce resource, and its mismanagement can lead to conflict between nations that share the same river. To address water issues, countries must work together to share data, knowledge, and best practices, and to establish treaties and agreements to allocate water resources equitably and sustainably. International organizations such as the United Nations and the World Bank can play a critical role in facilitating this cooperation by providing funding, technical assistance, and policy guidance. By working together, nations can ensure that all people have access to clean water and that water resources are used efficiently and effectively to promote economic growth and environmental sustainability.

① Conflict over water is increasingly pulling nations apart.
② International cooperation is needed to solve water problems.
③ Water shortage will worsen the economies of developing nations.
④ International organizations should have ownership of water resources.

18 (A)와 (B)에 들어갈 말로 가장 적절한 것은?

Polycarbonate is a transparent plastic material invented in 1898 which wasn't commercialized until 1953. It is prized for its tough, shatter-resistant strength and its resistance to heat and flame. __(A)__, polycarbonate is a safer choice than glass and other plastics, making it ideal for a wide range of products from baby bottles to Blu-ray disks. About one billion kilograms of polycarbonate are produced annually. __(B)__, although polycarbonate is not likely to shatter and physically harm users of these products, it is less clear whether the plastic might chemically harm them. Polycarbonate can contain traces of bisphenol A (BPA), a harmful chemical, from the manufacturing process and can release that BPA as the plastic ages or is exposed to heat, cleansers, or other substances.

(A)	(B)
① As a result	Yet
② Therefore	Thus
③ Nevertheless	Likewise
④ By contrast	Instead

19 밑줄 친 부분에 들어갈 말로 가장 적절한 것은?

In a recent book entitled *Scarcity*, Sendhil Mullainathan, an economist from Harvard University, and Eldar Shafir, a psychologist from Princeton University, detail what they refer to as the 'scarcity mindset.' When people experience resource pressures, whether they're short of money, time, friends or food, they tend to automatically focus their attention on making the most effective use of the resources they already have. While this focus may increase productivity and efficiency, it also comes at the cost of what they refer to as 'tunnelling.' That is, the tendency for people in a scarcity mindset to miss out on important peripheral details in their decision-making. In an effort to only give full consideration to that which is in the tunnel — and therefore to what appears to be the most pressing concern — they no longer attend to other, broader factors. Understood in this way, scarcity serves to _____.

① reduce trust
② identify details
③ narrow attention
④ sacrifice efficiency

[해설] 이 글은 사람들이 자원 압박을 받을 때, 즉 어떤 자원이 희소할 경우에 이미 가지고 있는 것을 최대한 효과적으로 이용하는 데에만 집중하게 되는 경향이 있는데, 이에 따라 다른 중요한 것들을 놓치게 된다는 내용의 글이다. 따라서 빈칸에 들어갈 말로 가장 적절한 것은 ③ '관심을 좁히는'이다.
① 신뢰를 감소시키는 → 희소성으로 인해 신뢰가 감소된다는 내용은 언급되지 않았다.
② 세부 사항을 파악하는 → 희소성으로 인해 의사 결정에서 중요한 주변 세부 사항을 놓치게 된다고 했으므로 반대된다.
④ 효율성을 희생시키는 → 오히려 희소성이 효율성을 높일 수 있다고 언급되므로 적절하지 않다.

[해석] Harvard 대학교의 경제학자 Sendhil Mullainathan과 Princeton 대학교의 심리학자 Eldar Shafir는 최근 출간한 <Scarcity>라는 제목의 책에서, 그들이 '희소성 마음가짐'이라고 부르는 것에 대해 상세히 설명한다. 사람들이 돈, 시간, 친구, 또는 음식이 부족하든 간에 자원 압박을 경험할 때, 이미 가지고 있는 자원을 최대한 효과적으로 이용하는 데 자동으로 주의를 집중하는 경향이 있다. 이러한 집중이 생산성과 효율성을 높일 수 있지만, 그것은 또한 그들이 '터널 파기'라고 부르는 것의 대가를 치르기도 한다. 즉, 이는 희소성 사고방식을 가진 사람들이 의사 결정에서 중요한 주변 세부 사항을 놓치는 경향이다. 터널 안에 있는 것, 즉 그러므로 가장 시급한 관심사로 보이는 것만 온전히 고려하려는 노력에서, 그들은 더 이상 다른 더 광범위한 요소에는 관심을 기울이지 않는다. 이렇게 (희소성을) 이해할 때, 희소성은 관심을 좁히는 역할을 한다.

[어휘] entitle 제목을 붙이다 detail 상세히 설명하다 refer to A as B A를 B라고 부르다 scarcity 희소성 mindset 마음가짐 pressure 압박 be short of ~이 부족하다 automatically 자동으로 make the most use of ~을 최대한 이용하다 at the cost of ~을 희생하여 miss out on ~을 놓치다 peripheral 주변(부)의 pressing 시급한, 긴급한 broad 광범위한

[정답] ③

20 밑줄 친 부분에 들어갈 말로 가장 적절한 것은?

If you believe in an afterlife, you have less reason to fear your own death than if you don't — provided, of course, that the afterlife is likely to be a pleasant one and not eternal damnation. For those who believe in an afterlife, death is not the end of everything. However, Greek philosopher Epicurus argued that those who don't believe in an afterlife and consider death as completely final also have no reason to fear death. According to Epicurus, fear of death arises from imagining that we will be there after our deaths to mourn our own loss. But when we are alive, death is absent; and when we are dead, we no longer exist to be harmed. So either we are alive, and death isn't harming us; or we are dead, and then there is nothing to be harmed. Furthermore, he argued, we don't worry about the eternity of our nonexistence before birth, so we shouldn't worry in the least about it after death. His conclusion was that fear of death is _____.

① harmless
② universal
③ irrational
④ beneficial

[해설] 사후세계를 믿지 않더라도 죽음을 두려워할 이유가 없다는 Epicurus의 주장에 관한 글이다. 그는 우리가 살아 있을 때 죽음은 존재하지 않으며 우리가 죽고 나서는 우리가 존재하지 않으므로 해를 입을 수 없다면서, 죽음을 두려워할 이유가 없음을 설명했다. 따라서 그는 죽음에 대한 두려움을 비합리적인 것으로 본 것을 알 수 있으므로, 빈칸에 들어갈 말로 가장 적절한 것은 ③ '비합리적인'이다.
① 무해한 → '죽음' 자체는 무해하다고 말하고 있으나, 이것이 '죽음에 대한 두려움'이 우리에게 해를 끼치지 않는다는 것을 의미하는 것은 아니다. 오히려 그것을 불필요하며 비합리적인 것으로 간주하고 있으므로, 죽음을 두려워해도 된다는 취지의 선지는 Epicurus의 주장을 나타내기에 적절하지 않다.
② 보편적인 → 죽음에 대한 두려움이 보편적이라는 점을 주장한 것이 아니다.
④ 유익한 → 오히려 죽음에 대한 두려움을 가질 이유가 없음을 설명하고 있으므로 적절하지 않다.

[해석] 당신이 사후세계를 믿는다면, 믿지 않는 경우보다 죽음을 두려워할 이유가 더 적다. 이것은 물론 그 사후세계가 영원한 지옥살이가 아니라 즐거운 것일 가능성이 크다는 전제하에서이다. 사후세계를 믿는 사람들에게 죽음은 모든 것의 끝이 아니다. 그러나 그리스 철학자 Epicurus는, 사후세계를 믿지 않고 죽음이 완전히 최종적인 것이라고 생각하는 사람들 또한 죽음을 두려워할 이유가 없다고 주장했다. Epicurus에 따르면, 죽음에 대한 두려움은 우리가 죽은 후에도 우리 자신의 죽음을 애도하기 위해 그곳에 있을 것이라고 상상하는 것에서 비롯된다. 하지만 우리가 살아 있을 때 죽음은 존재하지 않으며, 우리가 죽으면 더 이상 해를 입을 우리가 존재하지 않는다. 따라서 우리가 살아 있고 죽음이 우리를 해치지 않거나, 아니면 우리가 죽고 나서는 해를 입을 것이 없다. 게다가, 그는 우리가 태어나기 전에는 우리의 비존재의 영원성에 대해 걱정하지 않기 때문에 죽음 이후에도 그것에 대해 조금도 걱정하지 말아야 한다고 주장했다. 그의 결론은 죽음에 대한 두려움이 비합리적이라는 것이었다.

[어휘] afterlife 사후세계 eternal 영원한 damnation 지옥살이 mourn 애도하다 absent 없는 eternity 영원성 nonexistence 비존재 conclusion 결론

[정답] ③

Staff

Writer 심우철

Director 정규리

Researcher 강다비다 / 장은영

Design 강현구

Manufacture 김승훈

Marketing 윤대규 / 한은지 / 장승재 / 유경철

발행일 2024년 2월 19일 (2쇄)

Copyright ⓒ 2024
by Shimson English Lab.

All rights reserved. No part of this publication may be reproduced, stored in a retrieval system or transmitted in any form or by any means, electronic, mechanical, photocopying, recording or otherwise, without any prior written permission of the copyright owner.

본 교재의 독창적인 내용에 대한 일체의 무단 전재 · 모방은 법률로 금지되어 있습니다.
파본은 교환해 드립니다.

내용문의 http://cafe.naver.com/shimson2000